Serial Communications Programming in C and C++

MARK GOODWIN

MIS: PRESS

A Subsidiary of
Henry Holt and Co., Inc.

a subsidiary of Henry Holt and Company, Inc.
115 West 18th Street
New York, New York, 10011

First Edition—1992
ISBN 1-55828-128-3

Printed in the United States of America
10 9 8 7 6 5 4 3

MIS:Press books are available at special discounts for bulk purchases for sales promotions, premiums, fund-raising, or educational use. Special editions or book excerpts can also be created to specification.

For details contact: Special Sales Director
MIS:Press
a subsidiary of Henry Holt and Company, Inc.
115 West 18th Street
New York, New York 10011

TRADEMARKS

IBM is a trademark of IBM Corporation
Microsoft, MS, MS-DOS, and QuickC are trademarks of Microsoft Corporation

Dedication

To one of the sweetest and most lovable children in the whole world: my son, Matthew.

Acknowledgments

I would like to express my most sincere thanks to the following companies:

Borland International, Inc.

Intel Corporation

Microcom, Inc.

Microsoft Corporation

This book would not have been possible without their generous contributions.

Table of Contents

Introduction

Back when the IBM PC was first introduced, little thought was given to the new computer's serial interface. It could support two serial ports and the ROM BIOS provided a few routines that offered programmers a rudimentary interface between the computer's serial ports and application programs. Although the ROM BIOS serial communications routines were more than adequate to meet the demands of the then state-of-the-art 300-baud modems, they are grossly incapable of meeting the demands of today's high speed modems. Indeed, many of today's modems require serial communications ports to be locked at such high speeds as 38,400 baud to reach their maximum data throughput. Additionally, multitasking environments require UARTs with FIFO buffers to prevent characters from being lost during task switching. Consequently, it is quite evident that today's programmers can't rely on the ROM BIOS routines for serial communications tasks and instead must either write their own serial communications routines or purchase a commercially produced serial communications toolbox.

Although purchasing a commercially produced serial communications toolbox will certainly relieve programmers from writing their own serial communications routines, creating your own custom serial communications toolbox is a relatively easy chore for the experienced programmer. Many programmers are under the mistaken impression that serial communications programming is some arcane art, which can only be successfully performed by an elite group of programmers who specialize in the area. Nothing could be further from the truth. This book is devoted to showing the C programmer just how easy it is to roll your own serial communications toolbox. By the time you've turned this book's last page, you will be shown how a complete C and C++ library of serial communications routines (hereinafter referred to as the SERIAL toolbox) can be created to perform tasks such as opening and closing serial ports, sending and receiving characters; enabling and disabling FIFO buffers; performing XON/XOFF, RTS/CTS, and DTR/DSR flow control; and more.

Additionally, this book illustrates how the SERIAL toolbox's low-level serial communications routines can be used to transfer files using the Xmodem, Xmodem-1K, Ymodem, and Ymodem-G protocols. Although it doesn't use the SERIAL toolbox's low-level serial communications routines, the book does present a complete ANSI terminal emulator, which can be included in your own serial communications programs. Finally, the book presents a rather simple, yet complete, serial communications program that ties all of the book's many elements together. Thus, you can see how all of the SERIAL toolbox's many routines can be combined together to create a "real-world" application program.

Software and Hardware Requirements

To make the best use of the information provided in this book, you should be an intermediate-level programmer and must have a working knowledge of the C programming language. The programs in this book can be successfully compiled using Microsoft C, Microsoft QuickC, or Turbo C++. Either the Microsoft Macro Assembler or Turbo Assembler is required to assemble the book's low-level assembly language routines. (You should note that already assembled and compiled versions of the SERIAL toolbox are included on the book's companion disk.) Hardware requirements include an IBM PC or compatible computer, a serial port, and a modem.

Chapter 1

Serial Communications

To better understand how the serial communications routines contained in the SERIAL toolbox perform their intended functions, it is first necessary for the programmer to investigate topics such as serial vs. parallel communications, the RS-232 serial interface, and UARTs. Accordingly, this chapter takes an in-depth look at all of these topics and covers a number of other important points the programmer must be acquainted with to become an efficient serial communications programmer.

Parallel Communications

Before we look at serial communications, it is helpful to take a brief look at *parallel communications*. Parallel communications is where more than one data bit, usually eight data bits, can be sent either from or to a peripheral device and a computer. Probably the first example of a peripheral device that most people will think of is their printer. Figure 1.1 presents a very simplified diagram of the parallel interface that is used by an IBM PC to communicate with a parallel printer.

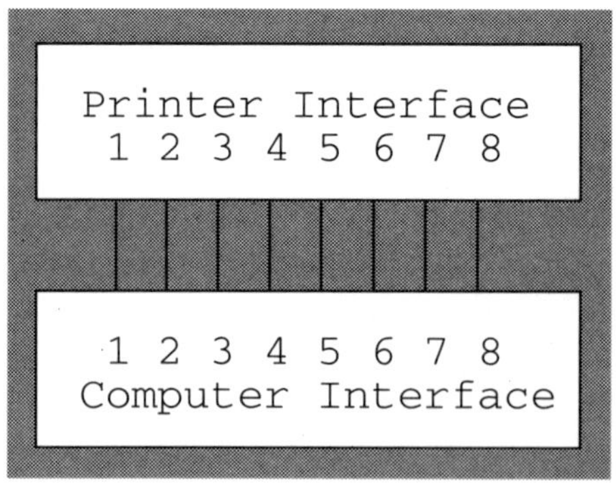

Figure 1.1 *A Parallel Printer-to-Computer Interface.*

Figure 1.1 clearly shows that the computer does indeed send eight data bits of information at a time to a parallel printer. Thus, the computer is effectively sending a character at a time to the printer. As you can well imagine, this is a highly efficient and fast way of sending data to a peripheral device. At this point you may be wondering if parallel communications is so efficient and fast, why use anything else? The answer to that question lies in the fact that any parallel communications system requires a separate wire for each data bit in the interface. This may be a very practical and desirable way to interface a peripheral device, such as a printer, which is always in close proximity with the computer; but for communications with a peripheral device or even another computer that is a considerable distance away from the computer the costs of parallel communications can be prohibitive. Thus, the **serial communications interface** comes into play.

Serial Communications

Although the parallel interface may be a more efficient and faster way of communicating data, the serial interface is a much more cost effective means for communicating data. Figure 1.2 presents a very simplified look at the way a computer would communicate with a printer that has a serial interface instead of a parallel interface.

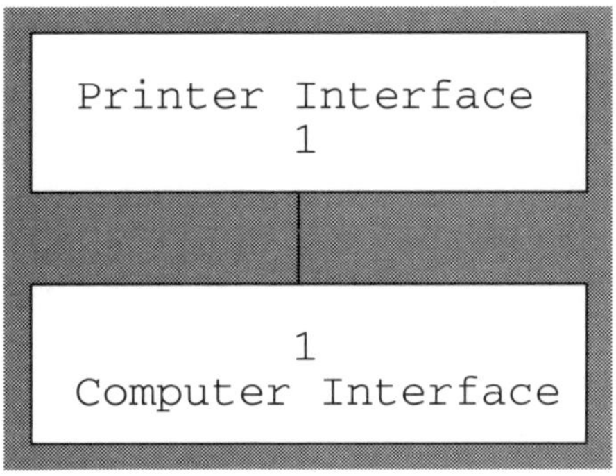

Figure 1.2 *A Serial Printer-to-Computer Interface.*

As Figure 1.2 illustrates, data is communicated between a peripheral device and the computer over a serial interface one data bit at a time. In a very simple serial interface, data can be transmitted back and forth over a single wire. Although such a simple serial interface might be desirable, it wouldn't be of much practical use in the real world. A more robust serial interface provides a number of other wires that are chiefly concerned with insuring that data is being sent back and forth in a fairly orderly fashion. The most widely used serial interface is the **RS-232 serial interface**. Although other serial interfaces do exist, the RS-232 serial interface is without a doubt the most universally accepted serial interface.

The RS-232 Serial Interface

The RS-232 serial interface is formally defined as *Recommended Standard Number 232, Revision C* from the Engineering Department of the Electronic Industries Association. This standard calls for a female connector on the Data Communications Equipment (DCE) and for a male connector on the Data Terminal Equipment (DTE). Simply put, the DTE is your computer and the DCE is the peripheral device that you are trying to communicate with. The RS-232 standard defines 25 communications lines. Figure 1.3 details the RS-232 serial interface's 25 lines and the pin numbers they are assigned to on their appropriate connectors.

Pin	***Abbreviation***	***Name***
1	AA	Protective Ground
2	BA	Transmitted Data
3	BB	Received Data
4	CA	Request to Send
5	CB	Clear to Send
6	CC	Data Set Ready
7	AB	Signal Common
8	CF	Received Line Signal Detect
9	—	Reserved for Testing
10	—	Reserved for Testing
11	—	Unassigned
12	SCF	Secondary Received Line Signal Detect
13	SCB	Secondary Clear to Send
14	SBA	Secondary Transmitted Data
15	DB	Transmission Signal Element Timing
16	SBB	Secondary Received Data
17	DD	Receiver Signal Element Timing
18	—	Unassigned
19	SCA	Secondary Request to Send
20	CD	Data Terminal Ready
21	CG	Signal Quality Detector
22	CE	Ring Indicator
23	CH/CI	Data Signal Rate Detector
24	DA	Transmit Signal Element Timing
25	—	Unassigned

Figure 1.3 *The 25 RS-232 Serial Interface Lines.*

The RS-232 standard also defines a number of electrical characteristics: total cable capacitance should be less than 2500 picofarads, a binary logic 1 is +5 to +15 volts for output lines and +3 to +15 volts for input lines, a binary logic 0 is –5 to –15 volts for output lines and –3 to –15 volts for input lines; voltages between –5 and +5 volts for output lines and –3 and +3 volts for input lines are undefined.

Although the EIA RS-232 specs are considered the standard, they aren't quite the way things are done in the microcomputer world. Figure 1.4 illustrates how the RS-232 interface is more commonly implemented on a microcomputer using a 25-pin connector.

Pin	*Abbreviation*	*Name*
1	—	Protective Ground
2	TD	Transmitted Data
3	RD	Received Data
4	RTS	Request to Send
5	CTS	Clear to Send
6	DSR	Data Set Ready
7	—	Signal Common
8	DCD	Data Carrier Detect
20	DTR	Data Terminal Ready
22	RI	Ring Indicator
23	DSRD	Data Signal Rate Detector

Figure 1.4 *A Real World 25-Pin RS-232 Microcomputer Serial Interface.*

As you can see from Figure 1.4, only a subset of the EIA RS-232 standard is typically used by microcomputers. Indeed, IBM AT-class machines use only a 9-pin RS-232 connector, which is illustrated in Figure 1.5.

Pin	*Abbreviation*	*Name*
1	DCD	Data Carrier Detect
2	RD	Received Data
3	TD	Transmit Data
4	DTR	Data Terminal Ready
5	—	Signal Common
6	DSR	Data Set Ready
7	RTS	Request to Send
8	CTS	Clear to Send
9	RI	Ring Indicator

Figure 1.5 *The IBM AT 9-Pin RS-232 Serial Interface.*

Although the IBM AT subset of the RS-232 serial interface may seem to be inadequate to perform its intended task, it is really all the programmer needs to carry out effective serial communications programming. To better understand what each of these RS-232 lines actually does, let's take a more detailed look a them.

Clear to Send (CTS)

The *CTS* line is asserted (logic state 1) by the DCE when it is ready to receive data.

Data Carrier Detect (DCD)

The *DCD* line is asserted (logic state 1) whenever there is a data link in progress.

Data Set Ready (DSR)

The *DSR* line is asserted (logic state 1) by the DCE when it is ready to communicate with the DTE.

Data Terminal Ready (DTR)

The *DTR* line is asserted (logic state 1) by the DTE when it is ready to communicate with the DCE.

Received Data (RD)

The *RD* line is used by the DCE to send data to the DTE.

Ring Indicator (RI)

The *RI* line is asserted (logic state 1) by the DCE when a ring is detected.

Request to Send (RTS)

The *RTS* line is asserted (logic state 1) by the DTE when it wants to transmit data to the DCE.

Transmit Data (TD)

The *TD* line is used by the DTE to send data to the DCE.

Baud Rate, Start Bits, Data Bits, Parity, and Stop Bits

Now that we have a standard interface to communicate through, we must use some sort of mutually agreeable convention to actually transmit the data through the serial interface. Because serial data is sent a bit at a time, there must be a way to synchronize the operation of sending data between the DTE and the DCE. The first thing that must be done is to agree upon a rate of speed for the data transfer. Speed on a serial communications line is expressed as the *baud rate*. Simply put, the baud rate is the number of bits per second that is being transferred between the DTE and the DCE. For example, two serial devices that are transferring data at a rate of 2400 baud are in reality transferring data at a rate of 2400 bits per second.

At this point, you might jump to the conclusion that the two example serial devices are transferring data at a rate of 300 characters per second (2400 baud/8 bits=300 bytes per second). Unfortunately, this assumption would be incorrect. Besides having to agree upon a baud rate, the two serial devices must format the data in such a way that they will be able to synchronize when a character of data starts and when it stops. We will call it a character instead of byte because not all data links send complete bytes of data. To perform this synchronization of transmitted data, the two serial devices will use start, parity, and stop bits with each character of data.

The Start Bit

When a serial device isn't transmitting, it asserts (logical 1) the TD line. To start the transmission of the character of data, the transmitting serial device sends a start bit. As you might suspect the start bit is a logical 0 and it lasts for the baud rate's time frame. By sending the start bit, the DCE is able to synchronize with the transmitter by simply waiting for the DTE's TD line to go from the logical 1 state to the logical 0 state. The DCE then pauses for half a bit time and then starts sampling the incoming data once every bit time until the character has been completely transferred. By pausing for half of the bit time, the DCE is able to maintain synchronization by always sampling the incoming data stream at or near the middle of each bit. If the DCE didn't provide this pause, it might get confused about the incoming bit stream because of minor differences between the DTE and DCE's clock rates. Figure 1.6 illustrates how a start bit is sent at 2400 baud. As this figure shows, the start bit lasts for 1/2400 of 1 second.

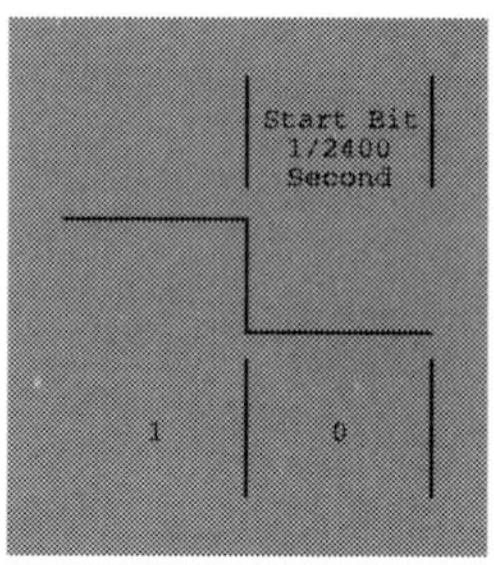

Figure 1.6 *The Start Bit.*

The Data Bits

After the transmitting serial device has sent the start bit, it will send five to eight data bits. For most data transmissions, either seven or eight data bits are sent. Figure 1.7 illustrates how the character A (41H) could be transmitted using eight data bits.

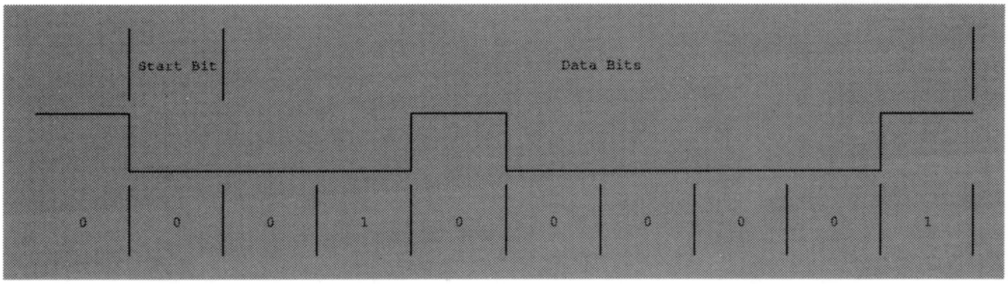

Figure 1.7 *The Data Bits.*

Parity

Some data links require a parity bit for a crude and rather ineffective form of error detection. The five basic forms of parity are *NONE*, *EVEN*, *ODD*, *MARK*, and *SPACE*. As its name implies, NONE means that the character is transmitted without a parity bit. This is a very common setting when eight data bits are being transmitted. With EVEN parity, the transmitting serial device will send a logical 1 parity bit after the character's data bits if there are an odd number of logical 1 bits in the character's data bits. Otherwise, the transmitting serial device will send a logical 0 parity bit after the data character's bits if there are an even number of logical 1 bits in the character's data bits. Thus, EVEN parity insures that there will always be an even number of logical 1 bits sent with each character and will indicate an error if an odd number of logical 1 bits is received by the receiving serial device. With ODD parity, the transmitting serial device will send a logical 1 parity bit after the character's data bits if there is an even number of logical 1 bits in the character's data bits. Otherwise, the transmitting serial device will send a logical 0 bit after the data character's bits if there is an odd number of logical 1 bits in the character's data bits. Thus, ODD parity insures that there will always be an odd number of logical 0 bits sent with each character and will indicate an error if an even number of logical 1 bits is received by the receiving serial device. With MARK parity, the transmitting serial device will send a logical 1 parity bit after the character's data bits. With SPACE parity, the transmitting serial device will send a logical 0 parity bit after the character's data bits. Figure 1.8 illustrates how the character C (43H) would be transmitted by a serial device using seven data bits and EVEN parity. As this figure shows, the transmitting serial device has to send a logical 1 in the parity bit to maintain EVEN parity.

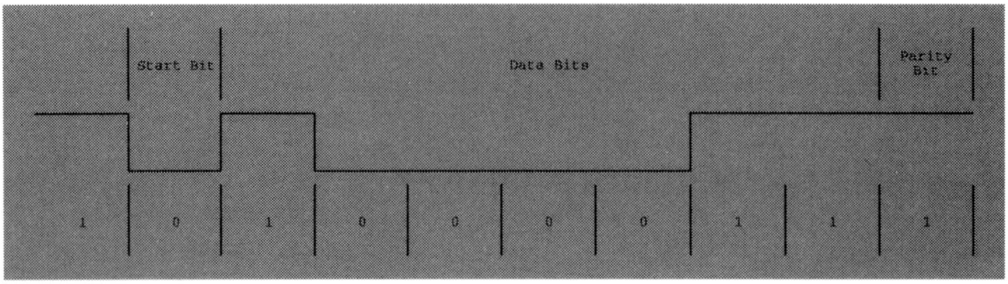

Figure 1.8 The Parity Bit.

The Stop Bit

As the start bit signifies the start of a character, the stop bit signifies the end of a character. The transmitting serial device always sends a logical 1 for the stop bit. This also asserts the TD line. Thus, the serial interface is put into its proper idle state by the stop bit. Figure 1.9 illustrates how a letter C (43H) is completely transmitted using eight data bits and no parity.

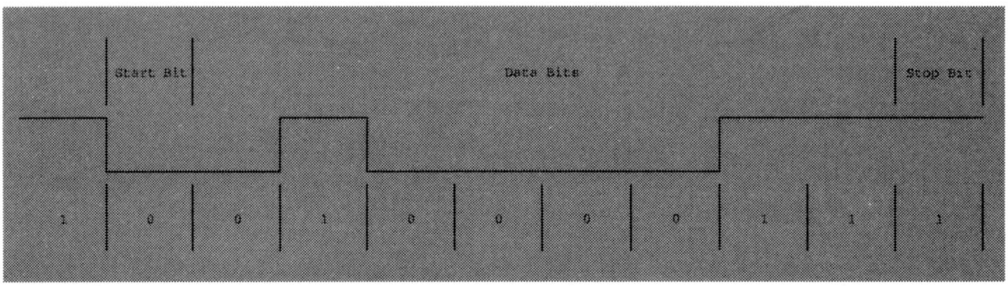

Figure 1.9 The Stop Bit.

A Two-Way Street?

It is easy to assume that all serial devices have both a receive and transmit line and can both send and receive data at the same time; however, this is not the case. There are four basic ways to transmit and receive serial data: simplex, half-duplex, full-duplex, and multiplex. With a simplex connection, serial communications is only taking place in one direction. With a half-duplex connection, serial communications can take place in both directions, but communications can only take place in one direction at a time. A full-duplex connection allows serial communications to take place in both directions at the same time. A multiplex connection allows multiple serial communications channels to occur over the same serial communications line. Multiplex operations are achieved by either allocating separate frequencies or time slices to the individual serial communications channels. You will find that most microcomputer serial communications are performed over a full-duplex connection.

UARTs

Now that you have a good working knowledge of the RS-232 serial interface and how serial data is actually transmitted over such an interface, it's time to take a detailed look at the hardware device that actually performs all of this for the computer. Almost all microcomputers use a special hardware device called a Universal Asynchronous Receiver Transmitter (hereinafter referred to as a UART) to implement an RS-232 serial interface. You should note that a UART is sometimes called an Asynchronous Communications Element (ACE). The IBM PC and compatibles use UARTs that are based on National Semiconductor's INS8250 family of UARTs. Although some PC serial interfaces still use the 8250 UART, most computers built today use the 16450 and 16550 UARTs. Basically, the 16450 UART is a higher speed version of the 8250 and the 16550 is a special version of the 16450 that has what are called FIFO buffers. With today's high speed modems and multi-tasking environments becoming more and more commonplace, the 16550 UART is gradually becoming the UART of choice in the PC world.

Addressing the UART

All UARTs have one or more registers to control their operations. These registers are read from and written to on an IBM PC or compatible computer through the use of **input/output ports**. The table in Figure 1.10 shows the address of a UART's base register (the UART's first register) for COM1 to COM4. Although some serial devices support serial ports greater than COM4, there really is no established standard for such ports and you should consult the serial device's accompanying literature to determine the port address the device's UART uses for its base register.

Serial Port	***Base Register Port Address***
COM1	3F8H
COM2	2F8H
COM3	3E8H
COM4	2E8H

Figure 1.10 *The Serial Port Base Register Ports.*

The 8250 UART

Now let's take a detailed look at the 8250's registers. As you will see, the 8250's registers perform a host of tasks that greatly simplify writing serial communications programs.

Register 0—The Receiver Buffer Register

When a character of data is received by the 8250 UART, it is assembled and placed in the UART's *Receiver Buffer Register* (*RBR*). The RBR is the UART's first register and can be addressed by reading the serial port's base register port. For COM1, the RBR can be read from by fetching a value from port **3F8H**. Figure 1.11 illustrates how the character of data is returned by the UART. Although the RBR will always hold an eight-bit value, you should mask out any bits not used for data links that are using less than eight data bits per character.

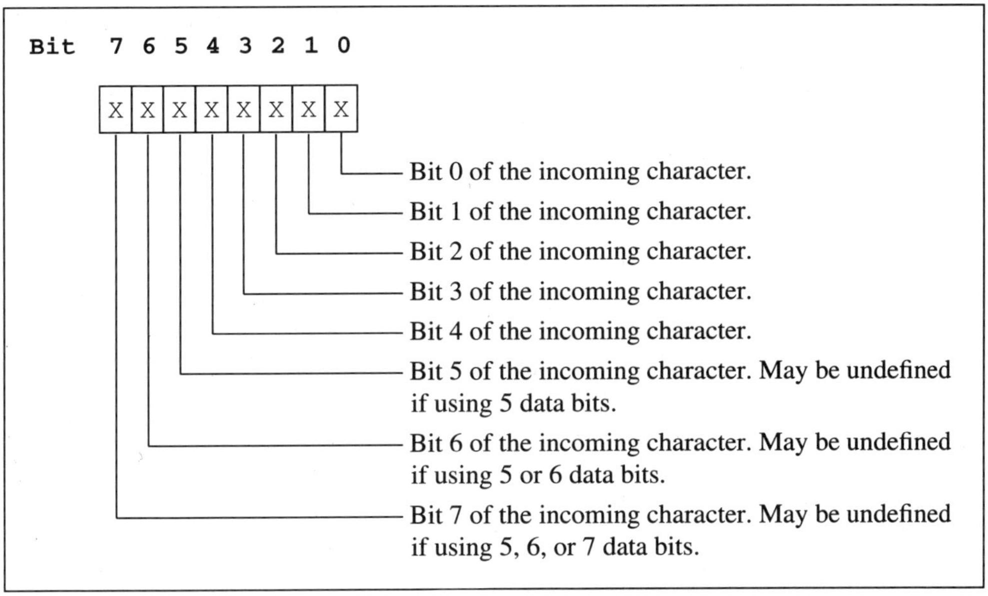

Figure 1.11 *The 8250 UART's Receiver Buffer Register (RBR).*

Register 0—The Transmitter Holding Register (THR)

The UART's *Transmitter Holding Register* (*THR*) is used to transmit a character of data out the serial interface. It shares the UART's first register with the RBR and can be addressed by writing to the serial port's base register port. For COM1, the THR can be written to by sending a value out port **3F8H**. Figure 1.12 illustrates how the character of data is sent to the UART.

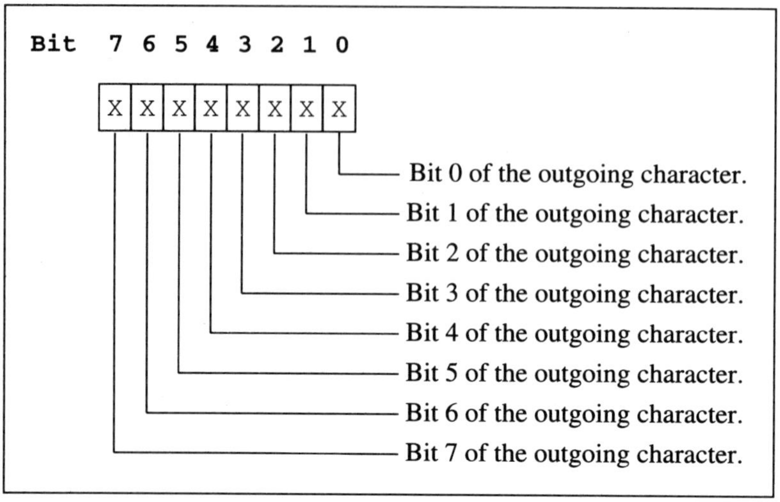

Figure 1.12 *The 8250 UART's Transmitter Holding Register (THR).*

Register 1—The Interrupt Enable Register (IER)

The UART's *Interrupt Enable Register* (*IER*) is used to enable interrupts. It can be addressed by either writing to or reading from the serial port's base register port plus one. For COM1, the IER can be written to or read from by sending a value out or fetching a value from port **3F9H**. Figure 1.13 illustrates the functions that are performed by the IER register's bits.

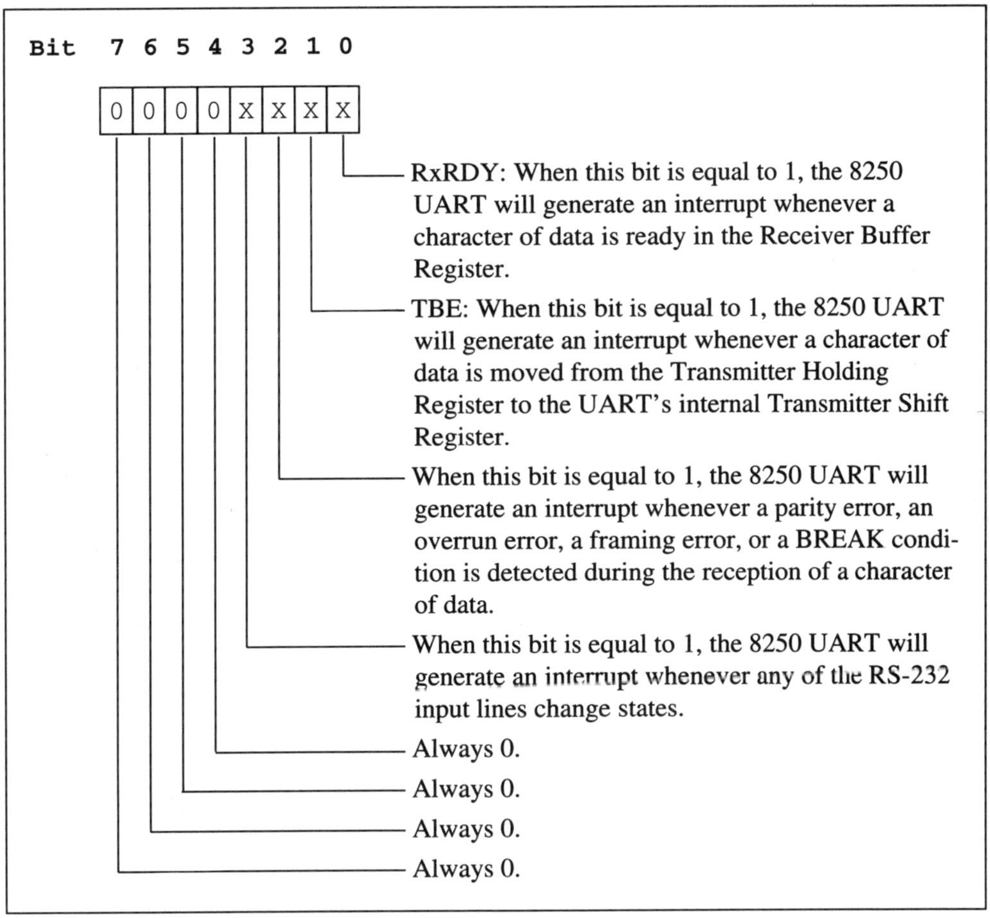

Figure 1.13 *The 8250 UART's Interrupt Enable Register (IER).*

Register 2—The Interrupt Identification Register (IIR)

The UART's *Interrupt Identification Register* (*IIR*) is used to determine what, if any, interrupts may have occurred. It can be addressed by reading from the serial port's base register port plus two. For COM1, The IIR can be read from by fetching a value from port **3FAH**. Figure 1.14 illustrates the interrupts that can be identified by reading the IIR.

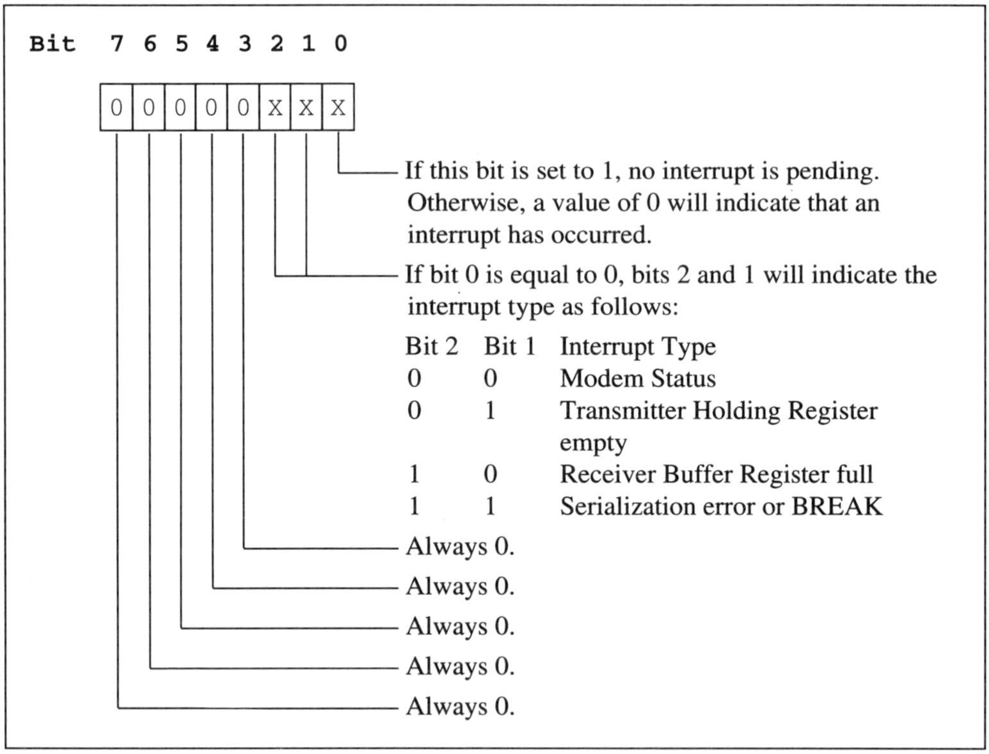

Figure 1.14 *The 8250 UART's Interrupt Identification Register (IIR).*

Register 3—The Line Control Register (LCR)

The UART's *Line Control Register* (*LCR*) is used to set such things as the number of data bits, the number of stop bits, the parity setting, and so on. It can be addressed by either writing to or reading from the serial port's base register plus three. For COM1, the LCR can be written to or read from by sending a value to or fetching a value from port **3FBH**. Figure 1.15 illustrates the functions that are performed by the LCR's bits.

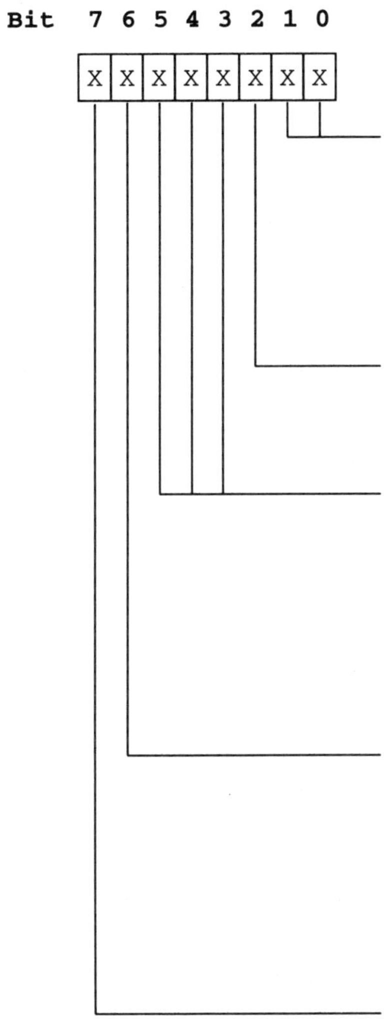

Bits 1 and 0 specify the number of data bits to be used as follows:

Bit 1	Bit 0	Number of Data Bits
0	0	5
0	1	6
1	0	7
1	1	8

If this bit is equal to 0, 1 stop bit will be used. Otherwise, a bit equal to 1 will generate 2 stop bits. **Note**: If 5 data bits are being used and this bit is equal to 1, the UART will use 1½ stop bits.

Bits 5, 4, and 3 specify the parity setting to be used as follows:

Bit 5	Bit 4	Bit 3	Parity
0	0	0	NONE
0	0	1	ODD
0	1	1	EVEN
1	0	1	MARK
1	1	1	SPACE

BREAK: If this bit is equal to 1, the UART will force the TD line to a logical 0 state. If this condition remains in effect for the length of time it would take to transmit one complete character of data, the serial device on the other end of the line will treat it as a BREAK condition. This bit should be left to a 0 value at all times unless a BREAK condition is desired.

Divisor Latch Access Bit (DLAB): When this bit is set to 1, the UART's RBR/THR register will act as the Baud Rate Divisor Latch's Least Significant Byte Register and the UART's IER register will act as the Baud Rate Divisor Latch's Most Significant Byte Register. The DLL and DLM registers will be explained in detail later on in this chapter. Unless the baud rate is being set, this bit should always be set to 0. Otherwise, there is no way to access the RBR/THR and IER registers.

Figure 1.15 *The 8250 UART's Line Control Register (LCR).*

Register 4—The Modem Control Register (MCR)

The UART's *Modem Control Register* (*MCR*) is used to set such things as the RTS line, the DTR line, enabling the UART's interrupts, and so on. It can be addressed by either writing to or reading from the serial port's base register plus four. For COM1, the MCR can be written to or read from by sending a value to or fetching a value from port **3FCH**. Figure 1.16 illustrates the functions that are performed by the MCR's bits.

```
Bit  7 6 5 4 3 2 1 0
     0 0 0 X X X X X
```

Data Terminal Ready (DTR): If this bit is equal to 1, the RS-232 serial interface's DTR line will be set to a logical 1. If this bit is equal to 0, the RS-232 serial interface's DTR line will be set to a logical 0.

Request To Send (RTS): If this bit is equal to 1, the RS-232 serial interface's RTS line will be set to a logical 1. If this bit is equal to 0, the RS-232 serial interface's RTS line will be set to a logical 0.

General Purpose Output #1 (GPO1): This is a user defined output. On the IBM PC, this can reset some internal modems by setting this bit to 1.

General Purpose Output #2 (GPO2): This is a user defined output. On the IBM PC, you must set this bit to 1 before any of the UART's interrupts that have been enabled by the IER will take effect. Actually, there are a few other steps that must be done to get a UART's interrupts working on a PC. The complete details about enabling serial communications-related interrupts are presented in Chapter 4.

Local Loopback Test: By setting this bit to 1, the 8250 UART will be placed in a local loopback state. Any data that is sent out through the transmitter will be returned by the UART as a received character. Under normal operation, this bit should always be set to 0.

Always 0.

Always 0.

Always 0.

Figure 1.16 *The 8250's Modem Control Register (MCR).*

Register 5—The Line Status Register (LSR)

The UART's *Line Status Register* (*LSR*) is used by the UART to report such things as the availability of received data, errors, and the completed transmission of data. It can be addressed by reading from the serial port's base register plus five. For COM1, the LSR can be read from by reading a value from port **3FDH**. Figure 1.17 illustrates the information that is provided by the LSR's bits.

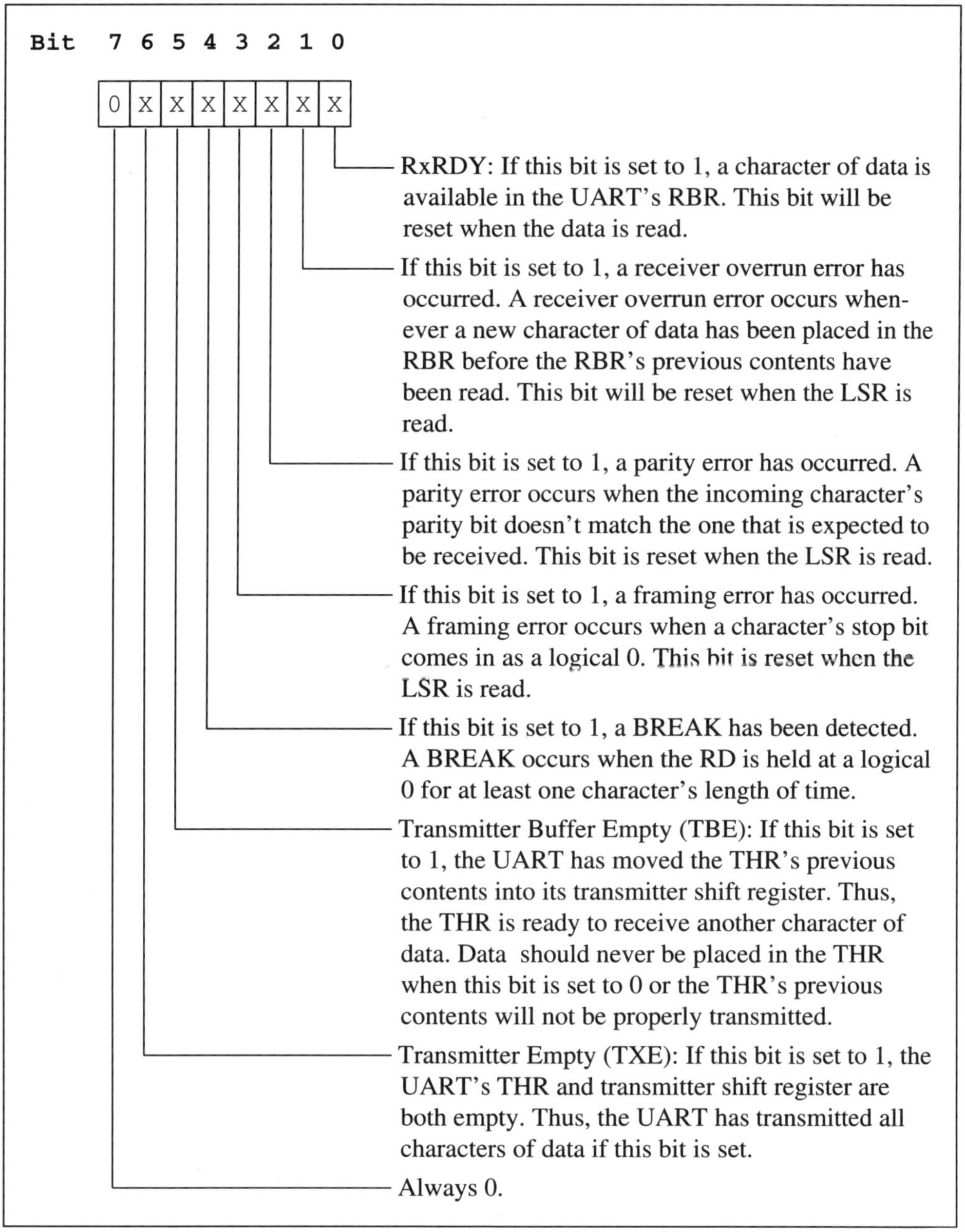

Figure 1.17 *The 8250's Line Status Register (LSR).*

Register 6—The Modem Status Register (MSR)

The UART's *Modem Status Register* (*MSR*) is used by the UART to report such things as the current state of the CTS and DSR lines, if a ring occurs, and if carrier is present. It can be addressed by reading from the serial port's base register plus six. For COM1, the MSR can be read from by reading a value from port **3FEH**. Figure 1.18 illustrates the information that is provided by the MSR's bits.

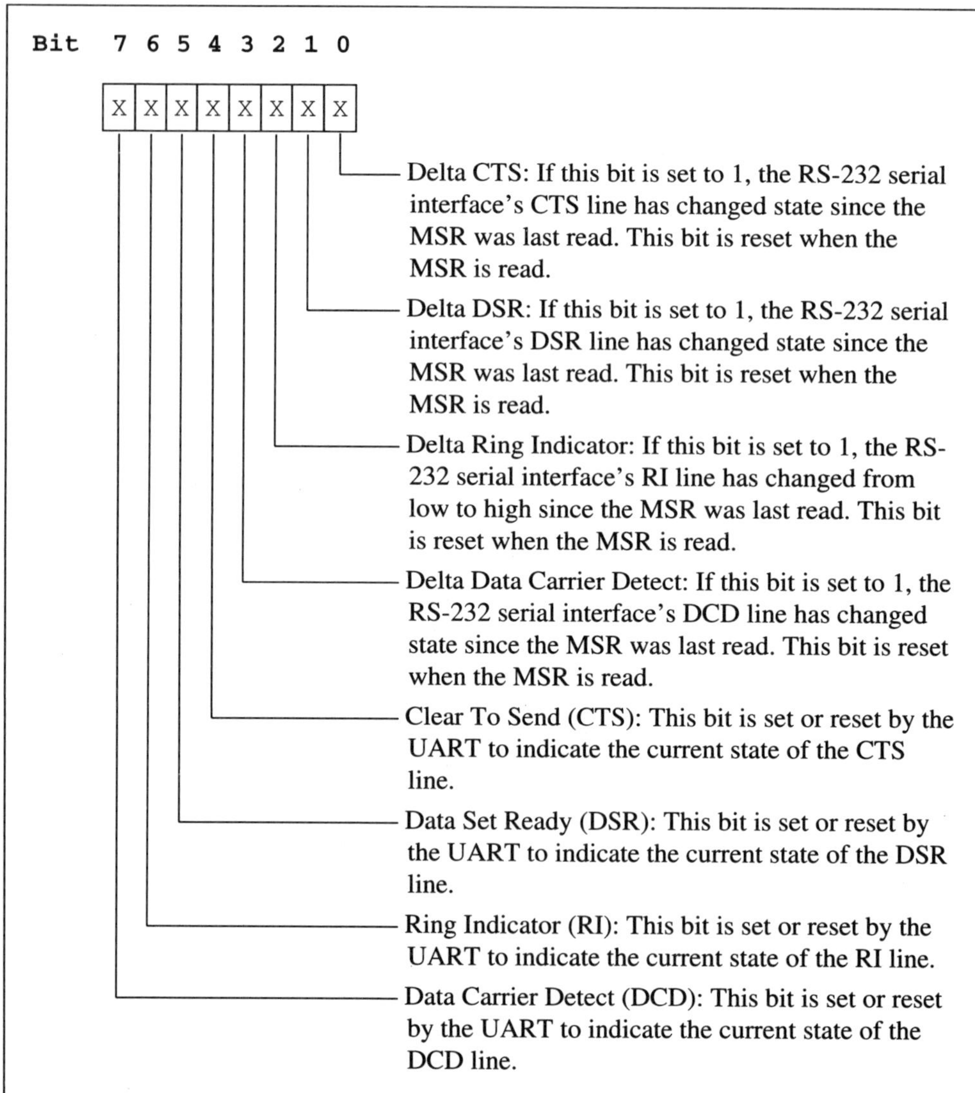

Figure 1.18 *The 8250's Modem Status Register (MSR).*

Register 7—The Scratch Pad

This register is not used by the 8250 UART and doesn't even exist on all versions of the 8250. For this reason, it is best to ignore that it even exists.

Register 8—The Baud Rate LSB Divisor Latch Register (DLL)

The UART's *Baud Rate LSB Divisor Latch Register* (*DLL*) is used to set the UART's least significant byte of the baud rate divisor. In order to read from or write to this register, you must first set the LCR's DLAB bit to 1. By setting the DLAB to 1, the DLL can be addressed by writing to or reading from the serial port's base register. For COM1, the DLL can be written to or read from by sending a value to or reading a value from port **3F8H**. It is vital that the DLAB bit be set back to 0 after access to the DLL is no longer needed. Failure to do so will effectively disable the UART's RBR/THR.

The UART's baud rate divisor is calculated by simply dividing 115,200 by the desired baud rate. The low order eight bits of the result are then placed in the DLL. Figure 1.19 illustrates how the LSB of the baud rate divisor is stored in the DLL.

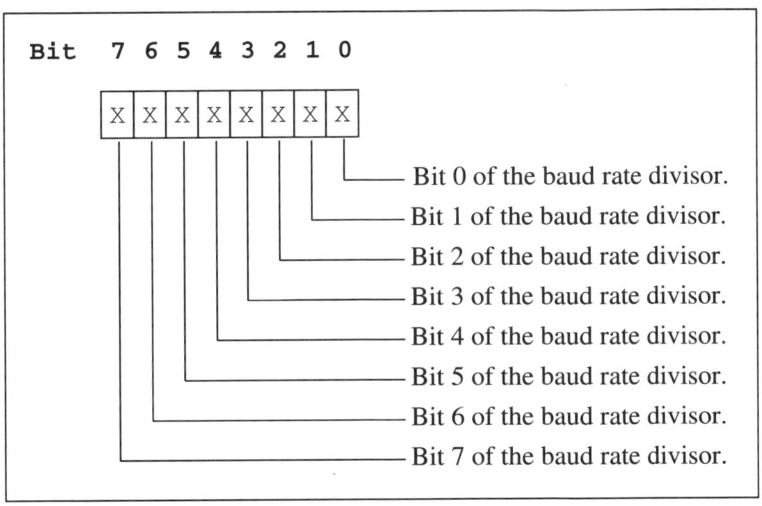

Figure 1.19 *The Baud Rate LSB Divisor Latch Register (DLL).*

Register 9—The Baud Rate MSB Divisor Latch Register (DLM)

The UART's *Baud Rate MSB Divisor Latch Register* (*DLM*) is used to set the UART's most significant byte of the baud rate divisor. In order to read from or write to this register, you must first set the LCR's DLAB bit to 1. By setting the DLAB to 1, the DLM can be addressed by writing to or reading from the serial port's base register plus one. For COM1, the DLM can be written to or read from by sending a value to or reading a value from port **3F9H**. It is vital that the DLAB bit be set back to 0 after access to the DLM is no longer needed. Failure to do so will effectively disable the UART's IER.

The UART's baud rate divisor is calculated by simply dividing 115,200 by the desired baud rate. The high order eight bits of the result are then placed in the DLM. Figure 1.20 illustrates how the MSB of the baud rate divisor is stored in the DLM.

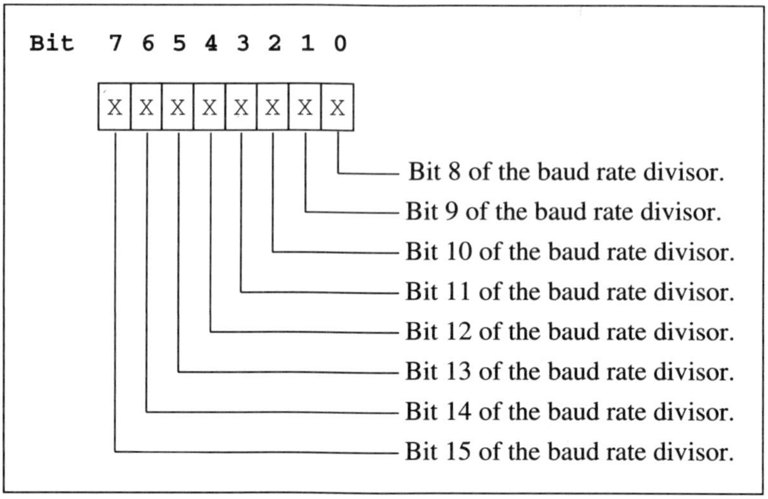

Figure 1.20 *The Baud Rate MSB Divisor Latch Register (DLM).*

The 16550 UART

Although the *16550 UART* is pretty much a pin compatible clone of the 8250 and the 16450 UARTs, it has internal FIFO buffers to buffer both incoming and outgoing characters. These buffers are extremely important when the serial device is being used in a multitasking environment. Let's suppose that a communications program is performing a file transfer as a background task under a multitasking environment. If the modem is slow enough and the CPU is fast enough, no characters will be lost by the CPU switching to and from the communications program. However, let's further suppose what would happen with either a high-speed data link or a slower CPU. It's fairly obvious that something has to give and unfortunately it means that the communications program will not have enough CPU time to grab all of the incoming characters from the UART. Consequently, the 16550 UART's FIFO buffers are important because the UART is able to store a limited number of bytes internally; thus, the communications program doesn't have to be quite so concerned with losing characters. The 16550 UART's transmitter FIFO buffer is 16 bytes in length. The 16550 receiver FIFO buffer is also 16 bytes long, but the receiver FIFO buffer has a software adjustable interrupt threshold. To utilize the 16550 UART's FIFO buffers, they must be enabled via a software command. It is important to note that if the programmer chooses to ignore the 16550 UART's FIFO buffers it is totally software compatible with the 8250 UART; however, utilizing a 16550's FIFO buffers is so easy to do it doesn't make sense not to use them. For the remainder of Chapter 1 we will examine the 16550 UART's registers. You will note that with a few exceptions that are necessary to provide support for its FIFO buffers, the 16550 UART's registers function, for the most part, the same as the 8250 UART's registers.

Register 0—The Receiver Buffer Register (RBR)

When a character of data is received by the 16550 UART, it is assembled and placed in the UART's *Receiver Buffer Register* (*RBR*). The RBR is the UART's first register and can be addressed by reading the serial port's base register port. For COM1, the RBR can be read by fetching a value from port **3F8H**. Figure 1.21 illustrates how a character of data is returned by the UART. Although the RBR will always hold an eight-bit value, you should mask out any bits not used for data links that are using less than eight data bits per character.

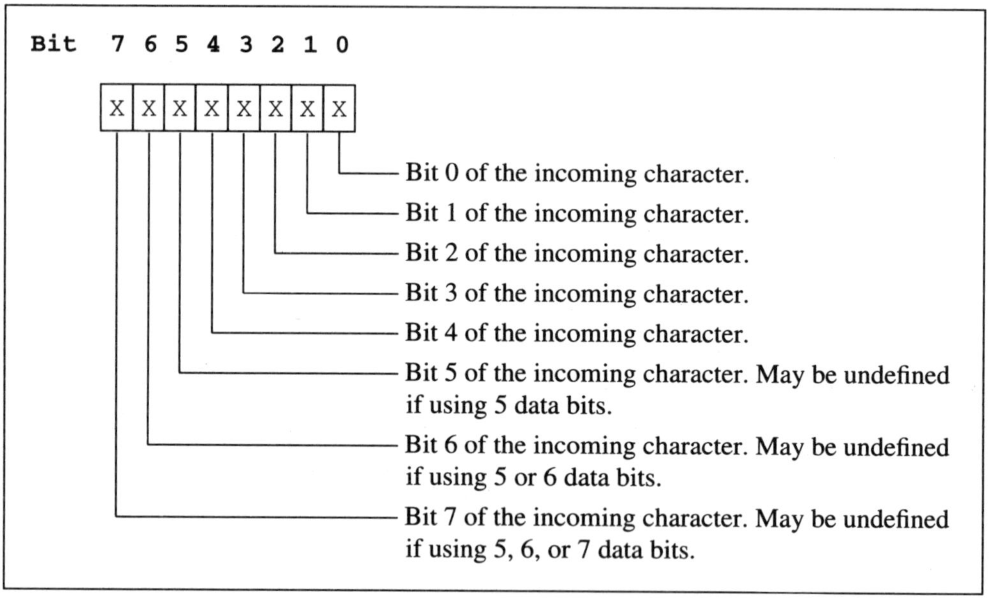

Figure 1.21 *The 16550 UART's Receiver Buffer Register (RBR).*

Register 0—The Transmitter Holding Register (THR)

The UART's *Transmitter Holding Register* (*THR*) is used to transmit a character of data out the serial interface. It shares the UART's first register with the RBR and can be addressed by writing to the serial port's base register port. For COM1, the THR can be written to by sending a value out port **3F8H**. Figure 1.22 illustrates how the character of data is sent to the UART.

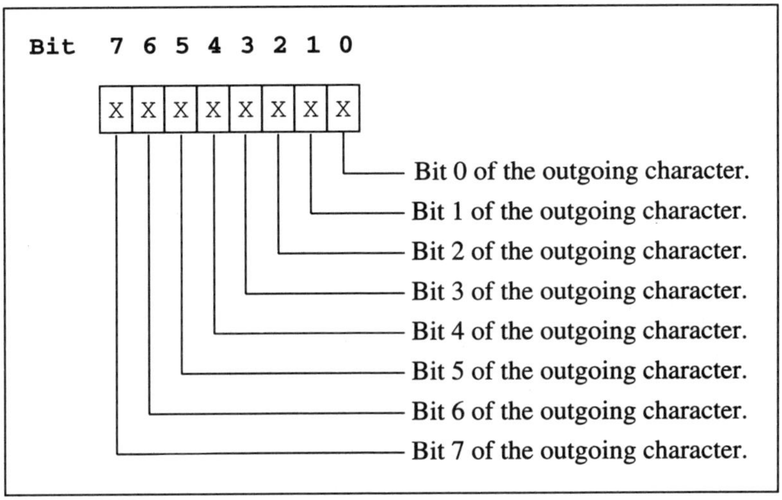

Figure 1.22 *The 16550 UART's Transmitter Holding Register (THR).*

Register 1—The Interrupt Enable Register (IER)

The UART's *Interrupt Enable Register* (*IER*) is used to enable interrupts. It can be addressed by either writing to or reading from the serial port's base register port plus one. For COM1, the IER can be written to or read from by sending a value out or fetching a value from port 3F9H. Figure 1.23 illustrates the functions that are performed by the IER's bits.

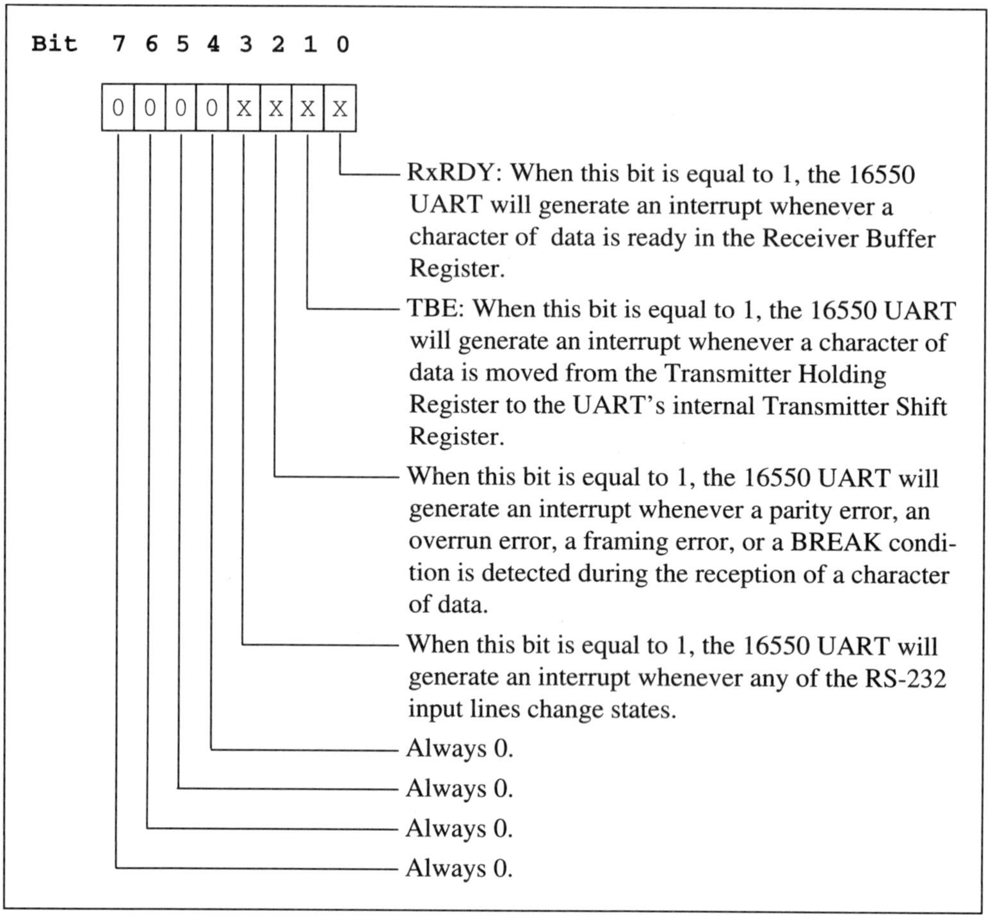

Figure 1.23 *The 16550 UART's Interrupt Enable Register (IER).*

Register 2—The Interrupt Identification Register (IIR)

The UART's *Interrupt Identification Register* (*IIR*) is used to determine what, if any, interrupts may have occurred and if the FIFO buffers are enabled. It can be addressed by reading from the serial port's base register port plus two. For COM1, The IIR can be read from by fetching a value from port **3FAH**. Figure 1.24 illustrates the interrupts that can be identified by reading the IIR.

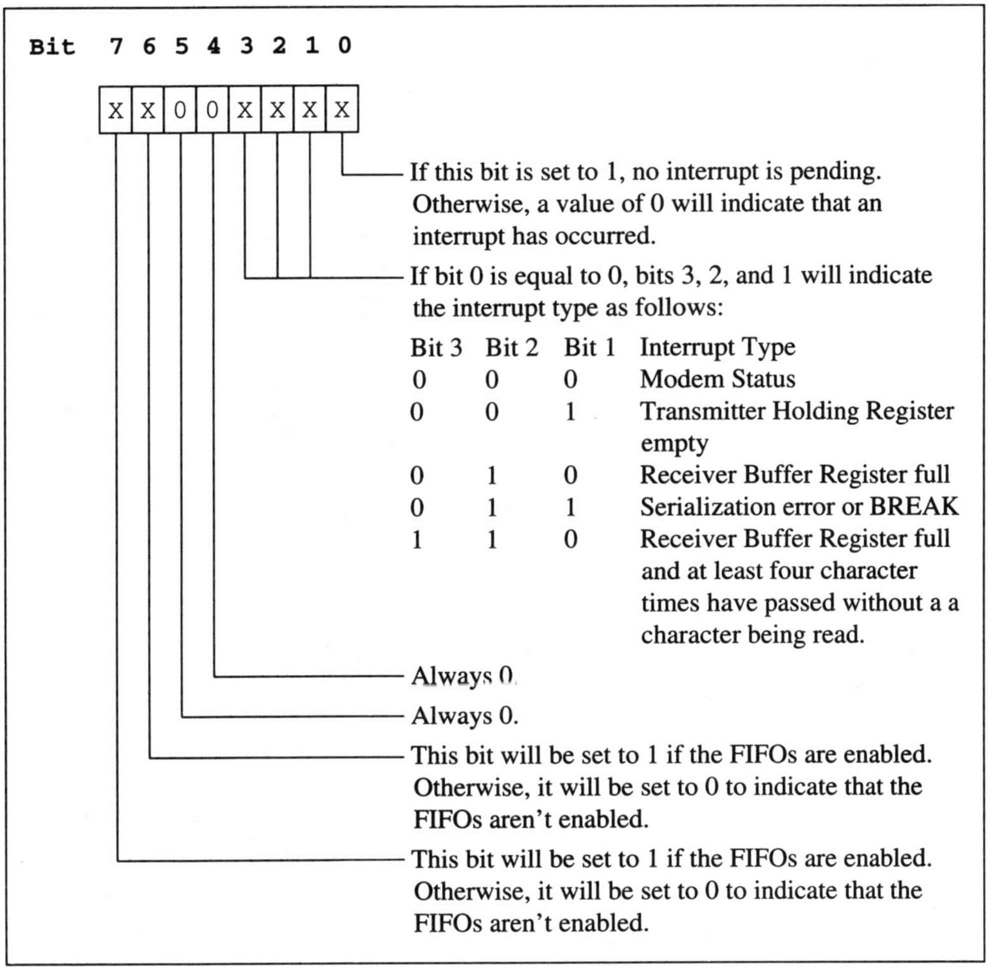

***Figure 1.24** The 16550 UART's Interrupt Identification Register (IIR).*

Register 2—The FIFO Control Register (FCR)

The UART's *FIFO Control Register* (*FCR*) is used to control the FIFO buffers. It can be addressed by writing to the serial port's base register port plus two. For COM1, the FCR can be written to by sending a value to port **3FAH**. Figure 1.25 illustrates the functions that can be performed by writing to the FCR.

```
Bit  7 6 5 4 3 2 1 0
    |X|X|X|X|X|X|X|X|
```

- Bit 0 — FIFO Enable: If this bit is set to 1, the 16550 UARTs FIFO buffers will be enabled. If this bit is set to 0, the 16550 UARTs FIFO will be disabled and the chip will function as a 16450 UART.
- Bit 1 — Receiver FIFO Reset: Setting this bit to 1 will clear the receiver FIFO buffer.
- Bit 2 — Transmitter FIFO Reset: Setting this bit to 1 will clear the transmitter FIFO buffer.
- Bit 3 — DMA Mode Select: This bit should always be set to 0 for the IBM PC and compatibles.
- Bit 4 — Reserved.
- Bit 5 — Reserved.
- Bits 7 and 6 — If the FIFOs are enabled, bits 7 and 6 set the receiver threshold for the receiver FIFO buffer. Simply put, the receiver threshold is the number of bytes that the UART will place in the FIFO buffer before generating a Receiver Buffer Register full interrupt. The receiver threshold can be set to any one of the following values:

Bit 7	Bit 6	Receiver Threshold
0	0	1 byte
0	1	4 bytes
1	0	8 bytes
1	1	14 bytes

Figure 1.25 *The FIFO Control Register (FCR).*

Register 3—The Line Control Register (LCR)

The UART's Line Control Register (LCR) is used to set such things as the number of data bits, the number of stop bits, the parity setting, and so on. It can be addressed by either writing to or reading from the serial port's base register plus three. For COM1, the LCR can be written to or read from by sending a value to or fetching a value from port 3FBH. Figure 1.26 illustrates the functions that are performed by the LCR register's bits.

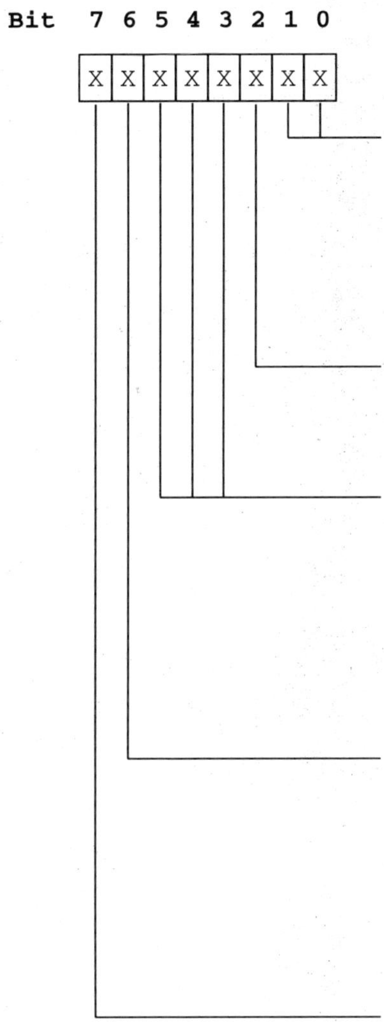

Bits 1 and 0 specify the number of data bits to be used as follows:

Bit 1	Bit 0	Number of Data Bits
0	0	5
0	1	6
1	0	7
1	1	8

If this bit is equal to 0, 1 stop bit will be used. Otherwise, a bit equal to 1 will generate 2 stop bits. **Note**: If 5 data bits are being used and this bit is equal to 1, the UART will use 1½ stop bits.

Bits 5, 4, and 3 specify the parity setting to be used as follows:

Bit 5	Bit 4	Bit 3	Parity
0	0	0	NONE
0	0	1	ODD
0	1	1	EVEN
1	0	1	MARK
1	1	1	SPACE

BREAK: If this bit is equal to 1, the UART will force the TD line to a logical 0 state. If this condition remains in effect for the length of time it would take to transmit one complete character of data, the serial device on the other end of the line will treat it as a BREAK condition. This bit should be left to a 0 value at all times unless a BREAK condition is desired.

Divisor Latch Access Bit (DLAB): When this bit is set to 1, the UART's RBR/THR register will act as the Baud Rate Divisor Latch's Least Significant Byte Register and the UART's IER register will act as the Baud Rate Divisor Latch's Most Significant Byte Register. The DLL and DLM registers will be explained in detail later on in this chapter. Unless the baud rate is being set, this bit should always be set to 0. Otherwise, there is no way to access the RBR/THR and IER registers.

Figure 1.26 *The 16550 UART's Line Control Register (LCR).*

Register 4—The Modem Control Register (MCR)

The UART's *Modem Control Register* (*MCR*) is used to set such things as the RTS line, the DTR line, enabling the UART's interrupts, and so on. It can be addressed by either writing to or reading from the serial port's base register plus four. For COM1, the MCR can be written to or read from by sending a value to or fetching a value from port **3FCH**. Figure 1.27 illustrates the functions that are performed by the MCR's bits.

Bit	7	6	5	4	3	2	1	0
	0	0	0	X	X	X	X	X

- Bit 0 — Data Terminal Ready (DTR): If this bit is equal to 1, the RS-232 serial interface's DTR line will be set to a logical 1. If this bit is equal to 0, the RS-232 serial interface's DTR line will be set to a logical 0.
- Bit 1 — Request To Send (RTS): If this bit is equal to 1, the RS-232 serial interface's RTS line will be set to a logical 1. If this bit is equal to 0, the RS-232 serial interface's RTS line will be set to a logical 0.
- Bit 2 — General Purpose Output #1 (GPO1): This is a user defined output. On the IBM PC, this can reset some internal modems by setting this bit to 1.
- Bit 3 — General Purpose Output #2 (GPO2): This is a user defined output. On the IBM PC, you must set this bit to 1 before any of the UART's interrupts that have been enabled by the IER will take effect. Actually, there are a few other steps that must be done to get a UART's interrupts working on a PC. The complete details about enabling serial communication related interrupts is presented in Chapter Four.
- Bit 4 — Local Loopback Test: By setting this bit to 1, the 16550 UART will be placed in a local loopback state. Any data that is sent out through the transmitter will be returned by the UART as a received character. Under normal operation, this bit should always be set to 0.
- Bit 5 — Always 0.
- Bit 6 — Always 0.
- Bit 7 — Always 0.

Figure 1.27 *The 16550's Modem Control Register (MCR).*

Register 5—The Line Status Register (LSR)

The UART's *Line Status Register* (*LSR*) is used by the UART to report such things as the availability of received data, errors, and the completed transmission of data. It can be addressed by reading from the serial port's base register plus five. For COM1, the LSR can be read from by reading a value from port **3FDH**. Figure 1.28 illustrates the information that is provided by the LSR's bits.

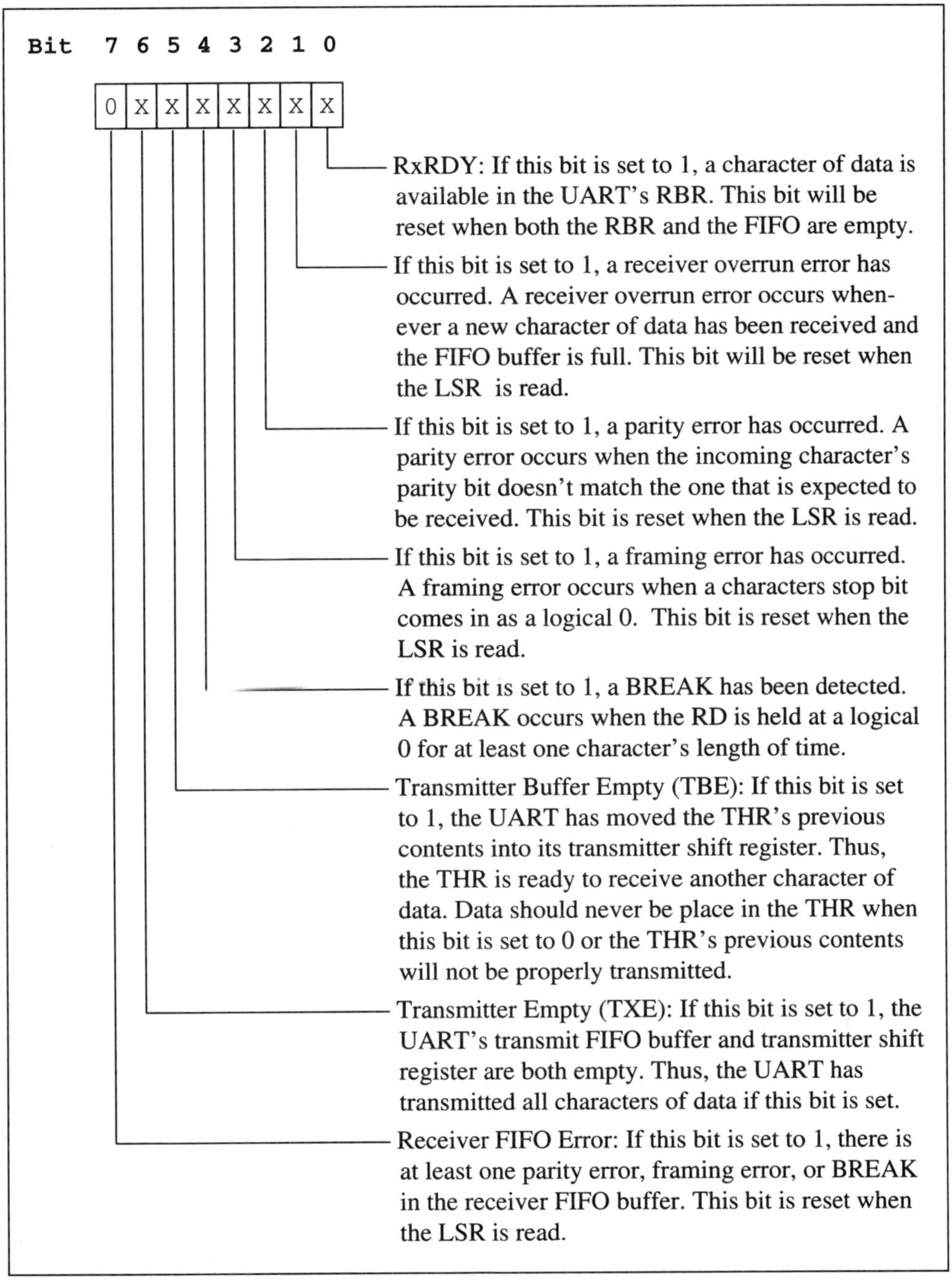

***Figure 1.28** The 16550's Line Status Register (LSR).*

Register 6—The Modem Status Register (MSR)

The UART's *Modem Status Register* (*MSR*) is used by the UART to report such things as the current state of the CTS and DSR lines, if a ring occurs, and if carrier is present. It can be addressed by reading from the serial port's base register plus six. For COM1, the MSR can be read by reading a value from port **3FEH**. Figure 1.29 illustrates the information that is provided by the MSR's bits.

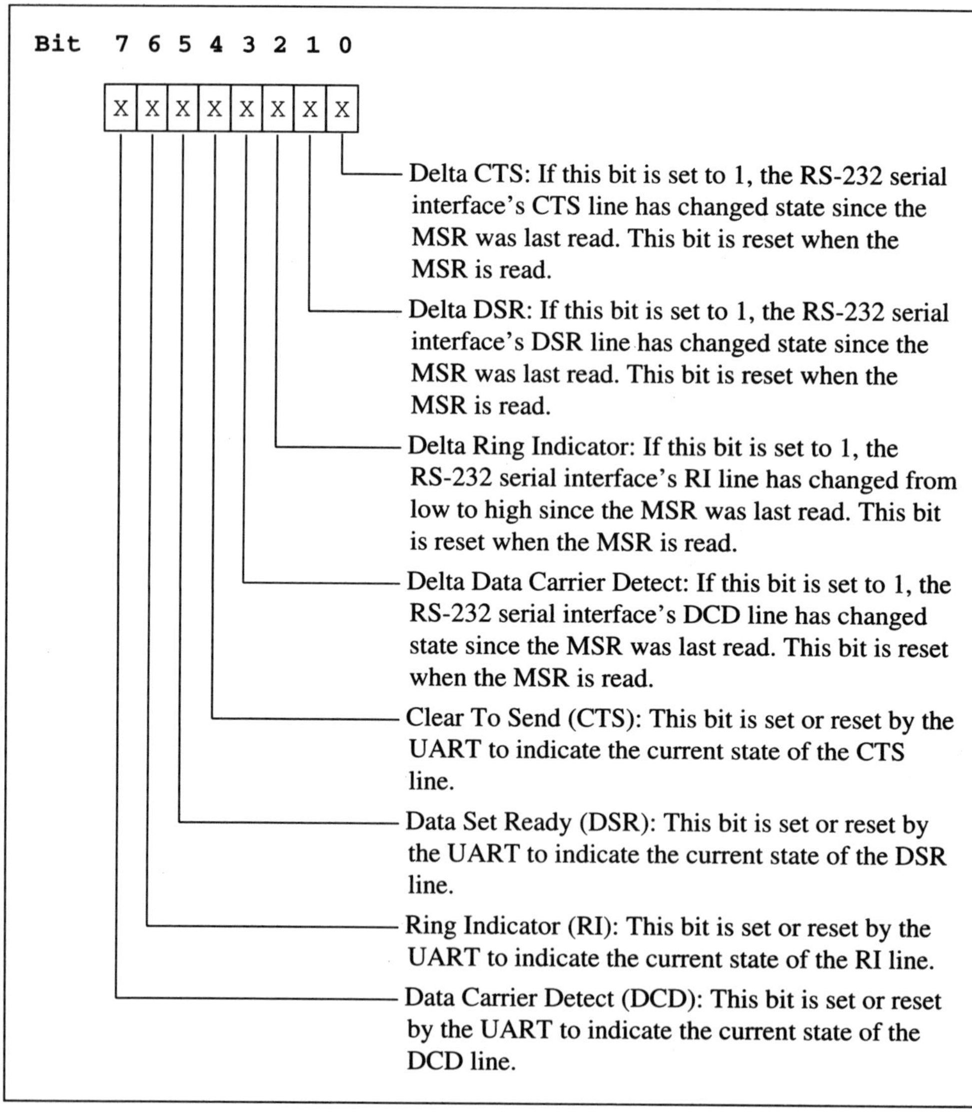

Figure 1.29 *The 16550's Modem Status Register (MSR).*

Register 7—The Scratch Pad

This register is not used by the 16550 UART. Because it doesn't exist on all versions of the 8250 UART, it is best to just ignore that it is even available.

Register 8—The Baud Rate LSB Divisor Latch Register (DLL)

The UART's *Baud Rate LSB Divisor Latch Register* (*DLL*) is used to set the UART's least significant byte of the baud rate divisor. In order to read or write to this register, you must first set the LCR's DLAB bit to 1. By setting the DLAB to 1, the DLL can be addressed by writing to or reading from the serial port's base register. For COM1, the DLL can be written to or read from by sending a value to or reading a value from port **3F8H**. It is vital that the DLAB bit be set back to 0 after access to the DLL is no longer needed. Failure to do so will effectively disable the UART's RBR/THR.

The UART's baud rate divisor is calculated by simply dividing 115,200 by the desired baud rate. The low order eight bits of the result are then placed in the DLL. Figure 1.30 illustrates how the LSB of the baud rate divisor is stored in the DLL.

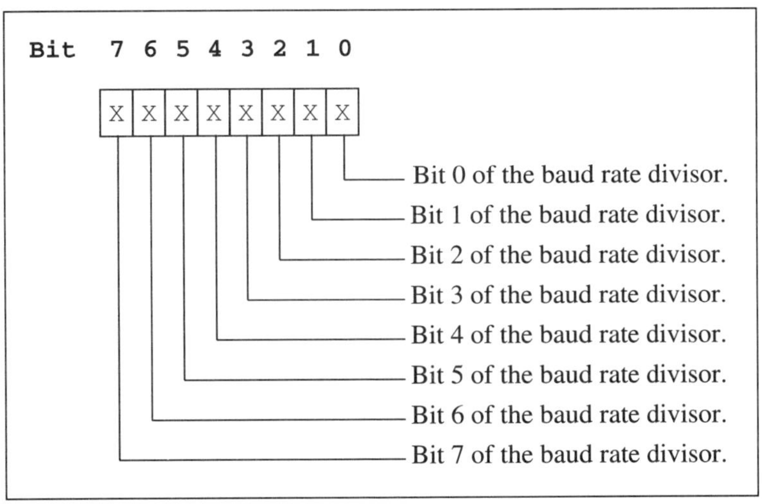

Figure 1.30 *The Baud Rate LSB Divisor Latch Register (DLL).*

Register 9—The Baud Rate MSB Divisor Latch Register (DLM)

The UART's *Baud Rate MSB Divisor Latch Register* (*DLM*) is used to set the UART's most significant byte of the baud rate divisor. In order to read from or write to this register, you must first set the LCR's DLAB bit to 1. By setting the DLAB to 1, the DLM can be addressed by writing to or reading from the serial port's base register plus one. For COM1, the DLM can be written to or read from by sending a value to or reading a value from port **3F9H**. It is vital that the DLAB bit be set back to 0 after access to the DLM is no longer needed. Failure to do so will effectively disable the UART's IER.

The UART's baud rate divisor is calculated by simply dividing 115,200 by the desired baud rate. The high order eight bits of the result are then placed in the DLM. Figure 1.31 illustrates how the MSB of the baud rate divisor is stored in the DLM.

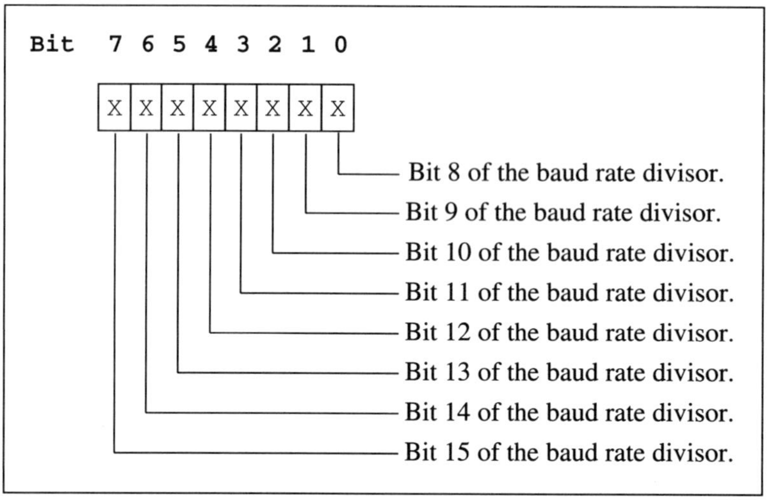

Figure 1.31 *The Baud Rate MSB Divisor Latch Register (DLM).*

Summary

Chapter 1 has discussed such topics as the RS-232 serial interface, start bits, data bits, parity bits, stop bits, and how serial data is actually transmitted. Additionally, an in-depth look at UARTs was presented with a complete register-by-register description of the 8250 and 16550 UARTs.

Chapter 2

The Modem

In Chapter 1, you saw how the RS-232 serial interface is used to communicate between a computer and a serial device. In this chapter, we will explore the most important serial device, the *modem*. This chapter explains the types of modems that are available, the international standards for transmitting data at certain baud rates, the **AT** command set, flow control, error correction, data compression, and more.

What is the Modem?

The word, *modem*, is derived from modulator/demodulator. Simply put, a modem converts digital computer signals into audio tones and is also able to reconvert incoming audio tones back into digital computer signals. Thus, the modem makes it possible to transmit serial data over great distances using simple everyday dial-up telephone lines.

Internal and External Modems

Modems for the IBM PC and compatibles come in two varieties: *internal modems* and *external modems*. An internal modem has a serial port built right into its circuit board. The internal modem's serial port is usually built around either an 8250 UART (or even more likely the high-speed 8250 clone, the 16450 UART) or a 16550 UART. The internal modem's circuit card is shaped as an 8-bit IBM PC XT compatible expansion card and can be plugged directly into a PC compatible computer's expansion slot.

An external modem is a completely self-contained unit with it's own power supply and RS-232 interface. It is connected to the computer via an RS-232 serial cable. Obviously, the computer must have a free serial port in order to be able to use an external modem with it.

What are the advantages of one type of modem over the other? An internal modem offers two very important advantages: (1) it's generally much cheaper than a comparable external modem and, (2) it has its own serial port built right in. The main advantage of an external modem is its versatility. It can be used with any computer that has a compatible RS-232 serial interface. Furthermore, it can be moved from one machine to another by simply unplugging it from one machine and replugging it into the new machine. Unlike an internal modem, which can only be used with IBM PCs and compatibles, an external modem can be used with virtually any type of computer.

International Baud Rate Standards

Back when the IBM PC was first introduced, 300-baud modems were considered state-of-the-art. Most 300-baud modems conform to the Bell 103 North American standard. This standard (as do all baud rate standards) sets guidelines for manufacturers to follow when building their modems to insure that a modem made by one manufacturer will be able to talk to a modem made by another manufacturer. Besides the Bell 103 300-baud standard, there is an international 300-baud standard specified by the Consultative Committee for International Telephone and Telegraph (CCITT) known as the *CCITT V.21 standard.* The 1200-baud North American standard is the Bell 212A standard and the international 600- and 1200-baud standard is the *CCITT V.22 standard.* All 2400-baud modems should conform to the CCITT V.22bis standard. The international standard for 4800- and 9600-baud modems is the *CCITT V.32 standard* and, finally, the international standard for 4800-, 7200-, 9600-, 12000-, and 14400-baud modems is the *CCITT V.32bis standard.* Although it isn't a true international standard, the *US Robotics HST specification* is in very wide spread use around the world. The USR-HST "standard" provides for communication at 4800, 7200, 9600, 12000, and 14400 baud; however, it is a proprietary communications standard and can only be used between two US Robotics HST or HST/Dual Standard modems. Although the new CCITT V.32bis standard is a superior method for high-speed communications, USR-HST modems are in such wide spread use throughout the world that they are still a very formidable force to be reckoned with.

Programming a Modem

Whenever a modem is turned on it is in one of two distinct states: the *online mode* or the *command mode*. The online mode is when a modem is connected with another modem. The command mode is when the modem will accept commands from the computer to instruct the modem as to what it should do next. Almost all modems that are manufactured today use the **AT** command set to send commands to a modem.

The **AT** command set was originally developed by Hayes Microcomputer Products, Inc. for their line of modems. Since it's introduction, it has become the defacto standard and you would be hard pressed to find a modem that doesn't understand the **AT** command set. The **AT** command set gets its name from the fact that all modem commands are preceded by **AT**, which stands for ATtention. For example, the command to reset a modem is **Z**. So you would issue the command **ATZ** to reset a modem that speaks the **AT** command set. You should note that the command could be issued by a user from the keyboard using a terminal program or could just as easily be sent to the modem by an application program.

If you are unfamiliar with the **AT** command set, you should review the material that is presented in Appendix B in this text, which presents detailed descriptions for the basic **AT** command set. You should note that many modems, in particular high-speed modems, have extensive **AT** command sets and vary a great deal from one manufacturer to the next. Consequently, it is beyond the scope of this book to even attempt to present a definitive description of every **AT** command you may run across in the read world of serial communications. However, Appendix B does cover all of the essential commands for a "Hayes-compatible modem."

Error-Correcting Modems

Many of today's modems are *error-correcting modems*, although, to call a modem an error-correcting modem is somewhat of a misnomer. Many people are under the mistaken impression that an error-correcting modem can detect an error in the incoming data and then magically correct it. In reality, an error-correcting modem can indeed detect an error, but it requests the sending modem to resend the incorrect data. This is accomplished by sending data in blocks. In addition to the data being sent, the blocks contain a *CRC* for each block. A *CRC* (*Cyclic Redundancy Check*) is a special mathematical algorithm that generates a very unique value for a block of data based on the block's contents. The receiving modem calculates a new CRC for the block of data it received and checks it against the CRC that was transmitted with the block. If the CRCs match, the receiving modem can safely assume the block of data was sent without error. Otherwise, the receiving modem will tell the transmitting modem to resend the block because nonmatching CRCs have indicated that a transmission error has occurred.

As with the international standards for baud rates, there are similar standards for error correcting modems. The most popular error correcting standard is the *Microcom Networking Protocol* (*MNP*), originally developed by Microcom, Inc. Most MNP modems provide four distinct error correcting classes as follows:

MNP Class 1. Data is transmitted in blocks in only one direction at a time. You should note that modems transmitting data using MNP Class 1 will only transmit data about 70 percent as fast as modems that are transmitting without error correction.

MNP Class 2. Data is transmitted in blocks in both directions at the same time. You should note that modems transmitting data using MNP Class 2 will only transmit data about 84 percent as fast as modems that are transmitting without error correction.

MNP Class 3. Like MNP Class 2, MNP Class 3 can send data in both directions at once. Furthermore, the start and stop bits are stripped from the data block by the transmitting modem and replaced by the receiving modem before they are passed to the UART. By stripping the start and stop bits, modems that are transmitting data using MNP Class 3 can transmit data 8 percent faster than modems that are transmitting without error correction.

MNP Class 4. MNP Class 4 is simply an enhanced version of MNP Class 3. MNP Class 4 can increase or decrease it's block size depending on the quality of the connection and MNP Class 4 uses a smaller header than MNP Class 3. Because of the improvements MNP Class 4 has to offer, it can be used to transmit data an astounding 20 percent faster than data that is being transmitted with nonerror-correcting modems.

The international standard for error correction is the *CCITT V.42 standard.* This standard specifies an error correction protocol called *Link Access Procedures for Modems (LAPM)* and is very similar to MNP Class 4. It is important to note that the CCITT V.42 standard supports MNP Classes 1 to 4 and will fall back to one of these classes if a modem with V.42 error correction can't establish a LAPM connection.

Data Compression

Besides providing an internal error correction ability, many of today's modems can actually compress data before transmission to even further increase a data link's throughput. The two most widely used standards for data compression are *MNP Class 5* and *CCITT V.42bis*. Both perform pretty much the same function: the transmitting modem compresses the data before sending it and the receiving modem uncompresses the data upon its receipt. However, CCITT V.42bis data compression is superior to MNP Class 5 because it monitors all data to see if it has grown in size after compressing it. You may be scratching your head at this point and wondering how compressed data can actually grow in size. This strange phenomena can occur when you try to compress data that has already been compressed. Simply put, compressing already compressed data will more often than not make it grow in size. Because most data that is transmitted today is already compressed by some type of compression utility, MNP Class 5 can take longer to transmit a compressed file than if the file was sent on a modem without using MNP Class 5. On the other hand, CCITT V.42bis data compression will send a block of data uncompressed if it grows in size after compression. Therefore, CCITT V.42bis will never increase a file's overall size and can greatly increase the data link's throughput on any data that hasn't been previously compressed. Under ideal conditions, MNP Class 5 and CCITT V.42bis can transmit data four times faster than a transmission that doesn't use data compression. You should note that in order to use MNP Class 5 the two modems must have an MNP Class 4 link established and to use CCITT V.42bis the two modems must have a LAPM link established.

Flow Control

When transmitting data over modems, serial communications programs will often use *flow control* to control the flow of data between the two serial devices. There are two basic forms of flow control: *software flow control* and *hardware flow control*. As its name implies, software flow control controls the flow of data through software. The two communications programs will usually use what is called *XON/XOFF* flow control to accomplish software flow control. When a receiving program needs to temporarily pause the transmitter it sends an XOFF character (13H) to the transmitting modem. When it wants the transmitter to resume with the data flow, it sends an XON (11H) character. You should note that many communications programs recognize the receipt of any character after an XOFF as an XON character. This can prevent the transmitter from being put on permanent hold due to an XON character that is corrupted during transmission and isn't properly recognized by the paused modem.

The most common form of hardware flow control that is used for serial communications is *RTS/CTS flow control*. Whenever the DTE wants to transmit data over the modem, the communications program asserts the RTS line and checks the status of the CTS line. If the modem sees that RTS is asserted and it is ready to transmit data, it will assert the CTS line and the DTE will be free to send the character of data through the serial interface to the modem. It is important to note that most error-correcting modems require RTS/CTS flow control. A similar form of hardware flow control is performed by using the DTR and DSR lines; however, *DTR/DSR flow control* is not used very often for transmitting data over a modem.

Locked Serial Ports

Before error-correcting and high-speed modems burst on the scene, a communications program would always set the DTE's (in the case of a PC, the UART's) baud rate to the connection rate of the modem. For example, a modem calls out at 2400 baud and makes a 1200-baud connection. The modem sends a CONNECT 1200-baud message to the DTE and lowers its own baud rate to 1200 baud. The DTE's communications program sees the CONNECT 1200-baud message and sets the UART's baud rate to 1200. Thus, everything will hum along just nicely at 1200 baud.

However, with error correction and data compression, it is possible for the modem to receive data at speeds that can reach four times the actual connection rate. Obviously, the UART is not going to be able to keep up with the modem if its baud rate is always set by the communication program to the connection rate. Although this may seem like an insurmountable problem, the solution is extremely simple. To account for the possibility of data being received so fast that the UART can't keep up with it, error-correcting modems and almost all serial communications programs allow the user to **lock** the serial port. By locking the serial port, the communications program sets the baud rate to a high value and leaves it there no matter what speed the actual connection may be made at. For example, it is quite common to lock a 9600-baud modem at 38400 baud. Therefore, when the modem makes a connection at 9600 baud, it will pass the normal CONNECT 9600-baud message to the DTE. Unlike before, however, the communication program will not set the UART's baud rate to the connection rate. Instead, the UART-to-modem rate will stay at the locked baud rate of 38400. The two modems will be sending data back and forth at 9600 baud, but should the receiving modem start receiving data faster than the connection rate (this is almost always the case with an MNP Class 4 or V.42 error-correcting connection) it will be able to pass the data to the DTE as fast as it comes in without worrying that data may be lost somewhere in the shuffle.

The Null Modem

Although modems can be used to communicate between computers in the same room as easily as they can be used to communicate between computers that are thousands of miles apart, high-speed modems don't come particularly cheap and obviously you are going to want to transfer data between two computers in close proximity as fast as possible. This type of need can usually be best addressed with a simple hardware device called the *null modem*. The null modem is simply a special connector that you plug serial cables from two computers into, which fools them into thinking that they are connected by two modems. Figure 2.1 illustrates a common method for wiring a null modem. As this illustration shows, the null modem functions mainly because the TD and RD lines are crossed and the hardware handshaking lines are all wired in a way that simulates how a modem would assert them if each of the two computers were actually connected with modems.

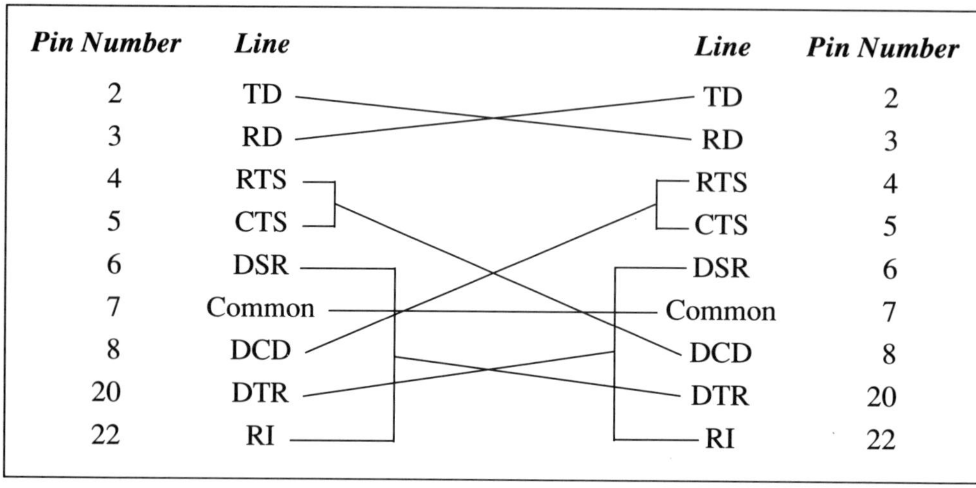

Figure 2.1 *The Null Modem.*

Summary

Chapter 2 introduced you to such topics as what a modem is, the international baud rate standards, the **AT** command set, error-correcting protocols, data compression protocols, locked serial ports, and the null modem.

Chapter 3

The ROM BIOS Routines

Before we start to build the **SERIAL** toolbox, it might be instructive to first look at how serial communications programs shouldn't be written. Accordingly, this chapter takes a look at the serial communications routines that are offered by the *ROM BIOS*. After examining how the ROM BIOS routines work, you will see how totally inadequate they are in meeting today's serial communications needs.

The Serial Routines

The ROM BIOS offers four routines for serial communications:

(1) A routine to initialize a serial port
(2) A routine to write a character to the serial port
(3) A routine to read a character from a serial port, and
(4) A routine to fetch the current status of a serial port.

As with all other ROM BIOS routines, the serial communication routines are called as a software interrupt. In this case, the call to the ROM BIOS serial communication routines is performed with an *INT 14H* interrupt call. Depending on the routine in question, the CPU's registers are loaded with certain parameters before making the INT 14H call. After completing their intended task, the serial communication routines return values in the CPU registers.

The first of the ROM BIOS serial communications routines is an *Initialize Serial Port routine*. Figure 3.1 illustrates how this routine is called and any values that are returned by this routine.

INT 14H, Function 00H – Initialize Serial Port

Description:

This ROM BIOS routine initializes a serial port's baud rate, number of data bits, parity setting, number of stop bits, and returns the serial port's current status.

Call With:

AH 00H (The function number.)

AL The serial port's initialization values as follows:

Bits 7 6 5 4 3 2 1 0

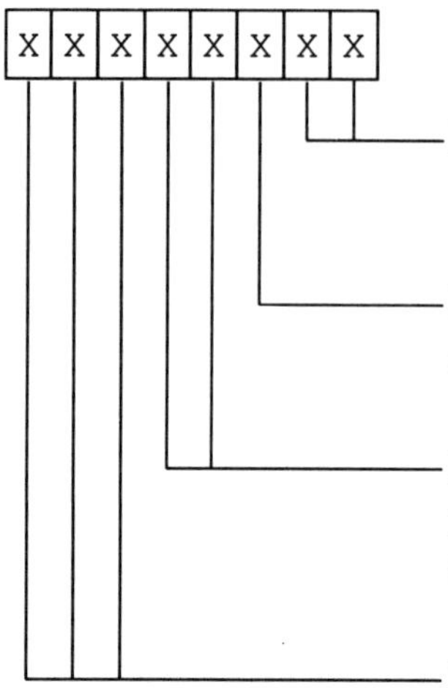

Number of data bits as follows:

1	0	7 Data Bits
1	1	8 Data Bits

Number of stop bits as follows:

0	1 Stop Bit
1	2 Stop Bits

Parity setting as follows:

X	0	No Parity
0	1	Odd Parity
1	1	Even Parity

Baud rate as follows:

0	0	0	110 Baud
0	0	1	150 Baud
0	1	0	300 Baud
0	1	1	600 Baud
1	0	0	1200 Baud
1	0	1	2400 Baud
1	1	0	4800 Baud
1	1	1	9600 Baud

DX 00H for COM1, 01H for COM2

continued...

...from previous page

Returns:

AH The port status as follows:

`Bit 7 6 5 4 3 2 1 0`

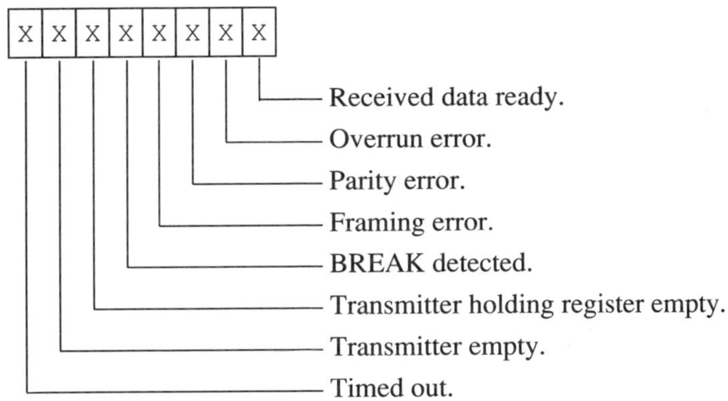

AL The modem status as follows:

`Bit 7 6 5 4 3 2 1 0`

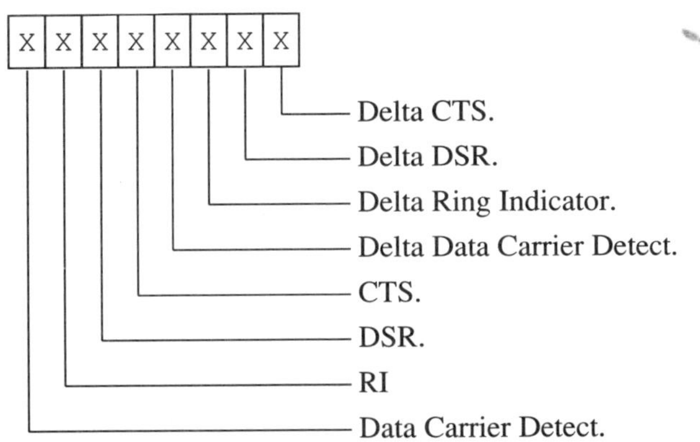

Figure 3.1 *ROM BIOS INT 14H, Function 00H.*

The second of the ROM BIOS serial communications routines is the *Write Character to Serial Port routine*. Figure 3.2 illustrates how this routine is called and any values that are returned by this routine.

INT 14H, Function 01H - Write Character to Serial Port

Description:

This ROM BIOS routine sends a character out a specified serial port and returns the port's current status.

Call With:

AH 01H (The function number.)

AL The character to be sent out the serial port.

DX 00H for COM1, 01H for COM2

If Successful, Returns:

AH Indicates a successful operation and returns the serial port's current status as follows:

Bits 7 6 5 4 3 2 1 0

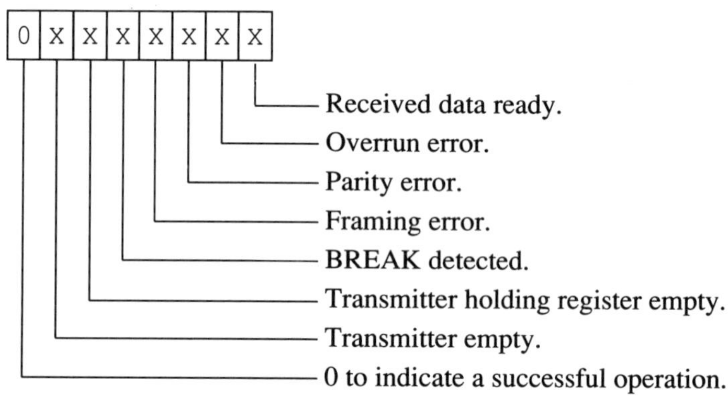

AL The character that was sent to the serial port.

If Not Successful, Returns:

AH Indicates an unsuccessful operation as follows:

Bits 7 6 5 4 3 2 1 0

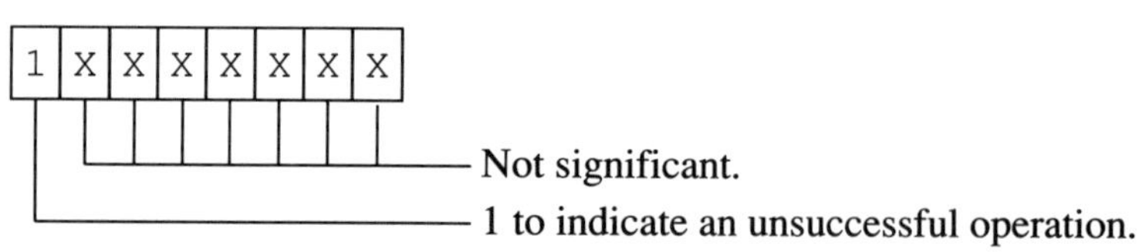

AL The character that was sent to the serial port.

***Figure 3.2** ROM BIOS INT 14, Function 01H.*

The third of the ROM BIOS serial communications routines is the *Read Character from Serial Port routine.* Figure 3.3 illustrates how this routine is called and any values that are returned by the routine.

INT 14H, FUNCTION 02H - Read Character from Serial Port

Description:

This ROM BIOS routine reads a character from a specified serial port. In addition to returning the character, this routine indicates any errors that may have occurred.

Call With:

AH 02H (The function number.)

DX 00H for COM1, 01H for COM2

If Successful, Returns:

AH Indicates a successful operation and returns the serial port's status as follows:

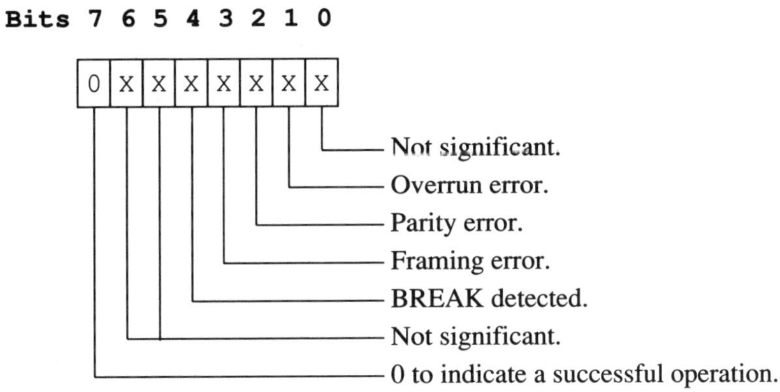

AL The character that was fetched from the serial port.

If Not Successful, Returns:

AH Indicates an unsuccessful operation as follows:

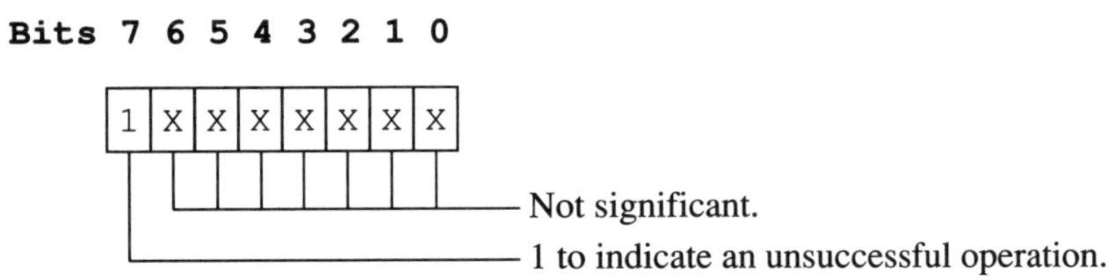

Figure 3.3 *ROM BIOS INT 14, Function 02H.*

The fourth and final ROM BIOS serial communications routine is the *Get Serial Port Status routine*. Figure 3.4 illustrates how this routine is called and the values that are returned by this routine.

INT 14, Function 03H - Get Serial Port Status

Description:

This ROM BIOS routine returns the serial port's current status.

Call With:

AH 03H (The function number.)

DX 00H for COM1, 01H for COM2

If Successful, Returns:

AH The port status as follows:

Bit 7 6 5 4 3 2 1 0

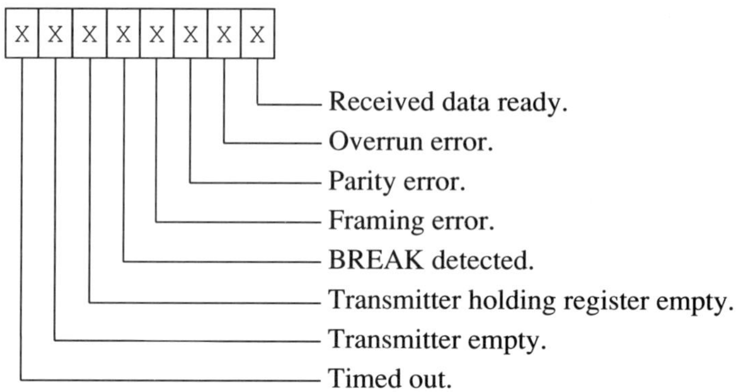

AL The modem status as follows:

Bit 7 6 5 4 3 2 1 0

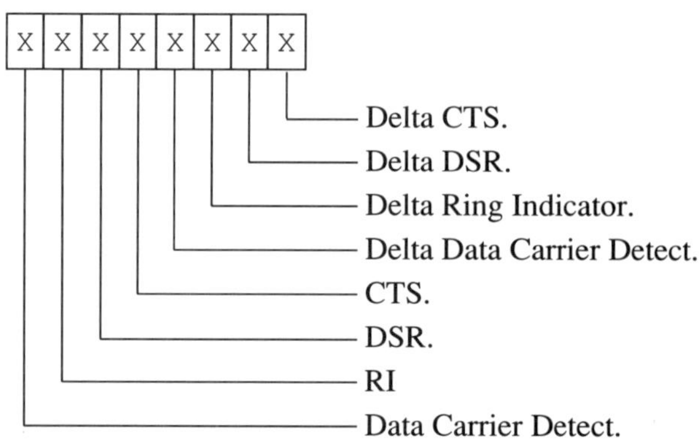

Figure 3.4 *ROM BIOS INT 14, Function 03H.*

A Dumb Terminal Program

Listing 3.1, **duh1.c**, presents a very simple and extremely dumb terminal program, which uses the ROM BIOS serial communications routines to perform input and output. Its lack of support for modems on both COM3 and COM4 and its restriction to baud rates of 9600 and below clearly illustrate just how inadequate the ROM BIOS serial communications routines really are. For that matter, the ROM BIOS routines are done so poorly that this program may not even work with some modems. To say the least, that shows just how inept the ROM BIOS serial communications routines really are.

Listing 3.1: duh1.c

```
/*********************************************************************
* duh1.c - An extremely dumb terminal program (ROM BIOS Version)
*          Copyright (c) 1992 By Mark Goodwin
*********************************************************************/
#include <stdio.h>
#include <stdlib.h>
#include <dos.h>

#define TRUE 1
#define FALSE 0

#define PORT 2                                   /* serial port */
#define BAUDRATE 2400                      /* baud rate */

/* function prototypes */
void open_port(int n, int b);
void put_serial(int n, int c);
int get_serial(int n);
int in_ready(int n);

void main(void)
{
      int c;

      printf("Duh No. 1 - An Extremely Dumb Terminal Program\n");
      printf("Copyright (c) 1992 By Mark Goodwin\n\n");

      /* open the serial port */
      open_port(PORT, BAUDRATE);
```

continued...

...from previous page (Listing 3.1)

```
	/* main program loop */
	while (TRUE) {
		/* process keyboard presses */
		if (kbhit()) {
			c = getch();
			switch (c) {
				case 0:                          /* exit on Alt-X */
					if (getch() == 45)
						exit(0);
					break;
				default:
					put_serial(PORT, c);     /* send to the serial port */
			}
		}
		/* process remote characters */
		if (in_ready(PORT)) {
			/* get character from serial port*/
			c = get_serial(PORT);
			/* display it if one was available */
			if (c != EOF)
				putch(c);
		}
	}
}

/* open serial port using ROM BIOS routine */
void open_port(int n, int b)
{
	union REGS regs;

	/* load AH with the function code */
	regs.h.ah = 0x00;
	/* load AL with the baud rate and 8-N-1 */
	switch (b) {
		case 9600:
			regs.h.al = 0xe3;
			break;
		case 4800:
			regs.h.al = 0xc3;
			break;
		case 2400:
			regs.h.al = 0xa3;
			break;
		case 1200:
			regs.h.al = 0x83;
			break;
		case 300:
			regs.h.al = 0x43;
			break;
		case 150:
			regs.h.al = 0x23;
			break;
```

continued...

...from previous page (Listing 3.1)

```
		default:
			regs.h.al = 0x03;
	}
	/* load DX with the port number */
	if (n == 1)
		regs.x.dx = 0;
	else
		regs.x.dx = 1;
	/* call the ROM BIOS routine */
	int86(0x14, &regs, &regs);
}

/* put character to serial port */
void put_serial(int n, int c)
{
	union REGS regs;

	/* load AH with the function code */
	regs.h.ah = 0x01;
	/* load AL with the character */
	regs.h.al = c;
	/* load DX with the port number */
	if (n == 1)
		regs.x.dx = 0;
	else
		regs.x.dx = 1;
	/* call the ROM BIOS routine */
	int86(0x14, &regs, &regs);
}

/* get character from serial port */
int get_serial(int n)
{
	union REGS regs;

	/* load AH with the function code */
	regs.h.ah = 0x02;
	/* load DX with the port number */
	if (n == 1)
		regs.x.dx = 0;
	else
		regs.x.dx = 1;
	/* call the ROM BIOS routine */
	int86(0x14, &regs, &regs);
	/* return EOF if timed out */
	if (regs.h.ah & 0x80)
		return EOF;
	return regs.h.al;
}
```

continued...

...from previous page (Listing 3.1)

```
/* check to see if a character is ready */
int in_ready(int n)
{
      union REGS regs;

      /* load AH with the function code */
      regs.h.ah = 0x03;
      /* load DX with the port number */
      if (n == 1)
            regs.x.dx = 0;
      else
            regs.x.dx = 1;
      /* call the ROM BIOS routine */
      int86(0x14, &regs, &regs);
      /* check for received data ready */
      if (regs.h.ah & 1)
            return TRUE;
      return FALSE;
}
```

Function Definition: main

As with all C programs, the **main** function is the main program loop. Its implementation is illustrated by the following pseudocode:

```
display the sign on message
open the serial port
while (TRUE) {
        if (key pressed) {
                switch (the key that was pressed) {
                        case extended key pressed:
                                exit if Alt-X
                                ignore all other extended keys
                        default:
                                send the character out the serial port
                }
        }
        if (character received) {
                get the character from the serial port
                display it if one was available
        }
}
```

Function Definition: open_port

The **open_port** function opens a serial port by calling ROM BIOS INT 14H, Function 00H. Its implementation is illustrated by the following pseudocode:

```
put the function code into AH
set register AL to the specified baud rate, eight data bits, no parity and one stop bit
set register DX to the appropriate serial port
call the ROM BIOS routine
```

Function Definition: put_serial

The **put_serial** function writes a character to a serial port by calling ROM BIOS INT 14H, Function 01H. Its implementation is illustrated by the following pseudocode:

```
put the function code in AH
put the character in AL
set register DX to the appropriate serial port
call the ROM BIOS routine
```

Function Definition: get_serial

The **get_serial** function gets a character from a serial port by calling ROM BIOS INT 14H, Function 02H. Its implementation is illustrated by the following pseudocode:

```
put the function code in AH
set register DX to the appropriate serial port
call the ROM BIOS routine
if (an error occurred)
        return EOF
return the character
```

Function Definition: in_ready

The **in_ready** function checks the serial port to see if a character is available by calling ROM BIOS INT 14H, Function 03H. Its implementation is illustrated by the following pseudocode:

```
put the function code in AH
set register DX to the appropriate serial port
call the ROM BIOS routine
if (a character is available)
        return TRUE
return FALSE
```

Summary

Chapter 3 has explained how the ROM BIOS serial communications routines can be used to initialize a serial port, write a character out a serial port, fetch a character from a serial port, and retrieve a serial port's current status. To illustrate how these ROM BIOS serial communications routines are used in an actual program, this chapter presented a complete ROM BIOS-based dumb terminal program. This dumb terminal program also served to illustrate just how inadequate the ROM BIOS routines are for performing serial communications programming.

Chapter 4

An Interrupt Driven Serial Communications Toolbox

Now that we've seen how ineffective it is to use the **ROM BIOS** routines to write a serial communications program, let's take a look at how the **SERIAL toolbox** uses interrupts to create an extremely efficient collection of serial communications routines. The first step in building the **SERIAL toolbox** is to understand how interrupts are used to handle communication with the **UART** to avoid the loss of any incoming characters.

Serial Communications Interrupt Routines

In Chapter 1, you learned that to enable a UART's interrupts the appropriate interrupt(s) must first be selected by setting their proper bits in the UART's Interrupt Enable Register (IER). For example, to have the UART generate an interrupt whenever there is a character available in the UART's Receiver Buffer Register, the IER's bit 0 would be set to 1. Next, the program would have to set the UART's GPO2 bit in the Modem Control Register (MCR) to 1. Although the UART is now fully ready to start generating an interrupt every time it places a character in the RBR, these interrupts won't as yet be recognized by the CPU. To fully enable the UART's interrupts, the computer's *8259 Peripheral Interrupt Controller* (*PIC*) must be set to recognize the UART's interrupts. Once it is set up to recognize the UART's interrupts, the 8259 will generate an appropriate CPU interrupt. Thus, the CPU will halt its current task and call the desired *Interrupt Service Routine* (*ISR*).

To set the PIC to recognize the UART's interrupts, the serial communications program must enable an appropriate IRQ line in the PIC's Interrupt Mask Register (IMR). The IMR is addressed by either writing to or reading from port **21H**. Figure 4.1 illustrates the IRQ lines that can be set by the IMR. You will note from this illustration that COM1 and COM3 share IRQ4 and COM2 and COM4 share IRQ3. Perhaps one of the most common communication problems occurs when two serial devices share the same interrupt line. For example, it is a common mistake to have a mouse on COM1 and then attempt to put a modem on COM3. Most people don't realize it and many manuals for serial devices ignore it, but configuring a system in this manner will cause the mouse-related interrupts to interfere with the serial communications program and the serial port-related interrupts to interfere with the mouse driver. Obviously, the only way to correct such a situation would be to move one of the devices to either COM2 or COM4.

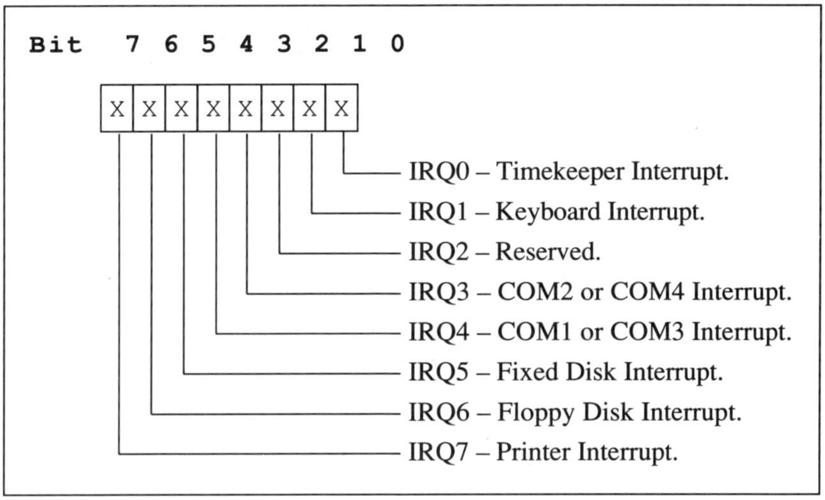

Figure 4.1 *The 8259's Interrupt Mask Register.*

Once the serial communications program has set the appropriate IMR line, the serial port's interrupts will be fully enabled. Whenever an interrupt occurs on COM1 or COM3, the CPU calls the IRQ4 ISR routine at INT 0CH. Whenever an interrupt occurs on either COM2 or COM3, the CPU calls the IRQ3 ISR routine at INT 0BH. Upon entry into the ISR routine, the serial communications program should examine the UART's Interrupt Identification Register (IIR) to see what type of interrupt has occurred. In the case of the SERIAL toolbox, the IIR indicates that a character is ready in the UART's RBR and will fetch this character and save it in an appropriate buffer area. You should note that the SERIAL toolbox ignores all other interrupts. You will find that setting up receiver-only interrupts is usually the easiest method for implementing most serial communications programs. Although receiver interrupts are essential to implementing an efficient serial communications program, the other interrupts the 8250 UART has to offer are rarely, if ever, needed. Ah, but what about transmit interrupts? Transmit interrupts aren't as essential to an efficient serial communications program because the program is well aware of when it needs to transmit a character and can simply proceed without having to add the complexity of an transmit interrupt handler.

After processing or ignoring an interrupt, the ISR must re-enable the 8259 PIC. Whenever an interrupt occurs, the 8259 PIC will continue to recognize interrupts, but it will not tell the CPU that another interrupt has occurred until an *End of Interrupt* (*EOI*) command has been written to the 8259 PIC's *Interrupt Control Register* (*ICR*). The ICR is addressed as port **20H** and coincidentally enough an EOI command is equal to 20H. Consequently, the serial communications program should always write an EOI to the ICR before it returns control back to the CPU.

Keeping Track of Time

Many routines in the SERIAL toolbox require an accurate time clock to time certain functions. Wherever possible, the SERIAL toolbox uses the C run time library routines to perform time-related functions. However, these run time library routines are not always the best choice for performing certain functions. Accordingly, the SERIAL toolbox uses the computer's internal clock to keep track of some time-related functions.

When a PC or compatible computer is turned on, the system clock generates an interrupt at a rate of 18.2 times per second. The ROM BIOS has an ISR that handles this interrupt and keeps track of each clock "tick" by maintaining a 32-bit counter starting at memory location 0000:004CH. By examining the first 16 bits of this counter, the SERIAL toolbox can easily determine if a clock tick has occurred since it's last check; therefore, the SERIAL toolbox can very accurately time a function whenever it is necessary.

Source File Listing: serasm.asm

Listing 4.1, **serasm.asm**, contains all of the SERIAL toolbox's low-level assembly language functions. These assembly language functions perform such tasks as interrupt handling, getting a character from the serial port's input buffer, and sending a character out the serial port. Although these functions could have been written in C, equivalent C functions just can't keep up with high-speed modems on a slow computer. However, this source listing's assembly language functions should be able to keep up with today's fastest modems on even the slowest XT-type computer. You should note that the assembly language routines presented in Listing 4.1 all use the large memory model as does the rest of the SERIAL toolbox. The reason for using the large memory model is because most real-world serial communications programs use extensive amounts of memory to run as efficiently as possible. By implementing the SERIAL toolbox using the large memory model, it will easily meet the needs of even the most memory hungry of serial communications programs.

Listing 4.1: serasm.asm

```
;
; serasm.asm - Low Level Communications Routines
;              Copyright (c) 1992 by Mark Goodwin
;

;
; UART register constants
;
IIR                 equ     2
MCR                 equ     4
LSR                 equ     5
MSR                 equ     6

;
; UART bit mask constants
;
RX_RDY              equ     1
TX_RDY              equ     20H
INT_MASK            equ     7
RX_ID               equ     4
MC_INT              equ     8
DTR                 equ     1
RTS                 equ     2
CTS                 equ     10H
DSR                 equ     20H
DCD                 equ     80H
ICR                 equ     20H
EOI                 equ     20H

;
; XON/XOFF constants
;
XON                 equ     11H
XOFF                equ     13H

;
; system clock location
;
CLOCK               equ     46cH

;
; boolean values
;
TRUE                equ     1
FALSE               equ     0
```

continued...

...from previous page (Listing 4.1)

```
;
; data segment
;
DGROUP              group   _DATA
_DATA               segment word public 'DATA'
                    assume  ds:DGROUP

;
; declare all variables as public
;
                    public  _sibuff,_eibuff,_ilen,_inbuff
                    public  _rx_flow,_rx_rts,_rx_dtr,_rx_xon
                    public  _tx_rts,_tx_dtr,_tx_xon,_tx_xonoff
                    public  _fon,_foff
                    public  _base

;
; varibles
;
_sibuff             dw      ?               ;start of input buffer ptr
_eibuff             dw      ?               ;end of input buffer ptr
_ilen               dw      ?               ;input buffer length
_inbuff             dd      ?               ;input buffer ptr
_rx_flow            dw      ?               ;input buffer full flag
_rx_rts             dw      ?               ;receive RTS/CTS flag
_rx_dtr             dw      ?               ;receive DTR/DSR flag
_rx_xon             dw      ?               ;receive XON/XOFF flag
_tx_rts             dw      ?               ;xmit RTS/CTS flag
_tx_dtr             dw      ?               ;xmit DTR/DSR flag
_tx_xon             dw      ?               ;xmit XON/XOFF flag
_tx_xonoff          dw      ?               ;xmit XOFF flag
_fon                dw      ?               ;point to turn receive flow on
_foff               dw      ?               ;point to turn receive flow off
_base               dw      ?               ;UART base ptr

_DATA               ends

;
; code segment
;
SERASM_TEXT         segment    para public 'CODE'
                    assume     cs:SERASM_TEXT

;
; declare procedures public
;
                    public  _get_serial,_put_serial,_handler,_mpeek
```

continued...

...from previous page (Listing 4.1)

```
;
; get character from the serial port
;
_get_serial         proc    far
                    push    di                  ;save di
                    push    es                  ;save es
                    mov     ax,-1               ;ax=character not available
                    push    ax                  ;save it on stack
                    mov     bx,_sibuff          ;bx=next character ptr
                    cmp     bx,_eibuff          ;buffer empty?
                    je      gs4                 ;jump if it is
                    pop     ax                  ;remove dummy return value
                    les     di,_inbuff          ;es:di=input buffer ptr
                    mov     al,es:[di][bx]      ;al=next character
                    xor     ah,ah               ;ax=next character
                    push    ax                  ;save it on stack
                    inc     bx                  ;bump the next character ptr
                    cmp     bx,_ilen            ;wrap ptr?
                    jne     gs1                 ;jump if not
                    xor     bx,bx               ;point it to start of buffer
gs1:                mov     _sibuff,bx          ;save the new ptr
                    cmp     _rx_flow,TRUE       ;receive flow?
                    jne     gs4                 ;jump if not
                    call    chars_in_buff       ;ax=number of chars in buffer
                    cmp     ax,_fon             ;turn back on?
                    jg      gs4                 ;jump if not
                    mov     _rx_flow,FALSE      ;flag receive flow off
                    cmp     _rx_rts,TRUE        ;RTS/CTS?
                    jne     gs2                 ;jump if not
                    mov     dx,_base            ;dx=base ptr
                    add     dx,MCR              ;dx=modem control register
                    in      al,dx               ;get current value
                    or      al,RTS              ;assert RTS
                    out     dx,al               ;send new value to UART
gs2:                cmp     _rx_dtr,TRUE        ;DTR/DSR?
                    jne     gs3                 ;jump if not
                    mov     dx,_base            ;dx=base ptr
                    add     dx,MCR              ;dx=modem control register
                    in      al,dx               ;get current value
                    or      al,DTR              ;assert DTR
                    out     dx,al               ;send new value to UART
gs3:                cmp     _rx_xon,TRUE        ;XON/XOFF?
                    jne     gs4                 ;Jump if not
                    cli                         ;disable the interrupts
                    mov     dx,_base            ;dx=xmit register
                    mov     al,XON              ;al=XON value
                    out     dx,al               ;send it to remote
                    sti                         ;enable the interrupts
```

continued...

...from previous page (Listing 4.1)

```
gs4:                pop     ax              ;get the character
                    pop     es              ;restore es
                    pop     di              ;restore di
                    ret                     ;return
_get_serial         endp

;
; send a byte out through the serial port
;
_put_serial         proc    far
char                equ     <[bp + 6]>      ;char parameter
                    push    bp              ;save bp
                    mov     bp,sp           ;bp=stack frame ptr
                    push    di              ;save di
                    push    es              ;save es
                    xor     ax,ax           ;ax=segment 0000h
                    mov     es,ax           ;es=segment 0000h ptr
                    mov     di,CLOCK        ;es:di=system clock ptr
                    mov     bx,es:[di]      ;bx=current value
                    mov     cx,18           ;cx=1 second timeout value
                    mov     dx,_base        ;dx=base register
                    mov     dx,MCR          ;dx=modem control register
                    in      al,dx           ;al=current value
                    or      al,MC_INT or DTR or RTS ;assert GPO2, DTR, RTS
                    out     dx,al           ;send it to UART
                    cmp     _tx_rts,TRUE    ;RTS/CTS?
                    jne     ps2             ;Jump if not
                    mov     dx,_base        ;dx=base register
                    add     dx,MSR          ;dx=modem status register
ps1:                in      al,dx           ;al=current value
                    and     al,CTS          ;CTS asserted?
                    jnz     ps2             ;jump if it is
                    cmp     bx,es:[di]      ;system clock changed?
                    je      ps1             ;loop if not
                    mov     bx,es:[di]      ;bx=new system clock value
                    loop    ps1             ;loop till time out
                    jmp     ps9             ;jump for time out
ps2:                cmp     _tx_dtr,TRUE    ; DTR/DSR?
                    jne     ps4             ;jump if not
                    mov     dx,_base        ;dx=base register
                    add     dx,MSR          ;dx=modem status register
ps3:                in      al,dx           ;al=current value
                    and     al,DSR          ;DSR asserted?
                    jnz     ps4             ;jump if it is
                    cmp     bx,es:[di]      ;system clock changed?
                    je      ps3             ;loop if not
                    mov     bx,es:[di]      ;bx=new system clock value
                    loop    ps3             ;loop till time out
                    jmp     ps9             ;jump for time out
```

continued...

...from previous page (Listing 4.1)

```
ps4:            cmp     _tx_xon,TRUE     ;XON/XOFF?
                jne     ps6              ;jump if not
ps5:            cmp     _tx_xonoff,TRUE  ;XOFF?
                jne     ps6              ;jump if not
                mov     dx,_base         ;dx=base register
                add     dx,MSR           ;dx=modem status register
                in      al,dx            ;al=current value
                and     al,DCD           ;carrier?
                jnz     ps5              ;loop if it is
ps6:            mov     dx,_base         ;dx=base register
                add     dx,LSR           ;dx=line status register
ps7:            in      al,dx            ;al=current value
                and     al,TX_RDY        ;xmitter ready?
                jnz     ps8              ;jump if it is
                cmp     bx,es:[di]       ;system clock changed?
                je      ps3              ;loop if not
                mov     bx,es:[di]       ;bx=new system clock value
                loop    ps7              ;loop till time out
                jmp     ps9              ;jump for time out
ps8:            cli                      ;disable the interrupts
                mov     dx,_base         ;dx=xmitter register
                mov     ax,char          ;al=character to send
                out     dx,al            ;send it
                sti                      ;enable the interrupts
ps9:            pop     es               ;restore es
                pop     di               ;restore di
                mov     sp,bp            ;restore the stack ptr
                pop     bp               ;restore bp
                ret                      ;return
_put_serial     endp

;
; calculate number of character in input buffer
;
chars_in_buff   proc    near
                mov     ax,_eibuff       ;ax=end of buffer ptr
                sub     ax,_sibuff       ;figure number of chars
                jae     cibl             ;jump if ptrs haven't crossed
                mov     ax,_ilen         ;ax=buffer size
                sub     ax,_sibuff       ;ax=number chars to end of buffer
                add     ax,_eibuff       ;ax=number chars in buffer
cibl:           ret                      ;return
chars_in_buff   endp
```

continued...

...from previous page (Listing 4.1)

```
;
; interrupt handler
;
_handler            proc    far
                    push    ax                  ;save ax
                    push    bx                  ;save bx
                    push    cx                  ;save cx
                    push    dx                  ;save dx
                    push    si                  ;save si
                    push    di                  ;save di
                    push    bp                  ;save bp
                    push    es                  ;save es
                    push    ds                  ;save ds
                    mov     ax,seg _base        ;ax=segment address
                    mov     ds,ax               ;ds=segment address
                    mov     dx,_base            ;dx=base register
                    add     dx,IIR              ;dx=interrupt id register
                    in      al,dx               ;al=current value
                    and     al,INT_MASK         ;mask it
                    cmp     al,RX_ID            ;receive interrupt?
                    je      h1                  ;jump if it is
                    jmp     h8                  ;jump if not
h1:                 mov     dx,_base            ;dx=receive register
                    in      al,dx               ;al=new character
                    cmp     _tx_xon,TRUE        ;XON/XOFF?
                    jne     h3                  ;jump if not
                    cmp     al,XOFF             ;XOFF?
                    jne     h2                  ;jump if not
                    mov     _tx_xonoff,TRUE     ;flag XOFF
                    jmp     h5                  ;jump
h2:                 cmp     al,XON              ;XON?
                    jne     h3                  ;jump if not
                    mov     _tx_xonoff,FALSE    ;flag not XOFF
                    jmp     h5                  ;jump
h3:                 mov     _tx_xonoff,FALSE    ;flag not XOFF
                    mov     bx,_eibuff          ;bx=next char ptr
                    les     di,_inbuff          ;es:di=input buffer ptr
                    mov     es:[di][bx],al      ;save the char
                    inc     bx                  ;bump the buffer ptr
                    cmp     bx,_ilen            ;wrap it?
                    jne     h4                  ;jump if not
                    xor     bx,bx               ;point to start of buffer
h4:                 mov     _eibuff,bx          ;save new ptr
```

continued...

...from previous page (Listing 4.1)

```
h5:             mov     dx,_base            ;dx=base register
                add     dx,LSR              ;dx=line status register
                in      al,dx               ;al=current value
                and     al,RX_RDY           ;another character available
                jnz     h1                  ;loop if it is
                cmp     _rx_flow,TRUE       ;receive flow on?
                je      h8                  ;jump if it is
                call    chars_in_buff       ;ax=no chars in buffer
                cmp     ax,_foff            ;turn receive off?
                jb      h8                  ;jump if not
                mov     _rx_flow,TRUE       ;flag receive flow on
                cmp     _rx_rts,TRUE        ;RTS/CTS?
                jne     h6                  ;jump if not
                mov     dx,_base            ;dx=base register
                add     dx,MCR              ;dx=modem control register
                in      al,dx               ;al=current value
                and     al,not RTS          ;unassert RTS
                out     dx,al               ;send it to UART
h6:             cmp     _rx_dtr,TRUE        ;DTR/DSR?
                jne     h7                  ;jump if not
                mov     dx,_base            ;dx=base register
                add     dx,MCR              ;dx=modem control register
                in      al,dx               ;al=current value
                and     al,not DTR          ;unassert DTR
                out     dx,al               ;send it to UART
h7:             cmp     _rx_xon,TRUE        ;XON/XOFF?
                jne     h8                  ;jump if not
                mov     dx,_base            ;dx=xmit register
                mov     al,XOFF             ;al=XOFF
                out     dx,al               ;send it
h8:             mov     dx,ICR              ;dx=interrupt control register
                mov     al,EOI              ;al=end of interrupt command
                out     dx,al               ;send it
                pop     ds                  ;restore ds
                pop     es                  ;restore es
                pop     bp                  ;restore bp
                pop     di                  ;restore di
                pop     si                  ;restore si
                pop     dx                  ;restore dx
                pop     cx                  ;restore cx
                pop     bx                  ;restore bx
                pop     ax                  ;restore ax
                iret                        ;return
_handler        endp
```

continued...

...from previous page (Listing 4.1)

```
;
; get word of memory routine
;
_mpeek          proc    far
srcseg          equ     <[bp + 6]>        ;segment parameter
srcoff          equ     <[bp + 8]>        ;offset parameter
                push    bp                ;save bp
                mov     bp,sp             ;bp=stack frame ptr
                push    di                ;save di
                push    es                ;save es
                mov     es,srcseg         ;es=segment address
                mov     di,srcoff         ;di=offset address
                mov     ax,es:[di]        ;ax=memory word
                pop     es                ;restore es
                pop     di                ;restore di
                pop     bp                ;restore bp
                ret                       ;return;
_mpeek          endp


SERASM_TEXT     ends

                end
```

Function Description: get_serial

The **get_serial** function returns a character, if one is available, from the serial port's input buffer. If a character isn't available, the **get_serial** function returns a **–1**. The **get_serial** function's implementation is illustrated by the following pseudocode:

```
if (input buffer empty)
        return -1
get the next character from the input buffer
wrap the next character pointer if it's gone beyond the end of the buffer
save the new next character pointer
if (ISR has turned off the transmitter) {
        if (buffer is empty enough to start receiving again) {
                flag ISR hasn't turned off the transmitter
                if (RTS/CTS flow control)
                        assert RTS
                if (DTR/DSR flow control)
                        assert DTR
                if (XON/XOFF flow control)
                        send an XON
        }
}
return the character
```

Function Description: put_serial

The **put_serial** function sends a character out the serial port. Its implementation is illustrated by the following pseudocode:

```
assert GPO2, DTR, and RTS
if (RTS/CTS flow control) {
        while (not CTS) {
                if (1 second has elapsed)
                        abort
        }
}
if (DTR/DSR flow control) {
        while (not DSR) {
                if (1 second has elapsed)
                        abort
        }
}
if (XON/XOFF flow control) {
        while (XOFF && carrier is detected) ;
}
while (transmitter not ready) {
        if (1 second has elapsed)
                abort
}
disable the interrupts
send the character to the UART
enable the interrupts
```

Function Description: chars_in_buff

The **chars_in_buff** function is used internally to determine the number of characters, if any, that remain in the serial port's input buffer. Its implementation is illustrated by the following pseudocode:

```
figure the number of remaining characters
return the value if the buffer hasn't wrapped
refigure the number of remaining characters
return the result
```

Function Description: handler

The **handler** function is the Interrupt Service Routine (ISR) the CPU will call whenever a serial-related interrupt is generated. Its implementation is illustrated by the following pseudocode:

```
save the CPU's registers
set the data segment
if (RBR full interrupt) {
        do {
                get the character from the UART
                if (XON/XOFF flow control) {
                        if (character == XOFF)
                                flag XOFF
                        else {
                                if (character == XON)
                                        flag not XOFF
                        }
                }
                else
                        save the character in the buffer
        } until (RBR is empty)
        if (flow control not asserted) {
                if (buffer is getting too full) {
                        if (RTS/CTS flow control)
                                unassert RTS
                        if (DTR/DSR flow control)
                                unassert DTR
                        if (XON/XOFF flow control)
                                send an XOFF
                }
        }
}
send EOI to the 8259's ICR
restore the registers
return from the interrupt
```

Function Description: mpeek

The **mpeek** function fetches an unsigned 16-bit value from a specified memory location. Its implementation is illustrated by the following pseudocode:

```
get the word of memory
return the word of memory to the calling program
```

Header File Listing: serial.h

Listing 4.2, **serial.h**, is the SERIAL toolbox header file. Like most other C header files, the chief purpose of serial.h is to define constants, global variables, macros, and function prototypes. To achieve correct program compilation, serial.h should be included in all of your programs that utilize the SERIAL toolbox.

Listing 4.2: serial.h

```
/*******************************************************************
* serial.h - Header file for Serial Comm Prog in C and C++        *
*            Copyright (c) 1992 By Mark D. Goodwin                *
*******************************************************************/
#ifndef __SERIALH__
#define __SERIALH__

#ifndef __TURBOC__
#include <time.h>
#endif

/* boolean constants */
#define TRUE 1
#define FALSE 0

/* parity constants */
#define NO_PARITY 0                     /* no parity constant */
#define EVEN_PARITY 1                   /* even parity constant */
#define ODD_PARITY 2                    /* odd parity constant */

/* file transfer constants */
#define XMODEM 1
#define XMODEM1K 2
#define YMODEM 3
#define YMODEMG 4

/* file error handler constants */
#define SENDING 1                       /* sending file code */
#define RECEIVING 2                     /* receiving file code */
#define SENT 3                          /* block sent ok code */
#define RECEIVED 4                      /* block received ok code */
#define ERROR 5                         /* error code */
#define COMPLETE 6                      /* completed transfer code */
```

continued...

...from previous page (Listing 4.2)

```
/* global variables */
extern int sibuff, eibuff, ilen;
extern unsigned char far *inbuff;
extern int rx_flow, rx_rts, rx_dtr, rx_xon;
extern int tx_rts, tx_dtr, tx_xon, tx_xonoff;
extern int fon, foff;
extern int base;
extern int ansi_dsr_flag;
extern int (*ansi_dsr)(unsigned char n);

/* function prototypes */
#ifdef __cplusplus
extern "C" {
#endif
void ansiout(int c);
int ansiprintf(char *f, ...);
void ansistring(char *s);
int carrier(void);
void close_port(void);
#ifndef __TURBOC__
void delay(clock_t n);
#endif
void fifo(int n);
long get_baud(void);
int get_bits(void);
int get_parity(void);
int get_rx_dtr(void);
int get_rx_rts(void);
int get_rx_xon(void);
int get_serial(void);
int get_stopbits(void);
int get_tx_dtr(void);
int get_tx_rts(void);
int get_tx_xon(void);
#ifdef __TURBOC__
void interrupt handler(void);
#else
void _interrupt _far handler(void);
#endif
char *ibmtoansi(int att, char *s);
int in_ready(void);
unsigned mpeek(unsigned seg, unsigned off);
void open_port(int port, int inlen);
int port_exist(int port);
void purge_in(void);
int put_serial(unsigned char n);
int recv_file(int xtype, int(*error_handler)(int c, long p, char *s), char *path);
void set_baud(long baud);
void set_data_format(int bits, int parity, int stopbit);
void set_dtr(int n);
void set_port(long baud, int bits, int parity, int stopbit);
void set_rx_dtr(int n);
```

continued...

...from previous page (Listing 4.2)

```
void set_rx_rts(int n);
void set_rx_xon(int n);
void set_tx_dtr(int n);
void set_tx_rts(int n);
void set_tx_xon(int n);
int xmit_file(int xtype, int (*error_handler)(int c, long p, char *s), char *files[]);
#ifdef __cplusplus
}
#endif

#endif
```

Source File Listing: serial.c

Listing 4.3, **serial.c**, contains all of the low-level C functions for the SERIAL toolbox. These functions perform such diverse operations as opening and closing the serial port, setting the serial port's baud rate, setting the serial port's number of data bits, setting the serial port's parity setting, setting the serial port's number of stop bits, retrieving the serial port's baud rate, retrieving the serial port's number of data bits, retrieving the serial port's parity setting, retrieving the serial port's number of stop bits, and so on.

Listing 4.3: serial.c

```
/**************************************************************************
* serial.c - Low-Level Serial Communications Routines                    *
*            Copyright (c) 1992 By Mark D. Goodwin                       *
**************************************************************************/
#include <stdio.h>
#include <stdlib.h>
#include <dos.h>
#include <conio.h>
#ifdef __TURBOC__
#include <alloc.h>
#else
#include <malloc.h>
#endif
#include <time.h>
#include "serial.h"
```

continued...

...from previous page (Listing 4.3)

```
#ifndef __TURBOC__
#define enable _enable
#define inportb inp
#define outportb outp
#define getvect _dos_getvect
#define disable _disable
#define setvect _dos_setvect
#define farmalloc _fmalloc
#endif

/* UART register constants */
#define TX 0                            /* transmit register */
#define RX 0                            /* receive register */
#define DLL 0                           /* divisor latch low */
#define IER 1                           /* interrupt enable register */
#define DLH 1                           /* divisor latch high */
#define IIR 2                           /* interrupt id register */
#define LCR 3                           /* line control register */
#define MCR 4                           /* modem control register */
#define LSR 5                           /* line status register */
#define MSR 6                           /* modem status register */

/* interrupt enable register constants */
#define RX_INT 1                        /* received data bit mask */

/* interrupt id register constants */
#define INT_MASK 7                      /* interrupt mask */
#define RX_ID 4                         /* received data interrupt */

/* line control register constants */
#define DLAB 0x80                       /* DLAB bit mask */

/* modem control register constants */
#define DTR 1                           /* Date Terminal Ready bit mask */
#define RTS 2                           /* Request To Send bit mask */
#define MC_INT 8                        /* GPO2 bit mask */

/* line status register constants */
#define RX_RDY 0x01
#define TX_RDY 0x20

/* modem status register constants */
#define CTS 0x10
#define DSR 0x20
#define DCD 0x80

/* 8259 PIC constants */
#define IMR 0x21                        /* interrupt mask register */
#define ICR 0x20                        /* interrupt control register */
```

continued...

...from previous page (Listing 4.3)

```
/* interrupt mask register constants */
#define IRQ3 0xf7                          /* IRQ 3 interrupt mask */
#define IRQ4 0xef                          /* IRQ 4 interrupt mask */

/* interrupt control register constants */
#define EOI 0x20                           /* end of interrupt mask */

/* XON/XOFF flow control constants */
#define XON 0x11
#define XOFF 0x13

int port_open = FALSE, irq;
#ifdef __TURBOC__
void interrupt (*oldvect)();
#else
void (_interrupt _far *oldvect)();
#endif

/* Check for a Port's Existence */
int port_exist(int port)
{
    return mpeek(0, 0x400 + (port - 1) * 2);
}

/* Open a Serial Port */
void open_port(int port, int inlen)
{
    long i;

    /* make sure a port isn't already open */
    if (port_open) {
        printf("Unable to open port: A port is already open!\n");
        exit(1);
    }

    /* make sure the port if valid */
    if (port < 1 || port > 4 || !port_exist(port)) {
        printf("Unable to open port: Invalid port number!\n");
        exit(1);
    }

    /* allocate the space for the buffers */
    ilen = inlen;
    if ((inbuff = farmalloc(ilen)) == NULL) {
        printf("Unable to open port: Not enough memory for the buffer!\n");
        exit(1);
    }

    /* calculate the flow control limits */
    foff = (int)((long)ilen * 90L / 100L);
    fon = (int)((long)ilen * 80L / 100L);
    rx_flow = FALSE;
```

continued...

...from previous page (Listing 4.3)

```
    /* set the base address and IRQ*/
    switch (port) {
        case 1:
            base = 0x3f8;
            irq = 0x0c;
            break;
        case 2:
            base = 0x2f8;
            irq = 0x0b;
            break;
        case 3:
            base = 0x3e8;
            irq = 0x0c;
            break;
        case 4:
            base = 0x2e8;
            irq = 0x0b;
            break;
    }

    /* set up the interrupt handler */
    disable();                              /* disable the interupts */
    oldvect = getvect(irq);                 /* save the current vector */
    setvect(irq, handler);                  /* set the new vector */
    sibuff = eibuff = 0;                    /* set the buffer pointers */
    outportb(base + MCR,
        inportb(base + MCR) | MC_INT | DTR | RTS); /* assert GPO2, RTS, and DTR */
    outportb(base + IER, RX_INT);           /* set received data interrupt */
    outportb(IMR,
        inportb(IMR) & (irq == 0x0b ? IRQ3 : IRQ4)); /* set the interrupt */
    enable();                               /* enable the interrupts */
    fifo(14);                               /* set FIFO buffer for 14 bytes */
    set_tx_rts(FALSE);                      /* turn off RTS/CTS flow control */
    set_tx_dtr(FALSE);                      /* turn off DTR/DSR flow control */
    set_tx_xon(FALSE);                      /* turn off XON/XOFF flow control */
    set_rx_rts(FALSE);                      /* turn off RTS/CTS flow control */
    set_rx_dtr(FALSE);                      /* turn off DTR/DSR flow control */
    set_rx_xon(FALSE);                      /* turn off XON/XOFF flow control */
    port_open = TRUE;                       /* flag port is open */
}
```

continued...

...from previous page (Listing 4.3)

```
/* close serial port routine */
void close_port(void)
{
    /* check to see if a port is open */
    if (!port_open)
        return;

    port_open = FALSE;                          /* flag port not opened */

    disable();                                  /* disable the interrupts */
    outportb(IMR,
        inportb(IMR) | (irq == 0x0b ? ~IRQ3 : ~IRQ4)); /* clear the interrupt */
    outportb(base + IER, 0);                    /* clear recceived data int */
    outportb(base + MCR,
        inportb(base + MCR) & ~MC_INT);         /* unassert GPO2 */
    setvect(irq, oldvect);                      /* reset the old int vector */
    enable();                                   /* enable the interrupts */
    outportb(base + MCR,
        inportb(base + MCR) & ~RTS);            /* unassert RTS */
}

/* purge input buffer */
void purge_in(void)
{
    disable();                                  /* disable the interrupts */
    sibuff = eibuff = 0;                        /* set the buffer pointers */
    enable();                                   /* enable the interrupts */
}

/* set the baud rate */
void set_baud(long baud)
{
    int c, n;

    /* check for 0 baud */
    if (baud == 0L)
        return;
    n = (int)(115200L / baud);                  /* figure the divisor */
    disable();                                  /* disable the interrupts */
    c = inportb(base + LCR);                    /* get line control reg */
    outportb(base + LCR, (c | DLAB));           /* set divisor latch bit */
    outportb(base + DLL, n & 0x00ff);           /* set LSB of divisor latch */
    outportb(base + DLH, (n >> 8) & 0x00ff); /* set MSB of divisor latch */
    outportb(base + LCR, c);                    /* restore line control reg */
    enable();                                   /* enable the interrupts */
}
```

continued...

...from previous page (Listing 4.3)

```
/* get the baud rate */
long get_baud(void)
{
    int c, n;

    disable();                          /* disable the interrupts */
    c = inportb(base + LCR);            /* get line control reg */
    outportb(base + LCR, (c | DLAB));   /* set divisor latch bit */
    n = inportb(base + DLH) << 8;       /* get MSB of divisor latch */
    n |= inportb(base + DLL);           /* get LSB of divisor latch */
    outportb(base + LCR, c);            /* restore the line control reg */
    enable();                           /* enable the interrupts */
    return 115200L / (long)n;           /* return the baud rate */
}

/* get number of data bits */
int get_bits(void)
{
    return (inportb(base + LCR) & 3) + 5;   /* return number of data bits */
}

/* get parity */
int get_parity(void)
{
    switch ((inportb(base + LCR) >> 3) & 7) {
        case 0:
            return NO_PARITY;
        case 1:
            return ODD_PARITY;
        case 3:
            return EVEN_PARITY;
    }
    return -1;
}

/* get number of stop bits */
int get_stopbits(void)
{
    if (inportb(base + LCR) & 4)
        return 2;
    return 1;

 {
```

continued...

...from previous page (Listing 4.3)

```
void set_data_format(int bits, int parity, int stopbit)
{
    int n;

    /* check parity value */
    if (parity < NO_PARITY || parity > ODD_PARITY)
        return;

    /* check number of bits */
    if (bits < 5 || bits > 8)
        return;

    /* check number of stop bits */
    if (stopbit < 1 || stopbit > 2)
        return;

    n = bits - 5;                           /* figure the bits value */
    n |= ((stopbit == 1) ? 0 : 4);          /* figure the stop bit value */
    /* figure the parity value */
    switch (parity) {
        case NO_PARITY:
            break;
        case ODD_PARITY:
            n |= 0x08;
            break;
        case EVEN_PARITY:
            n |= 0x18;
            break;
    }

    disable();                              /* disable the interrupts */
    outportb(base + LCR, n);                /* set the port */
    enable();                               /* enable the interrupts */
}

void set_port(long baud, int bits, int parity, int stopbit)
{
    /* check for open port */
    if (!port_open)
        return;

    set_baud(baud);                         /* set the baud rate */
    set_data_format(bits, parity, stopbit); /* set the data format */
}

/* check for byte in input buffer */
int in_ready(void)
{
    return !(sibuff == eibuff);
}
```

continued...

...from previous page (Listing 4.3)

```
/* check for carrier routine */
int carrier(void)
{
    return inportb(base + MSR) & DCD ? TRUE : FALSE;
}

/* set DTR routine */
void set_dtr(int n)
{
    if (n)
        outportb(base + MCR, inportb(base + MCR) | DTR); /* assert DTR */
    else
        outportb(base + MCR, inportb(base + MCR) & ~DTR); /* unassert RTS */
}

/* 16550 FIFO routine */
void fifo(int n)
{
    int i;

    switch (n) {
        case 1:
            i = 1;                          /* 1 byte FIFO buffer */
            break;
        case 4:
            i = 0x41;                       /* 4 byte FIFO buffer */
            break;
        case 8:
            i = 0x81;                       /* 8 byte FIFO buffer */
            break;
        case 14:
            i = 0xc1;                       /* 14 byte FIFO buffer */
            break;
        default:
            i = 0;                          /* turn FIFO off for all others */
    }
    outportb(base + IIR, i);                /* set the FIFO buffer */
}

#ifndef __TURBOC__
void delay(clock_t n)
{
    clock_t i;

    i = n + clock();
    while (i > clock()) ;
}
#endif
```

continued...

...from previous page (Listing 4.3)

```
/* set transmit RTS/CTS flag */
void set_tx_rts(int n)
{
    tx_rts = n;
}

/* set transmit DTR/DSR flag */
void set_tx_dtr(int n)
{
    tx_dtr = n;
}

/* set transmit XON/XOFF flag */
void set_tx_xon(int n)
{
    tx_xon = n;
    tx_xonoff = FALSE;
}

/* set receive RTS/CTS flag */
void set_rx_rts(int n)
{
    rx_rts = n;
}

/* set receive DTR/DSR flag */
void set_rx_dtr(int n)
{
    rx_dtr = n;
}

/* set receive XON/XOFF flag */
void set_rx_xon(int n)
{
    rx_xon = n;
}

/* get transmit RTS flag */
int get_tx_rts(void)
{
    return tx_rts;
}

/* get transmit DTR/DSR flag */
int get_tx_dtr(void)
{
    return tx_dtr;
}
```

continued...

...from previous page (Listing 4.3)

```
/* get transmit XON/XOFF flag */
int get_tx_xon(void)
{
    return tx_xon;
}

/* get receive RTS/CTS flag */
int get_rx_rts(void)
{
    return rx_rts;
}

/* get receive DTR/DSR flag */
int get_rx_dtr(void)
{
    return rx_dtr;
}

/* get receive XON/XOFF flag */
int get_rx_xon(void)
{
    return rx_xon;
}
```

Function Description: port_exist

The **port_exist** function checks the ROM BIOS data area to see if a serial port actually exists. Its implementation is illustrated by the following pseudocode:

```
return the serial port's base register address from the ROM BIOS data area
```

Function Description: open_port

The **open_port** function opens a serial port for communication. Its implementation is illustrated by the following pseudocode:

```
if (port is already open)
        abort
if (invalid port number)
        abort
allocate the serial port's input buffer
if (not enough memory for input buffer)
        abort
set the input buffer's flow control limits
flag flow control not asserted
```

continued...

...from previous page

figure the UART's base register address and INT number
disable the interrupts
save the current interrupt handler
set the INT to the SERIAL toolbox's ISR
empty the buffer
assert GPO2, RTS, and DTR
enable the received data interrupt
enable the IRQ with the 8259 PIC's IMR
enable the interrupts
enable the FIFO buffers
turn off transmit RTS/CTS flow control
turn off transmit DTR/DSR flow control
turn off transmit XON/XOFF flow control
turn off receive RTS/CTS flow control
turn off receive DTR/DSR flow control
turn off receive XON/XOFF flow control
flag the port as opened

Function Description: close_port

The **close_port** function closes a previously opened serial port. Its implementation is illustrated by the following pseudocode:

flag the port as closed
disable the interrupts
disable the IRQ with the 8259 PIC's IMR
disable the UART's interrupts
unassert GPO2
restore the old INT vector
enable the interrupts
unassert RTS

Function Description: purge_in

The **purge_in** function purges the serial port's input buffer of any characters that may be in the buffer. Its implementation is illustrated by the following pseudocode:

disable the interrupts
empty the serial port's input buffer
enable the interrupts

Function Description: set_baud

The **set_baud** function sets the serial port's baud rate. Its implementation is illustrated by the following pseudocode:

```
if (baud rate == 0)
        return
figure the baud rate divisor
disable the interrupts
set the LCR's divisor latch bit
set the baud rate divisor's least significant byte
set the baud rate divisor's most significant byte
restore the LCR to its previous state
enable the interrupts
```

Function Description: get_baud

The **get_baud** function calculates and returns the serial port's current baud rate setting. Its implementation is illustrated by the following pseudocode:

```
disable the interrupts
set the LCR's divisor latch bit
get the baud rate divisor's most significant byte
get the baud rate divisor's least significant byte
restore the LCR to its previous state
enable the interrupts
calculate and return the serial port's current baud rate setting
```

Function Description: get_bits

The **get_bits** function calculates and returns the serial port's current number of data bits. Its implementation is illustrated by the following pseudocode:

```
calculate and return the serial port's current number of data bits
```

Function Description: get_parity

The **get_parity** function calculates and returns the serial port's current parity setting. Its implementation is illustrated by the following pseudocode:

```
calculate and return the current parity setting for no parity, even parity, or odd parity
return -1 for all other parity settings
```

Function Description: get_stopbits

The **get_stopbits** function calculates and returns the serial port's current number of stop bits. Its implementation is illustrated by the following pseudocode:

```
calculate and return the serial port's current number of stop bits
```

Function Description: set_data_format

The **set_data_format** function sets a serial port's number of data bits, parity setting, and number of stop bits. Its implementation is illustrated by the following pseudocode:

```
if (invalid parity setting)
        return
if (invalid number of data bits)
        return
if (invalid number of stop bits)
        return
figure the bit mask for the number of data bits
adjust the bit mask for the number of stop bits
adjust the bit mask for the parity setting
disable the interrupts
set the serial port's new data format
enable the interrupts
```

Function Description: set_port

The **set_port** function sets a serial port's baud rate, number of data bits, parity setting, and number of stop bits. It's implementation is illustrated by the following pseudocode:

```
if (serial port isn't open)
        return
set the serial port's baud rate
set the serial port's new data format
```

Function Description: in_ready

The **in_ready** function indicates if there are any characters available in the serial port's input buffer. Its implementation is illustrated by the following pseudocode:

```
return TRUE if there are characters in the serial port's input buffer or FALSE if the
input
        buffer is empty
```

Function Description: carrier

The **carrier** function indicates if there is carrier present or not. Its implementation is illustrated by the following pseudocode:

```
return TRUE if carrier is present or FALSE if carrier isn't present
```

Function Description: set_dtr

The **set_dtr** function sets the UART's DTR line. Its implementation is illustrated by the following pseudocode:

```
if (argument is TRUE)
        assert DTR
else
        unassert DTR
```

Function Description: fifo

The **fifo** function enables and disables the 16550 UART's FIFO buffers: Its implementation is illustrated by the following pseudocode:

```
if (valid FIFO buffer setting)
        calculate the bit mask to enable the FIFO buffers
else
        calculate the bit mask to disable the FIFO buffers
enable or disable the FIFO buffers
```

Function Description: delay

The **delay** function delays program execution for a specified number of milliseconds. Its implementation is illustrated by the following pseudocode:

```
figure the ending clock value
while (ending clock value not yet reached) ;
```

Function Description: set_tx_rts

The **set_tx_rts** function sets the transmit RTS/CTS flow control on and off. Its implementation is illustrated by the following pseudocode:

```
if (argument is TRUE)
        enable transmit RTS/CTS flow control
else
        disable transmit RTS/CTS flow control
```

Function Description: set_tx_dtr

The **set_tx_dtr** function sets the transmit DTR/DSR flow control on and off. Its implementation is illustrated by the following pseudocode:

```
if (argument is TRUE)
        enable transmit DTR/DSR flow control
else
        disable transmit DTR/DSR flow control
```

Function Description: set_tx_xon

The **set_tx_xon** function sets the transmit XON/XOFF flow control on or off. Its implementation is illustrated by the following pseudocode:

```
if (argument is TRUE)
        enable transmit XON/XOFF flow control
else
        disable transmit XON/XOFF flow control
flag XON/XOFF flow control isn't asserted
```

Function Description: set_rx_rts

The **set_rx_rts** function sets the receive RTS/CTS flow control on or off. Its implementation is illustrated by the following pseudocode:

```
if (argument is TRUE)
        enable receive RTS/CTS flow control
else
        disable receive RTS/CTS flow control
```

Function Description: set_rx_dtr

The **set_rx_dtr** function sets the receive DTR/DSR flow control on or off. Its implementation is illustrated by the following pseudocode:

```
if (argument is TRUE)
        enable receive DTR/DSR flow control
else
        disable receive DTR/DSR flow control
```

Function Description: set_rx_xon

The **set_rx_xon** function sets the receive XON/XOFF flow control on or off. Its implementation is illustrated by the following pseudocode:

```
if (argument is TRUE)
        enable receive XON/XOFF flow control
else
        disable receive XON/XOFF flow control
```

Function Description: get_tx_rts

The **get_tx_rts** function returns the current state of the transmit RTS/CTS flow control. Its implementation is illustrated by the following pseudocode:

```
return the current state of the transmit RTS/CTS flow control
```

Function Description: get_tx_dtr

The **get_tx_dtr** function returns the current state of the transmit DTR/DSR flow control. Its implementation is illustrated by the following pseudocode:

```
return the current state of the transmit DTR/DSR flow control
```

Function Description: get_tx_xon

The **get_tx_xon** function returns the current state of the transmit XON/XOFF flow control. Its implementation is illustrated by the following pseudocode:

```
return the current state of the transmit XON/XOFF flow control
```

Function Description: get_rx_rts

The **get_rx_rts** function returns the current state of the receive RTS/CTS flow control. Its implementation is illustrated by the following pseudocode:

```
return the current state of the receive RTS/CTS flow control
```

Function Description: get_rx_dtr

The **get_rx_dtr** function returns the current state of the receive DTR/DSR flow control. Its implementation is illustrated by the following pseudocode:

```
return the current state of the receive DTR/DSR flow control
```

Function Description: get_rx_xon

The **get_rx_xon** function returns the current state of the receive XON/XOFF flow control. Its implementation is illustrated by the following pseudocode:

```
return the current state of the receive XON/XOFF flow control
```

Another Dumb Terminal Program

Chapter 3 presented a dumb terminal program, which was implemented using the ROM BIOS serial communications routines. Listing 4.4, **duh2.c**, presents a newer version of the dumb terminal program. Unlike the version that was presented in Chapter 3, this revised dumb terminal program ignores the ROM BIOS serial communications routines and in their place uses the SERIAL toolbox to implement the program. Because **duh2.c** uses the SERIAL toolbox, it fully supports both COM3 and COM4, baud rates greater than 9600, and full FIFO buffering for serial ports equipped with 16550 UARTs. Additionally, **duh2.c** is a much shorter program than its predecessor.

Listing 4.4: duh2.c

```
/**********************************************************************
* duh2.c - An extremely dumb terminal program (Interrupt Version)
*         Copyright (c) 1992 By Mark Goodwin
**********************************************************************/
#include <stdio.h>
#include <stdlib.h>
#include <dos.h>
#include "serial.h"

#define PORT 2                      /* serial port */
#define BAUDRATE 2400               /* baud rate */

void main(void)
{
    int c;

    printf("Duh No. 2 - An Extremely Dumb Terminal Program\n");
    printf("Copyright (c) 1992 By Mark Goodwin\n\n");

    /* open the serial port */
    open_port(PORT, 1024);
    set_port(BAUDRATE, 8, NO_PARITY, 1);

    /* main program loop */
    while (TRUE) {
        /* process keyboard presses */
        if (kbhit()) {
            c = getch();
            switch (c) {
                case 0:                 /* exit on Alt-X */
                    if (getch() == 45) {
                        close_port();
                        exit(0);
                    }
                    break;
                default:
                    put_serial(c);      /* send to the serial port */
            }
        }
        /* process remote characters */
        if (in_ready()) {
            c = get_serial();           /* get the character */
            putch(c);                   /* display it */
        }
    }
}
```

Function Description: main

As with all C programs, the **main** function is the main program loop. Its implementation is illustrated by the following pseudocode:

```
display sign on message
open the serial port
set the serial port's baud rate and data format
while (TRUE) {
        if (key pressed) {
                switch (the key that was pressed) {
                        case extended key pressed:
                                if (Alt-X) {
                                        close the serial port
                                        exit the program
                                }
                        default:
                                send the character out the serial port
                }
        }
        if (character received) {
                get the character from the serial port
                display the character
        }
}
```

Summary

In this chapter, you learned how a UART's interrupts can be fully enabled by setting the computer's 8259 Peripheral Interrupt Controller (PIC) and how time-related functions can be accurately implemented using the computer's clock ticks. Furthermore, this chapter presented the complete source code for the SERIAL toolbox's interrupt-driven serial communications routines. Finally, the chapter presented a rather simple dumb terminal program, which demonstrated how the SERIAL toolbox's serial communications routines are put into practical use in an application program.

Chapter 5

A C++ Serial Communications Object Class

Chapter 4 presented all of the SERIAL toolbox's low-level assembly language and C serial communications functions. To take advantage of C++'s object-oriented programming extensions, this chapter presents a C++ object class that essentially performs the same functions as the previous chapter's assembly language and C routines. Because of the ability to inline functions with C++, the serial communications object class can be fully implemented with a rather simple header file.

Header File: sercpp.h

Listing 5.1, **sercpp.h**, is the C++ header file for the SERIAL toolbox. Its main purpose is to define a C++ object class, **SERIALPORT**, for the SERIAL toolbox's many serial communications routines. Additionally, **sercpp.h** includes the **serial.h** header file; therefore, it isn't necessary to specifically include serial.h in C++ programs that use the SERIAL toolbox. However, to achieve correct program compilation, **sercpp.h** must be included in all of your C++ programs, which utilize the SERIAL toolbox.

Listing 5.1: sercpp.h

```
/*******************************************************************
* sercpp.h - C++ Header File for Serial Comm Prog in C and C++      *
*               Copyright (c) 1992 By Mark D. Goodwin               *
*******************************************************************/
#ifndef __SERCPPH__
#define __SERCPPH__

#include "serial.h"

class SERIALPORT {
    int port;
public:
    SERIALPORT(int n, int l) { open_port(n, l); }
    ~SERIALPORT(void) { close_port(); }
    int carrier(void) { return ::carrier(); }
    void fifo(int n) { ::fifo(n); }
    long get_baud(void) { return ::get_baud(); }
    int get_bits(void) { return ::get_bits(); }
    int get_parity(void) { return ::get_parity(); }
    int get_rx_dtr(void) { return ::get_rx_dtr(); }
    int get_rx_rts(void) { return ::get_rx_rts(); }
    int get_rx_xon(void) { return ::get_rx_xon(); }
    int get(void) { return get_serial(); }
    int get_stopbits(void) { return ::get_stopbits(); }
    int get_tx_dtr(void) { return ::get_tx_dtr(); }
    int get_tx_rts(void) { return ::get_tx_rts(); }
    int get_tx_xon(void) { return ::get_tx_xon(); }
    int in_ready(void) { return ::in_ready(); }
    void purge_in(void) { ::purge_in(); }
    int put(unsigned char n) { return put_serial(n); }
    void set_baud(long baud) { ::set_baud(baud); }
    void set_data_format(int bits = 8, int parity = NO_PARITY,
        int stopbit = 1) { ::set_data_format(bits, parity, stopbit); }
    void set_dtr(int n) { ::set_dtr(n); }
    void set_port(long baud, int bits = 8, int parity = NO_PARITY,
        int stopbit = 1) { ::set_port(baud, bits, parity, stopbit); }
    void set_rx_dtr(int n) { ::set_rx_dtr(n); }
    void set_rx_rts(int n) { ::set_rx_rts(n); }
    void set_rx_xon(int n) { ::set_rx_xon(n); }
    void set_tx_dtr(int n) { ::set_tx_dtr(n); }
    void set_tx_rts(int n) { ::set_tx_rts(n); }
    void set_tx_xon(int n) { ::set_tx_xon(n); }
};

#endif
```

Yet Another Dumb Terminal Program

Listing 5.2, **duh3.cpp**, is a C++ version of the dumb terminal program, which appeared in the previous chapter. The only major difference between the two programs is that this chapter's version of the program utilizes the SERIALPORT object class to incorporate the SERIAL toolbox's serial communications routines into the terminal program.

Listing 5.2: duh3.cpp

```
/*********************************************************************
* duh3.cpp - An extremely dumb terminal program (C++ Interrupt Version)
*            Copyright (c) 1992 By Mark Goodwin
*********************************************************************/
#include <stdio.h>
#include <stdlib.h>
#include <dos.h>
#include <conio.h>
#include "sercpp.h"

#define PORT 2                          /* serial port */
#define BAUDRATE 2400                   /* baud rate */

SERIALPORT port(PORT, 1024);

void main(void)
{
    int c;

    printf("Duh No. 3 - An Extremely Dumb Terminal Program\n");
    printf("Copyright (c) 1992 By Mark Goodwin\n\n");

    /* open the serial port */
    port.set_port(BAUDRATE);

    /* main program loop */
    while (TRUE) {
        /* process keyboard presses */
        if (kbhit()) {
            c = getch();
            switch (c) {
                case 0:                 /* exit on Alt-X */
                    if (getch() == 45)
                        exit(0);
```

continued...

...from previous page (Listing 4.2)

```
                    break;
                default:
                    port.put(c);             /* send to the serial port */
            }
        }
        /* process remote characters */
        if (port.in_ready()) {
            c = port.get();                  /* get the character */
            putch(c);                            /* display it */
        }
    }
}
```

Function Description: main

As with all C++ programs, the main function is the main program loop. Its implementation is illustrated by the following pseudocode:

```
display sign on message
open the serial port
while (TRUE) {
        if (key pressed) {
                switch (the key that was pressed) {
                        case extended key pressed:
                                if (Alt-X)
                                        exit the program
                        default:
                                send the character out the serial port
                }
        }
        if (character received) {
                get the character from the serial port
                display the character
        }
}
```

Summary

This chapter presented a **C++ object class** for the SERIAL toolbox's many serial communications routines. Additionally, this chapter presented a **dumb terminal program**, which demonstrated how the SERIALPORT object class is used in an actual serial communications program.

Chapter 6

The File Transfer Protocols

Perhaps the most important task a serial communications program must perform is the transferring of files from one computer to another. In the early days of personal computers, people just sent files byte-by-byte and hoped nothing interfered with them along the way. Unfortunately, such things as line noise can wreak havoc with this type of file transfer. So the pioneering serial communications programmers realized that standards needed to be developed to successfully transfer files. These file transfer standards are known as *file transfer protocols* and this chapter will review some of the most popular file transfer protocols in use today.

The Xmodem Protocol

The **Xmodem protocol** was developed in 1977 by Ward Christensen. Essentially, the Xmodem protocol transmits data in 128-byte data blocks. Because the receiving computer controls when blocks are actually transmitted, the Xmodem protocol is called a *receiver-driven protocol.* The transfer of a file using Xmodem is started by the receiver sending a NAK character (15H). If the transmitter actually receives the NAK, it will send a data block to the receiver. If the NAK isn't acknowledged by the transmitter sending a data block within one second, the receiver will send another NAK to the transmitter. The receiver will continue to send up to 10 NAKs to the transmitter. If after sending 10 NAKs the transmitter has yet to respond by sending a data block, the receiver will **timeout** and abort the file transfer. If the transmitter did receive the NAK correctly, it transmits a data block using the format illustrated in Figure 6.1.

Byte Transmitted	***Description***
SOH	01H to indicate to the receiver the start of a data block.
Block Number	The eight-bit block number. The first block is block 1 and block 255 wraps to block 0.
Complement of Block	This is the eight-bit one's complement of the block number.
Data Byte 1	The first byte of data.
•	
•	
•	
Data Byte 128	The last byte of data.
Checksum	This is the least significant byte of the sum of the block's data bytes.

Figure 6.1 *A 128-Byte Xmodem Data Block.*

You should note from Figure 6.1 that an **Xmodem data block** has a block number, a complement of the block number, and a checksum for the data block. All three of these bytes are handy for catching transmission errors. First of all, the block number should always match the block number the receiver expected next and when complemented it should match the next byte in the block. Furthermore, the receiver will calculate a checksum for the data it actually received and if it matches the transmitter's checksum, the receiver can be reasonably sure that the data was received without error. If a block is received without error, the receiver sends an ACK (06H) to the transmitter and the transmitter will in turn either send the file's next data block or send an EOT (04H) to indicate the file transfer is complete. If a block is erroneously received, the receiver will send a NAK to the transmitter and the transmitter will retransmit the block.

You may be wondering about files that aren't evenly divisible by 128. Because Xmodem expects all data blocks to be 128 bytes in length, the final data block is padded with end-of-file characters (1AH). You should note that it is optional to send a final 128-byte data block of EOF characters if a file is evenly divisible by 128.

Finally, there must be a method of aborting a file transfer by either end. Sending a series of CAN (18H) characters is the standard way of aborting an Xmodem transfer. Unfortunately, there is no agreed upon number of CANs that is universally recognized as an aborted transfer. Due to line noise, a single CAN character isn't sufficient; therefore, most Xmodem implementations use from two to five CAN characters received in succession as a request from the remote computer to abort the transfer.

The Xmodem-CRC Protocol

Although the Xmodem was a great step forward for performing file transfers, it's use of an 8-bit checksum to detect errors is not very efficient. Indeed, the 8-bit checksum version of Xmodem is notorious for letting transmission errors slip by. Consequently, the 8-bit checksum was replaced with a more efficient *16-bit CRC*. CRCs are calculated using modulo two arithmetic and fortunately for the serial communications programmer there are a number of public domain routines for calculating CRCs. The following **C** code can be used to calculate a 16-bit CRC and is called for each of the block's data bytes:

```
unsigned updatecrc(int c, unsigned crc)
{
    int i;

    for (i = 8; —i >= 0; ) {
        if (crc & 0x8000) {
            crc <<= 1;
            crc += ((c <= 1) & 0400) != 0);
            crc ^= 0x1021;
    }
    else {
        crc <<= 1;
        crc += (((c <<= 1) & 0400) != 0);
    }
    return crc;
}
```

Although the previous routine is very useful, most Xmodem-CRC implementations (as does the one in this book) use a fast table-driven macro to calculate CRCs. The actual code for a table-driven 16-bit CRC generator is presented in this chapter's program listing. You should note that both the previous CRC routine and the table-driven routine used in this book are derived from the routines in the public domain **Zmodem source code** by Chuck Forsberg of Omen Technologies.

In order to be able to transfer files using Xmodem-CRC and still maintain compatibility with older version of Xmodem that only use checksums, the Xmodem-CRC protocol starts by having the receiver send a C character instead of a NAK to begin the transmission. If the transmitter supports CRCs, it will respond to the C character by sending a data block. If the receiver doesn't receive a data block after sending three Cs with a one second delay between each character, it will assume that the transmitter doesn't support CRCs and start sending NAKs to initiate an Xmodem checksum transmission. Figure 6.2 illustrates how a Xmodem data block, which uses a 16-bit CRC, would be transmitted.

Byte Transmitted	***Description***
SOH	01H to indicate to the receiver the start of a data block.
Block Number	The eight-bit block number. The first block is block 1 and block 255 wraps to block 0.
Complement of Block	This is the eight-bit one's complement of the block number.
Data Byte 1	The first byte of data.
•	
•	
•	
Data Byte 128	The last byte of data.
MSB of CRC	The 16-bit CRC's most significant byte.
LSB of CRC	The 16-bit CRC's least significant byte.

Figure 6.2 *A 128-Byte Xmodem-CRC Data Block.*

The Xmodem-1K Protocol

Although the Xmodem-CRC protocol is more reliable than its checksum counterpart, both protocols are extremely slow protocols. Their slowness is a direct result of only transmitting data in 128-byte data blocks. This was adequate back when 300 baud modems were state-of-the-art, but such a block size is a very poor choice for even a 1200-baud modem. A much more practical block size is 1024 bytes. Because a 1024-byte data block is eight times larger than a 128-byte data block, it only requires one-eighth as much header and CRC information. Furthermore, the delays caused by the transmitter waiting for the receiver to acknowledge the previously transmitted block are also eight times fewer. Because of all of these efficiency advantages a larger data block would offer, a 1024-byte data block version of Xmodem was created and was called, appropriately enough, *Xmodem-1K*.

Basically, there are only two differences between Xmodem-CRC and Xmodem-1K. The first and most obvious is that Xmodem-1K can transmit 1024 bytes per data block. The second difference is that Xmodem-1K uses an STX (02H) for the a 1024-byte data block's header byte. In addition to 1024-byte data block's, the Xmodem-1K transmitter can also transmit 128-byte data blocks; therefore, the Xmodem-1K receiver should be implemented so it can handle any combination of 1024-byte and 128-byte data blocks. Figure 6.3 illustrates a 1024-byte Xmodem-1K data block.

Byte Transmitted	***Description***
STX	02H to indicate to the receiver the start of a 1024-byte data block.
Block Number	The eight-bit block number. The first block is block 1 and block 255 wraps to block 0.
Complement of Block	This is the eight-bit one's complement of the block number.
Data Byte 1	The first byte of data.
•	
•	
•	
Data Byte 1024	The last byte of data.
MSB of CRC	The 16-bit CRC's most significant byte.
LSB of CRC	The 16-bit CRC's least significant byte.

Figure 6.3 *A 1024-Byte Xmodem-1K Data Block.*

The Ymodem Protocol

Certainly the Xmodem-1K protocol greatly increased Xmodem's efficiency, but it did little for its ease of use. For example, both Xmodem and Xmodem-1K require that the receiver's operator manually enter the file name. Furthermore, using either 128-byte or 1024-byte data blocks almost always changes a file's size and neither Xmodem nor Xmodem-1K preserve the file's modification date. Also, wouldn't it be nice to be able to transmit more than one file at a time? To provide all of these bells and whistles, the *Ymodem protocol* was born. Not only is it a batch protocol (able to transmit more than one file at a time) it sends each file's name and can optionally send other file-related information like the file's size and its modification date.

Essentially, the *Ymodem protocol* is a variant of the Xmodem-1K protocol. Unlike Xmodem and Xmodem-1K, the Ymodem protocol starts each file transfer off by transmitting a block number 0. Figure 6.4 illustrates how the Ymodem Block0 is constructed. As this figure shows, a Ymodem Block0 can be used to pass a number of optional parameters to the receiver. However, it is important to note that to pass a specific optional parameter all preceding optional parameters must also be passed. It is quite common for Ymodem implementations to use both the file name and file size parameters. If the transmitter does pass these two parameters, it is very easy for the receiver to utilize them to adjust the received file's length and date.

You should also note that Figure 6.4 shows that Ymodem passes a null string (" ") to indicate the end of a batch transfer. During a normal batch transfer, Ymodem will send the Block0 for each file. After the receiver properly acknowledges the Block0 with an ACK, the transmitter will send the file just like an Xmodem-1K file transfer. It is important to note that the receiver initiates the file transfer as it would for an Xmodem-1K by sending a C character. Like it's predecessors, Ymodem is a receiver-driven protocol and will do nothing until the receiver tells it to. After the receiver properly acknowledges the EOT and initiates another transfer by sending a C character, Ymodem will send another Block0 to the receiver. If all files have been transferred, the transmitter will send a Block0 with a null string for the file name. Otherwise, Ymodem will send a Block0 for the next file as it did for the first file and the process of transferring the file with a Xmodem-1K-like file transfer would start anew.

Byte Transmitted	*Description*
SOH	01H to indicate to the receiver the start of a data block.
Block Number	00H to indicate to the receiver that it's a Ymodem Block0.
Complement of Block	This is the eight-bit one's complement of the block number. FFH in the case of a Ymodem Block0.
File Name	The file's name. Terminated with a 00H byte. A null string ("") indicates the end of the batch transfer.
File Size	Optional file size as a decimal string.
Modification Date	Optional date of the file's last modification as an octal string and is measured in the number of seconds from January 1, 1970 (GMT). If the modification date is to be passed, file size must also be passed and the two are separated by a space character.
File Mode	Optional file mode as an octal string. If the file mode is to be passed, the modification date must also be passed and the two are separated by a space character.
Serial Number	Optional serial number as an octal string. If the serial number is to be passed, the file mode must also be passed and the two are separated by a space character.
Nulls	The rest of the data block is null (00H) padded.
MSB of CRC	The 16-bit CRC's most significant byte.
LSB of CRC	The 16-bit CRC's least significant byte.

Figure 6.4 *A Ymodem Block0.*

The Ymodem-G Protocol

The *Ymodem-G protocol* is an extremely streamlined variant of the Ymodem protocol. To initiate a Ymodem-G transfer, the receiver sends a G character instead of the more familiar Xmodem/Ymodem C character. By receiving the G character, the transmitter will send all data blocks without waiting for acknowledgement from the receiver. To allow for file maintenance on both ends, the Ymodem-G transmitter does wait for an acknowledgment after sending each file's EOT. In all other respects, the Ymodem-G protocol is identical to the Ymodem protocol.

Because there is no way for the Ymodem-G receiver to request that a block be retransmitted, the receiver will usually abort the transfer whenever it detects a bad block number, a short block, or a CRC error by sending a series of CAN characters to the transmitter. Because of the Ymodem-G protocol's inability to retransmit data it is known as an **error-correcting protocol** and is only intended to be used with **error-correcting modems**. Remember from Chapter 2 that error-correcting modems have the ability to retransmit data between each other if a bad block is encountered. Consequently, it is somewhat redundant for the file transfer protocol to retransmit incorrect data. Indeed, over an ideal error-correcting connection, you will never see any errors during any file transfer. Unfortunately, that type of ideal condition doesn't exist in the real world. It is a common misperception that error-correcting modems will correct for all errors. Although error-correcting modems are extremely efficient at catching errors between themselves, they have no way of detecting if an error occurs between the modem itself and the serial communications program. There is a lot of hardware in between and sometimes things don't quite click. For example, multitasking can greatly increase the probability that an error can occur. Although the 16550 UART and its FIFO buffers are very good at picking up the slack on a multitasking system, it is not a perfect solution. Accordingly, don't be surprised to occasionally see aborted Ymodem-G file transfers even with an error-correcting data link.

Source Listing: protocol.c

Listing 6.1, **protocol.c**, contains the SERIAL toolbox routines that implement the Xmodem, Xmodem-1K, Ymodem, and Ymodem-G file transfer protocols. Because the four protocols are very similar, the SERIAL toolbox only needs one transmit routine and one receive routine to handle all four protocols. Obviously, this saves a great deal of space due to the elimination of an enormous amount of redundant code.

Note: Due to the physical constraints of this book, some lines in the following listing are shown wrapped. These should be entered as single lines.

Listing 6.1: protocol.c

```
/*******************************************************************
* protocol.c - Xmodem, Xmodem-1K, Ymodem, and Ymodem-G Protocols    *
*             Copyright (c) 1992 By Mark D. Goodwin                 *
*******************************************************************/
#include <stdio.h>
#include <stdlib.h>
#include <string.h>
#include <time.h>
#ifdef __TURBOC__
#include <dir.h>
#else
#include <dos.h>
#endif
#include <stdarg.h>
#include <io.h>
#include "serial.h"

/* protocol constants */
#define SOH 0x01
#define STX 0x02
#define EOT 0x04
#define ACK 0x06
#define NAK 0x15
#define CAN 0x18
#define CPMEOF 0x1A
#define TIMED_OUT 3
#define BAD_BLOCK 5
#define CRC_ERROR 7

/* calculate elapsed time */
#define elapsed ((clock() - start) / CLK_TCK)

/* buffer for data packets */
unsigned char buffer[1024];

/* CRC table */
unsigned short crctab[256] = {
    0x0000, 0x1021, 0x2042, 0x3063, 0x4084, 0x50a5, 0x60c6, 0x70e7,
    0x8108, 0x9129, 0xa14a, 0xb16b, 0xc18c, 0xd1ad, 0xe1ce, 0xf1ef,
    0x1231, 0x0210, 0x3273, 0x2252, 0x52b5, 0x4294, 0x72f7, 0x62d6,
    0x9339, 0x8318, 0xb37b, 0xa35a, 0xd3bd, 0xc39c, 0xf3ff, 0xe3de,
    0x2462, 0x3443, 0x0420, 0x1401, 0x64e6, 0x74c7, 0x44a4, 0x5485,
    0xa56a, 0xb54b, 0x8528, 0x9509, 0xe5ee, 0xf5cf, 0xc5ac, 0xd58d,
    0x3653, 0x2672, 0x1611, 0x0630, 0x76d7, 0x66f6, 0x5695, 0x46b4,
    0xb75b, 0xa77a, 0x9719, 0x8738, 0xf7df, 0xe7fe, 0xd79d, 0xc7bc,
    0x48c4, 0x58e5, 0x6886, 0x78a7, 0x0840, 0x1861, 0x2802, 0x3823,
    0xc9cc, 0xd9ed, 0xe98e, 0xf9af, 0x8948, 0x9969, 0xa90a, 0xb92b,
    0x5af5, 0x4ad4, 0x7ab7, 0x6a96, 0x1a71, 0x0a50, 0x3a33, 0x2a12,
    0xdbfd, 0xcbdc, 0xfbbf, 0xeb9e, 0x9b79, 0x8b58, 0xbb3b, 0xab1a,
    0x6ca6, 0x7c87, 0x4ce4, 0x5cc5, 0x2c22, 0x3c03, 0x0c60, 0x1c41,
    0xedae, 0xfd8f, 0xcdec, 0xddcd, 0xad2a, 0xbd0b, 0x8d68, 0x9d49,
```

continued...

...from previous page (Listing 6.1)

```
    0x7e97,  0x6eb6,  0x5ed5,  0x4ef4,  0x3e13,  0x2e32,  0x1e51,  0x0e70,
    0xff9f,  0xefbe,  0xdfdd,  0xcffc,  0xbf1b,  0xaf3a,  0x9f59,  0x8f78,
    0x9188,  0x81a9,  0xb1ca,  0xa1eb,  0xd10c,  0xc12d,  0xf14e,  0xe16f,
    0x1080,  0x00a1,  0x30c2,  0x20e3,  0x5004,  0x4025,  0x7046,  0x6067,
    0x83b9,  0x9398,  0xa3fb,  0xb3da,  0xc33d,  0xd31c,  0xe37f,  0xf35e,
    0x02b1,  0x1290,  0x22f3,  0x32d2,  0x4235,  0x5214,  0x6277,  0x7256,
    0xb5ea,  0xa5cb,  0x95a8,  0x8589,  0xf56e,  0xe54f,  0xd52c,  0xc50d,
    0x34e2,  0x24c3,  0x14a0,  0x0481,  0x7466,  0x6447,  0x5424,  0x4405,
    0xa7db,  0xb7fa,  0x8799,  0x97b8,  0xe75f,  0xf77e,  0xc71d,  0xd73c,
    0x26d3,  0x36f2,  0x0691,  0x16b0,  0x6657,  0x7676,  0x4615,  0x5634,
    0xd94c,  0xc96d,  0xf90e,  0xe92f,  0x99c8,  0x89e9,  0xb98a,  0xa9ab,
    0x5844,  0x4865,  0x7806,  0x6827,  0x18c0,  0x08e1,  0x3882,  0x28a3,
    0xcb7d,  0xdb5c,  0xeb3f,  0xfb1e,  0x8bf9,  0x9bd8,  0xabbb,  0xbb9a,
    0x4a75,  0x5a54,  0x6a37,  0x7a16,  0x0af1,  0x1ad0,  0x2ab3,  0x3a92,
    0xfd2e,  0xed0f,  0xdd6c,  0xcd4d,  0xbdaa,  0xad8b,  0x9de8,  0x8dc9,
    0x7c26,  0x6c07,  0x5c64,  0x4c45,  0x3ca2,  0x2c83,  0x1ce0,  0x0cc1,
    0xef1f,  0xff3e,  0xcf5d,  0xdf7c,  0xaf9b,  0xbfba,  0x8fd9,  0x9ff8,
    0x6e17,  0x7e36,  0x4e55,  0x5e74,  0x2e93,  0x3eb2,  0x0ed1,  0x1ef0
};

/* update CRC routine */
#define updcrc(d, s) (crctab[((s >> 8) & 0xff)] ^ (s << 8) ^ d)

/* get a character, but time out after a specified time limit */
static int timed_get(int n)
{
    clock_t start;

    start = clock();                    /* get current time */
    while (TRUE) {
        if (in_ready())                 /* char available? */
            return get_serial();        /* return it if one is */
        if (!carrier() || elapsed >= n) /* break out of loop if time out */
            break;
    }
    return -1;                          /* return time out error */
}

/* build a data packet */
static int build_block(int l, FILE *file)
{
    int i, j;

    i = fread(buffer, 1, l, file);      /* read in the next block */
    if (!i)                             /* return if EOF */
        return FALSE;
    for (j = i; j < l; j++)             /* save CPMEOF for rest of block */
        buffer[j] = CPMEOF;
    return TRUE;
}
```

continued...

...from previous page (Listing 6.1)

```
/* build Ymodem header block */
static void header_block(char *fname, FILE *file)
{
    int i;
    long length;
    #ifdef __TURBOC__
    struct ftime ft;
    #else
    unsigned fd, ft;
    #endif
    struct tm t;

    for (i = 0; i < 128; i++)           /* zero out the buffer */
        buffer[i] = 0;
    if (fname != NULL) {
        sprintf(buffer, fname);         /* save the filename */
        fseek(file, 0L, SEEK_END);      /* get the length */
        length = ftell(file);
        fseek(file, 0L, SEEK_SET);
        #ifdef __TURBOC__
        getftime(fileno(file), &ft);    /* figure the file mod date */
        t.tm_year = ft.ft_year + 80;
        t.tm_mon = ft.ft_month - 1;
        t.tm_mday = ft.ft_day;
        t.tm_hour = ft.ft_hour;
        t.tm_min = ft.ft_min;
        t.tm_sec = ft.ft_tsec * 2;
        t.tm_isdst = FALSE;
        #else
        _dos_getftime(fileno(file), &fd, &ft);
        t.tm_year = (fd >> 9) + 80;
        t.tm_mon = ((fd >> 5) & 0xf) - 1;
        t.tm_mday = (fd & 0x1f);
        t.tm_hour = (ft >> 11);
        t.tm_min = (ft >> 5) & 0x3f;
        t.tm_sec = (ft & 0x1f) * 2;
        t.tm_isdst = FALSE;
        #endif
        putenv("TZ=GMT0GMT");           /* adjust for time zones */
        tzset();
        /* save the length and mod date */
        sprintf(buffer + strlen(buffer) + 1, "%ld %lo", length, mktime(&t));
    }
}
```

continued...

...from previous page (Listing 6.1)

```
/* abort transfer routine */
static void abort_transfer(void)
{
    int i;

    for (i = 0; i < 8; i++)             /* send 8 CANs */
        put_serial(CAN);
}

/* parse the filename */
static void parse(char *p, char *f)
{
    int i;
    char *s;

    if ((s = strrchr(p, ':')) != NULL)  /* bump past drive spec */
        p = s + 1;
    if ((s = strrchr(p, '\\')) != NULL) /* bump past path spec */
        p = s + 1;
    *f = 0;                             /* save the filename */
    for (i = 0; i < 12; i++) {
        if (!*p)
            break;
        *f = *p;
        f++;
        *f = 0;
        p++;
    }
}

/* file transmit routine */
int xmit_file(int xtype, int (*error_handler)(int c, long p, char *s), char *files[])
{
    int i, tries, block = 0, bsize, cancel, retrans, crc, batch, nfiles = 0;
    int obits, oparity, ostop, oxon;
    unsigned int sum;
    long length, bsent;
    clock_t start;
    char *fname;
    FILE *file;
    char path[13];
```

continued...

...from previous page (Listing 6.1)

```
switch (xtype) {                    /* set block size and batch flag */
    case XMODEM:
        bsize = 128;
        batch = FALSE;
        break;
    case XMODEM1K:
        bsize = 1024;
        batch = FALSE;
        break;
    case YMODEM:
        bsize = 1024;
        batch = TRUE;
        break;
    case YMODEMG:
        bsize = 1024;
        batch = TRUE;
        break;
    default:
        return FALSE;
}
obits = get_bits();                 /* save current settings */
oparity = get_parity();
ostop = get_stopbits();
oxon = get_tx_xon();
set_data_format(8, NO_PARITY, 1);   /* set for 8-N-1 */
set_tx_xon(FALSE);
while (TRUE) {
    fname = files[nfiles];          /* get the next filename */
    nfiles++;
    /* return if none and if not a batch transfer */
    if (fname == NULL && !batch) {
        set_data_format(obits, oparity, ostop);
        set_tx_xon(oxon);
        return TRUE;
    }
    start = clock();                /* get clock */
    cancel = FALSE;                 /* no CAN */
    while (TRUE) {
        /* abort if loss of carrier */
        if (!carrier()) {
            (*error_handler)(ERROR, block, "Loss of Carrier Detected!");
            set_data_format(obits, oparity, ostop);
            set_tx_xon(oxon);
            return FALSE;
        }
```

continued...

...from previous page (Listing 6.1)

```
            /* get a character from the receiver */
            if (in_ready()) {
                switch (get_serial()) {
                    case NAK:           /* Use no CRCs */
                        crc = FALSE;
                        break;
                    case 'C':           /* Use CRCs */
                        if (xtype == YMODEMG)
                            xtype = YMODEM;
                        crc = TRUE;
                        break;
                    case 'G':           /* Ymodem-G */
                        if (xtype != YMODEMG)
                            continue;
                        crc = TRUE;
                        break;
                    case CAN:
                        /* abort if second cancel */
                        if (cancel) {
                            (*error_handler)(ERROR, block, "Transfer Cancelled By
Receiver");
                            set_data_format(obits, oparity, ostop);
                            set_tx_xon(oxon);
                            return FALSE;
                        }
                        cancel = TRUE;
                        continue;
                    default:
                        cancel = FALSE;
                        continue;
                }
                break;
            }
            /* abort if time out */
            if (elapsed >= 60) {
                set_data_format(obits, oparity, ostop);
                set_tx_xon(oxon);
                return FALSE;
            }
        }
        if (fname != NULL) {
            /* open the file */
            if ((file = fopen(fname, "rb")) == NULL) {
                abort_transfer();
                set_data_format(obits, oparity, ostop);
                set_tx_xon(oxon);
                return FALSE;
            }
```

continued...

...from previous page (Listing 6.1)

```
            /* parse filename */
            parse(fname, path);
            fseek(file, 0L, SEEK_END);
            length = ftell(file);
            fseek(file, 0L, SEEK_SET);
            /* send filename and length to the error handler */
            if (!(*error_handler)(SENDING, length, fname)) {
                abort_transfer();
                fclose(file);
                set_data_format(obits, oparity, ostop);
                set_tx_xon(oxon);
                return FALSE;
            }
            /* set number of bytes sent */
            bsent = 0L;
        }
        /* send header if Ymodem or Ymodem-G */
        if (batch) {
            /* build header block */
            header_block(fname, file);
            while (TRUE) {
                /* figure CRC */
                for (i = sum = 0; i < 128; i++)
                    sum = updcrc(buffer[i], sum);
                /* send the block */
                put_serial(SOH);
                put_serial(0);
                put_serial(0xff);
                for (i = 0; i < 128; i++)
                    put_serial(buffer[i]);
                sum = updcrc(0, sum);
                sum = updcrc(0, sum);
                put_serial((unsigned char)((sum >> 8) & 0xff));
                put_serial((unsigned char)(sum & 0xff));
                cancel = retrans = FALSE;
                start = clock();
                while (TRUE) {
                    /* abort if loss of carrier */
                    if (!carrier()) {
                        (*error_handler)(ERROR, block, "Loss of Carrier Detected!");
                        if (fname != NULL)
                            fclose(file);
                        set_data_format(obits, oparity, ostop);
                        set_tx_xon(oxon);
                        return FALSE;
                    }
                    /* don't wait if Ymodem-G */
                    if (xtype == YMODEMG)
                        break;
```

continued...

...from previous page (Listing 6.1)

```
                /* get ACK */
                if (in_ready()) {
                    switch (get_serial()) {
                        case NAK:    /* retransmit the block */
                            cancel = FALSE;
                            retrans = TRUE;
                            break;
                        case ACK:    /* block received ok */
                            cancel = FALSE;
                            break;
                        case CAN:
                            /* abort if second CAN */
                            if (cancel) {
                                if (fname != NULL)
                                    fclose(file);
                                set_data_format(obits, oparity, ostop);
                                set_tx_xon(oxon);
                                return FALSE;
                            }
                            cancel = TRUE;
                            continue;
                        default:
                            cancel = FALSE;
                            continue;
                    }
                    break;
                }
                /* abort if time out */
                if (elapsed >= 60) {
                    if (fname != NULL)
                        fclose(file);
                    set_data_format(obits, oparity, ostop);
                    set_tx_xon(oxon);
                    return FALSE;
                }
            }
            /* do it again if NAK */
            if (retrans)
                continue;
            /* exit if end of batch transmission */
            if (fname == NULL) {
                timed_get(10);
                set_data_format(obits, oparity, ostop);
                set_tx_xon(oxon);
                return TRUE;
            }
            break;
        }
```

continued...

...from previous page (Listing 6.1)

```
        start = clock();                /* get clock */
        cancel = FALSE;                 /* flag no CAN */
        while (TRUE) {
            /* abort if loss of carrier */
            if (!carrier()) {
                (*error_handler)(ERROR, block, "Loss of Carrier Detected!");
                set_data_format(obits, oparity, ostop);
                set_tx_xon(oxon);
                fclose(file);
                return FALSE;
            }
            if (in_ready()) {
                switch (get_serial()) {
                    case NAK:           /* no CRCs */
                        crc = FALSE;
                        break;
                    case 'C':           /* use CRCs */
                        if (xtype == YMODEMG)
                            xtype = YMODEM;
                        crc = TRUE;
                        break;
                    case 'G':           /* Ymodem-G */
                        if (xtype != YMODEMG)
                            continue;
                        crc = TRUE;
                        break;
                    case CAN:
                        /* abort if second CAN */
                        if (cancel) {
                            (*error_handler)(ERROR, block, "Transfer Cancelled By
Receiver");

                            set_data_format(obits, oparity, ostop);
                            set_tx_xon(oxon);
                            fclose(file);
                            return FALSE;
                        }
                        cancel = TRUE;
                        continue;
                    default:
                        cancel = FALSE;
                        continue;
                }
                break;
            }
            /* abort if time out */
            if (elapsed >= 60) {
                set_data_format(obits, oparity, ostop);
                set_tx_xon(oxon);
                fclose(file);
                return FALSE;
            }
        }
    }
```

continued...

...from previous page (Listing 6.1)

```
        block = 1;                      /* starting block number */
        retrans = FALSE;
        while (TRUE) {
            /* build the new block if not rexmit */
            if (!retrans) {
                if (bsize == 1024 && length - ftell(file) < 1024L)
                    bsize = 128;
                if (!build_block(bsize, file))
                    break;
            }
            /* figure CRC or checksum */
            for (i = sum = 0; i < bsize; i++) {
                if (crc)
                    sum = updcrc(buffer[i], sum);
                else
                    sum += buffer[i];
            }
            /* send the block */
            if (bsize == 128)
                put_serial(SOH);
            else
                put_serial(STX);
            put_serial((unsigned char)(block & 0xff));
            put_serial((unsigned char)((255 - block) & 0xff));
            for (i = 0; i < bsize; i++)
                put_serial(buffer[i]);
            if (crc) {
                sum = updcrc(0, sum);
                sum = updcrc(0, sum);
                put_serial((unsigned char)((sum >> 8) & 0xff));
                put_serial((unsigned char)(sum & 0xff));
            }
            else
                put_serial((unsigned char)(sum & 0xff));
            cancel = retrans = FALSE;
            start = clock();
            while (TRUE) {
                /* abort if loss of carrier */
                if (!carrier()) {
                    (*error_handler)(ERROR, block, "Loss of Carrier Detected!");
                    fclose(file);
                    set_data_format(obits, oparity, ostop);
                    set_tx_xon(oxon);
                    return FALSE;
                }
```

continued...

...from previous page (Listing 6.1)

```
            /* Ymodem-G */
            if (xtype == YMODEMG) {
                /* adjust no bytes sent */
                bsent += bsize;
                if (!(*error_handler)(SENT, bsent, "ACK")) {
                    abort_transfer();
                    fclose(file);
                    set_data_format(obits, oparity, ostop);
                    set_tx_xon(oxon);
                    return FALSE;
                }
                /* abort if two CANs received */
                if (in_ready() && get_serial() == CAN &&
                    in_ready() && get_serial() == CAN) {
                    (*error_handler)(ERROR, block, "Transfer Cancelled By
Receiver");
                    fclose(file);
                    set_data_format(obits, oparity, ostop);
                    set_tx_xon(oxon);
                    return FALSE;
                }
                break;
            }
            if (in_ready()) {
                switch (get_serial()) {
                    case NAK:       /* retransmit */
                        if (!(*error_handler)(ERROR, block, "NAK")) {
                            abort_transfer();
                            fclose(file);
                             set_data_format(obits, oparity, ostop);
                            set_tx_xon(oxon);
                            return FALSE;
                        }
                        cancel = FALSE;
                        retrans = TRUE;
                        break;
                    case ACK:       /* block received ok */
                        bsent += bsize;
                        if (!(*error_handler)(SENT, bsent, "ACK")) {
                            abort_transfer();
                            fclose(file);
                            set_data_format(obits, oparity, ostop);
                            set_tx_xon(oxon);
                            return FALSE;
                        }
```

continued...

...from previous page (Listing 6.1)

```
                        cancel = FALSE;
                        break;
                    case CAN:
                        /* abort if second CAN */
                        if (cancel) {
                            (*error_handler)(ERROR, block, "Transfer Cancelled By
Receiver");

                            fclose(file);
                            set_data_format(obits, oparity, ostop);
                            set_tx_xon(oxon);
                            return FALSE;
                        }
                        cancel = TRUE;
                        continue;
                    default:
                        cancel = FALSE;
                        continue;
                }
                break;
            }
            /* abort if time out */
            if (elapsed >= 60) {
                fclose(file);
                set_data_format(obits, oparity, ostop);
                set_tx_xon(oxon);
                return FALSE;
            }
        }
        /* bump block number if not retransmit */
        if (retrans)
            continue;
        block = (block + 1) & 0xff;
    }
    /* close the file */
    fclose(file);
    start = clock();
    /* flag end of transfer */
    put_serial(EOT);
    while (TRUE) {
        /* abort if loss of carrier */
        if (!carrier()) {
            (*error_handler)(ERROR, block, "Loss of Carrier Detected!");
            set_data_format(obits, oparity, ostop);
            set_tx_xon(oxon);
            return FALSE;
        }
```

continued...

...from previous page (Listing 6.1)

```
            /* get ACK */
            if (in_ready()) {
                if (get_serial() != ACK) {
                    put_serial(EOT);
                    continue;
                }
                break;
            }
            /* abort if time out */
            if (elapsed >= 60) {
                set_data_format(obits, oparity, ostop);
                set_tx_xon(oxon);
                return FALSE;
            }
        }
        (*error_handler)(COMPLETE, block, "Transfer Successfully Completed");
        /* exit if not Ymodem or Ymodem-G */
        if (!batch) {
            set_data_format(obits, oparity, ostop);
            set_tx_xon(oxon);
            return TRUE;
        }
        /* adjust block size */
        bsize = 1024;
    }
}

/* get a block from transmitter */
static int getblock(int block, int crc)
{
    int c, l, i, sum;

    /* get a character */
    if ((c = timed_get(10)) == -1)
        return TIMED_OUT;
    switch (c) {
        case CAN:                       /* two CANs? */
            if ((c = timed_get(1)) == CAN)
                return CAN;
            return TIMED_OUT;
        case SOH:                       /* 128 byte block header */
            l = 128;
            break;
        case STX:                       /* 1024 byte block header */
            l = 1024;
            break;
        case EOT:                       /* end of transfer */
            return EOT;
        default:
            return TIMED_OUT;           /* return timed out */
    }
```

continued...

...from previous page (Listing 6.1)

```
    if ((c = timed_get(1)) == -1)          /* get the block number */
        return TIMED_OUT;
    if (c != block)                       /* return if bad block number */
        return BAD_BLOCK;
    if ((c = timed_get(1)) == -1)         /* get complement */
        return TIMED_OUT;
    if (c != ((255 - block) & 0xff))      /* return if bad block number */
        return BAD_BLOCK;
    for (i = 0; i < l; i++)               /* get the block */
        if ((int)(buffer[i] = (unsigned char)timed_get(1)) == -1)
            return TIMED_OUT;
    /* get checksum */
    if (!crc) {
        if ((c = timed_get(1)) == -1)
            return TIMED_OUT;
        for (i = sum = 0; i < l; i++)
            sum += buffer[i];
    }
    /* get CRC */
    else {
        if ((sum = timed_get(1)) == -1)
            return TIMED_OUT;
        if ((c = timed_get(1)) == -1)
            return TIMED_OUT;
        c |= sum << 8;
        for (i = sum = 0; i < l; i++)
            sum = updcrc(buffer[i], sum);
        sum = updcrc(0, sum);
        sum = updcrc(0, sum);
    }
    /* check for checksum or CRC error */
    if (c != sum)
        return CRC_ERROR;
    /* return block size */
    if (l == 128)
        return SOH;
    return STX;
}

/* receive files routine */
int recv_file(int xtype, int(*error_handler)(int c, long p, char *s), char *path)
{
    int i, l, batch, block, crc;
    int obits, oparity, ostop, oxon;
    long length, received, moddate;
    char *fname, line[80];
    FILE *file;
    #ifdef __TURBOC__
    struct ftime ft;
    #else
    unsigned fd, ft;
    #endif
    struct tm *t;
```

continued...

...from previous page (Listing 6.1)

```
/* set batch flag */
switch (xtype) {
    case XMODEM:
    case XMODEM1K:
        batch = FALSE;
        break;
    case YMODEM:
    case YMODEMG:
        batch = TRUE;
        break;
    default:
        return FALSE;
}
obits = get_bits();                     /* save current settings */
oparity = get_parity();
ostop = get_stopbits();
oxon = get_tx_xon();
set_data_format(8, NO_PARITY, 1);   /* set to 8-N-1 */
set_tx_xon(FALSE);
while (TRUE) {
    crc = TRUE;                         /* use CRCs */
    /* get transmitter going */
    if (xtype == YMODEMG)
        put_serial('G');
    else
        put_serial('C');
    block = batch ? 0 : 1;
    for (i = 0; i < 10; i++) {
        /* get a block */
        l = getblock(block, crc);
        /* abort if CAN or loss of carrier */
        if (l == CAN || !carrier()) {
            set_data_format(obits, oparity, ostop);
            set_tx_xon(oxon);
            return FALSE;
        }
        /* get transmitter going again */
        if (l != SOH && l != STX && l != EOT) {
            switch (xtype) {
                case XMODEM:
                    if (i < 2)
                        put_serial('C');    /* use CRCs */
                    else {
                        put_serial(NAK);    /* no CRCs after two tries */
                        crc = FALSE;
                    }
```

continued...

...from previous page (Listing 6.1)

```
                    continue;
                case XMODEM1K:
                case YMODEM:
                    put_serial('C');        /* use CRCs */
                    continue;
                case YMODEMG:
                    put_serial('G');        /* Ymodem-G */
                    continue;
            }
        }
        break;
    }
    /* abort if transmitter doesn't respond after 10 tries */
    if (i == 10) {
        set_data_format(obits, oparity, ostop);
        set_tx_xon(oxon);
        return FALSE;
    }
    /* set filename, length, and number of bytes received */
    if (!batch) {
        fname = path;
        length = received = 0L;
    }
    else {
        if (!*buffer) {
            set_data_format(obits, oparity, ostop);
            set_tx_xon(oxon);
            return TRUE;
        }
        sprintf(line, "%s\\%s", path, buffer);
        fname = line;
        if (!buffer[strlen(buffer) + 1]) {
            length = 0L;
            moddate = 0L;
        }
        else {
            sscanf(buffer + strlen(buffer) + 1, "%ld%lo", &length, &moddate);
            received = 0;
        }
    }
    /* open the file */
    if ((file = fopen(fname, "wb")) == NULL) {
        abort_transfer();
        set_data_format(obits, oparity, ostop);
        set_tx_xon(oxon);
        return FALSE;
    }
```

continued...

...from previous page (Listing 6.1)

```
    /* send filename and length to the error handler */
    if (!(*error_handler)(RECEIVING, length, fname)) {
        abort_transfer();
        fclose(file);
        set_data_format(obits, oparity, ostop);
        set_tx_xon(oxon);
        return FALSE;
    }
    /* if batch signal get 1st block */
    if (batch) {
        crc = TRUE;
        put_serial(ACK);            /* ACK block 0 */
        /* tell tranmitter to send 1st block */
        if (xtype == YMODEMG)
            put_serial('G');
        else
            put_serial('C');
        block = 1;
        for (i = 0; i < 10; i++) {
            /* get a block */
            l = getblock(block, crc);
            /* abort if CAN or loss of carrier */
            if (l == CAN || !carrier()) {
                set_data_format(obits, oparity, ostop);
                set_tx_xon(oxon);
                fclose(file);
                return FALSE;
            }
            /* nudge transmitter again if no block */
            if (l != SOH && l != STX && l != EOT) {
                switch (xtype) {
                    case YMODEM:
                        put_serial('C');
                        continue;
                    case YMODEMG:
                        put_serial('G');
                        continue;
                }
            }
            break;
        }
        /* abort if failed after 10 attempts */
        if (i == 10) {
            abort_transfer();
            set_data_format(obits, oparity, ostop);
            set_tx_xon(oxon);
            fclose(file);
            return FALSE;
        }
    }
```

continued...

...from previous page (Listing 6.1)

```
    /* get file */
    while (TRUE) {
        /* break out of loop if end of file */
        if (l == EOT) {
            (*error_handler)(COMPLETE, 0, "Transfer Successfully Completed");
            break;
        }
        /* write the block to disk */
        if (!batch || (batch && !length)) {
            fwrite(buffer, 1, l == SOH ? 128 : 1024, file);
            received += (l == SOH ? 128 : 1024);
        }
        else {
            if (length - received >= (l == SOH ? 128 : 1024)) {
                fwrite(buffer, 1, l == SOH ? 128 : 1024, file);
                received += (l == SOH ? 128 : 1024);
            }
            else {
                if (length - received) {
                    fwrite(buffer, 1, (size_t)(length - received), file);
                        received = length;
                }
            }
        }
        if (!(*error_handler)(RECEIVED, received, "Block Received")) {
            abort_transfer();
            set_data_format(obits, oparity, ostop);
            set_tx_xon(oxon);
            fclose(file);
            return FALSE;
        }
        /* increment block number */
        block = (block + 1) & 255;
        /* ACK if not Ymodem-G */
        if (xtype != YMODEMG)
            put_serial(ACK);
        for (i = 0; i < 10; i++) {
            /* get a block */
            l = getblock(block, crc);
            if (l == SOH || l == STX || l == EOT)
                break;
            /* abort if loss of carrier */
            if (!carrier()) {
                (*error_handler)(ERROR, block, "Loss of Carrier Detected!");
                set_data_format(obits, oparity, ostop);
                set_tx_xon(oxon);
                fclose(file);
                return FALSE;
            }
```

continued...

...from previous page (Listing 6.1)

```
            switch (l) {
                case CAN:           /* abort if CAN */
                    (*error_handler)(ERROR, block, "Cancelled by Sender");
                    set_data_format(obits, oparity, ostop);
                    set_tx_xon(oxon);
                    fclose(file);
                    return FALSE;
                case TIMED_OUT:     /* TIMED OUT */
                    if (!(*error_handler)(ERROR, block, "Short Block")) {
                        abort_transfer();
                        set_data_format(obits, oparity, ostop);
                        set_tx_xon(oxon);
                        fclose(file);
                        return FALSE;
                    }
                    break;
                case BAD_BLOCK:     /* bad block number */
                    if (!(*error_handler)(ERROR, block, "Bad Block Number")) {
                        abort_transfer();
                        set_data_format(obits, oparity, ostop);
                        set_tx_xon(oxon);
                        fclose(file);
                        return FALSE;
                    }
                    break;
                case CRC_ERROR:     /* CRC error */
                    if (!(*error_handler)(ERROR, block, crc ? "CRC Error" :
"Checksum Error") || xtype == YMODEMG) {
                        abort_transfer();
                        set_data_format(obits, oparity, ostop);
                        set_tx_xon(oxon);
                        fclose(file);
                        return FALSE;
                    }
                    break;
            }
            /* send NAK if not Ymodem-G */
            if (xtype != YMODEMG)
                put_serial(NAK);
        }
        /* abort after 10 attempts */
        if (i == 10) {
            abort_transfer();
            set_data_format(obits, oparity, ostop);
            set_tx_xon(oxon);
            return FALSE;
        }
    }
```

continued...

...from previous page (Listing 6.1)

```
            /* ACK EOT */
            put_serial(ACK);
            /* close the file */
            fclose(file);
            /* exit if not Ymodem or Ymodem-G */
            if (!batch)
                return TRUE;
            /* adjust file mod date */
            if (moddate && (file = fopen(fname, "rb")) != NULL) {
                putenv("TZ=GMT0GMT");
                tzset();
                t = localtime(&moddate);
                #ifdef __TURBOC__
                ft.ft_year = t->tm_year - 80;
                ft.ft_month = t->tm_mon + 1;
                ft.ft_day = t->tm_mday;
                ft.ft_hour = t->tm_hour;
                ft.ft_min = t->tm_min;
                ft.ft_tsec = t->tm_sec / 2;
                setftime(fileno(file), &ft);
                #else
                fd = (t->tm_year - 80) << 9;
                fd |= (t->tm_mon + 1) << 5;
                fd |= t->tm_mday;
                ft = t->tm_hour << 11;
                ft |= t->tm_min << 5;
                ft |= t->tm_sec / 2;
                _dos_setftime(fileno(file), fd, ft);
                #endif
                fclose(file);
            }
        }
}
```

Function Description: timed_get

The timed_get function either retrieves a character from the serial port or times out after a specified number of seconds. Its implementation is illustrated by the following pseudocode:

```
get the current system clock setting
while (TRUE) {
        if (a character is available)
                return the character
        if (loss of carrier or the time interval has elapsed)
                break out of the loop
}
return -1
```

Function Description: build_block

The **build_block** function reads a portion of a disk file and saves it in a memory buffer. If the remaining portion of the file is shorter than the desired block length, the **build_block** routine will pad the remainder of the block with EOF characters. The **build_block** function's implementation is illustrated by the following pseudocode:

```
try to read in the desired number of characters
if (EOF)
        return FALSE
if (remainder of disk file < block length)
        pad the block with EOF characters
return TRUE
```

Function Description: header_block

The **header_block** function builds a Ymodem Block0. Its implementation is illustrated by the following pseudocode:

```
fill the buffer with all nulls
if (file name isn't a null string) {
        put the file name in the buffer
        put the file's length in the buffer
        put the file's modification date in the buffer
}
```

Function Description: abort_transfer

The **abort_transfer** function is used to abort a file transfer by sending a series of eight CAN characters. Its implementation is illustrated by the following pseudocode:

```
send eight CANs out the serial port
```

Function Description: parse

The **parse** function is used to parse a file name from a path name. Its implementation is illustrated by the following pseudocode:

```
bump the string pointer past any drive spec
bump the string pointer past any path spec
copy the file name to the desired buffer
```

Function Description: xmit_file

The **xmit_file** function is used to transmit one or more files using either the Xmodem, Xmodem-1K, Ymodem, or Ymodem-G protocol. Its implementation is illustrated by the following pseudocode:

```
set the block size and the batch flag
return if it's an invalid protocol
save the serial port's current data format
save the serial port's current transmit XON/XOFF flow control setting
set the serial port for 8-N-1
turn off the serial port's transmit XON/XOFF flow control
while (TRUE) {
        get the path name for the next file to be transmitted
        bump the number of files that have been transmitted
        if (file name is a null string and it isn't a batch transfer) {
                restore the serial port's previous data format
                restore the serial port's previous transmit XON/XOFF flow control setting
                return TRUE
        }
        get the current system clock setting
        flag no CAN
        while (TRUE) {
                if (loss of carrier detected) {
                        send message to the error handler
                        restore the serial port's previous data format
                        restore the serial port's previous transmit XON/XOFF flow control setting
                        return FALSE
                }
                if (a character is available) {
                        switch (the character) {
                                case NAK:
                                        flag don't use CRCs
                                case 'C':
                                        if (protocol is Ymodem-G)
                                                set protocol to Ymodem
                                        flag use CRCs
                                case 'G':
                                        if (protocol isn't Ymodem-G)
                                                go wait for another character
                                        flag use CRCs
```

continued...

...from previous page

```
                    case CAN:
                        if (second CAN) {
                            send message to the error handler
                            restore the serial port's previous data
    format
                            restore the serial port's previous
    transmit
                                XON/XOFF flow control
    setting
                            return FALSE
                        }
                        flag one CAN received
                    default:
                        flag no CAN received
                        go wait for another character
                }
            }
            if (60 seconds has elapsed) {
                restore the serial port's previous data format
                restore the serial port's previous transmit XON/XOFF flow
    control setting
                return FALSE
            }
        }
        if (not end of batch transfer) {
            open the file
            if (error opening the file) {
                abort the transfer
                restore the serial port's previous data format
                restore the serial port's previous transmit XON/XOFF flow
    control setting
                return FALSE
            }
            parse the file name
            determine the file's length
            send the file's name and length to the error handler
```

continued...

...from previous page

```
                if (transfer aborted by operator) {
                        abort the transfer
                        restore the serial port's previous data format
                        restore the serial port's previous transmit XON/XOFF flow
        control setting
                        return FALSE
                }
                set the number of bytes sent to 0
        }
        if (Ymodem or Ymodem-G) {
                build the Block0
                while (TRUE) {
                        figure the block's CRC
                        send an SOH
                        send the block number
                        send the complement of the block number
                        send the data block
                        send the CRC
                        flag no cancel and no retransmission
                        get the current system clock setting
                        while (TRUE) {
                                if (loss of carrier detected) {
                                        send message to the error handler
                                        if (a file is open)
                                                close the file
                                        restore the serial port's previous data format
                                        restore the serial port's previous transmit
        XON/XOFF flow control
                                        return FALSE
                                }
                                if (Ymodem-G)
                                        break out of the loop
                                if (a character is available) {
                                        switch (the character) {
                                                case NAK:
                                                        flag no cancel
```

continued...

...from previous page

```
                                    flag retransmit block
                                case ACK:
                                    flag no cancel
                                case CAN:
                                    if (second CAN) {
                                        send message to the
error handler
                                        if (a file is open)
                                            close the file
                                        restore the serial port's
previous data format
                                        restore the serial port's
previous transmit XON/XOFF flow control setting
                                        return FALSE
                                    }
                                    flag CAN received
                                default:
                                    flag no CAN received
                                    got wait for another character
                            }
                        }
                        if (60 seconds has elapsed) {
                            if (a file is open)
                                close the file
                            restore the serial port's previous data format
                            restore the serial port's previous transmit
XON/XOFF flow control setting
                            return FALSE
                        }
                    }
                    if (NAK was received)
                        retransmit the block
                    if (end of batch transmission) {
                        wait for the ACK
                        restore the serial port's previous data format
                        restore the serial port's previous transmit XON/XOFF
flow control setting
                        return TRUE
                    }
                }
```

continued...

...from previous page

```
                    get the current system clock setting
                    flag no CAN received
                    while (TRUE) {
                            if (loss of carrier detected) {
                                    send message to the error handler
                                    restore the serial port's previous data format
                                    restore the serial port's previous transmit XON/XOFF
        flow control setting
                                    close the file
                                    return FALSE
                            }
                            if (a character is available) {
                                    switch (the character) {
                                            case NAK:
                                                    flag don't use CRCs
                                            case 'C':
                                                    if (protocol is Ymodem-G)
                                                            set protocol to Ymodem
                                                    flag use CRCs
                                            case 'G':
                                                    if (protocol isn't Ymodem-G)
                                                            got wait for another character
                                                    flag use CRCs
                                            case CAN:
                                                    if (second CAN) {
                                                            send message to the error
        handler
                                                            restore the serial port's
        previous data format
                                                    restore the serial port's previous
        transmit XON/XOFF flow control setting
                                                            close the file
                                                            return FALSE
                                                    }
                                            default:
                                                    flag no CAN received
                                                    go wait for another character
                                    }
                            }
```

continued...

...from previous page

```
                        if (60 seconds has elapsed) {
                                restore the serial port's previous data format
                                restore the serial port's transmit XON/XOFF flow
control setting
                                close the file
                                return FALSE
                        }
                }
        }
        set the block number to 1
        flag no retransmit
        while (TRUE) {
                if (not a retransmission) {
                        if (current block size is 1024 and remaining file length is
< 1024)
                                set block size to 128
                        build the data block
                        if (EOF)
                                break out of the loop
                }
                figure the block's CRC or checksum
                if (block size is 128)
                        send a SOH
                else
                        send a STX
                send the block number
                send the complement of the block number
                send the block's data bytes
                send the CRC or checksum
                flag no CAN or retransmission
                get the current system clock setting
                while (TRUE) {
                        if (loss of carrier detected) {
                                send message to the error handler
                                close the file
                                restore the serial port's previous data format
                                restore the serial port's previous transmit XON/XOFF
flow control setting
                                return FALSE
                        }
```

continued...

...from previous page

```
                        if (Ymodem-G) {
                                update the number of bytes sent
                                send the updated number of bytes sent to the error
handler
                                if (transfer aborted from keyboard) {
                                        abort the transfer
                                        close the file
                                        restore the serial port's previous data format
                                        restore the serial port's previous transmit
XON/XOFF flow control setting
                                        return FALSE
                                }
                                if (two CANs received) {
                                        send message to the error handler
                                        close the file
                                        restore the serial port's previous data format
                                restore the serial port's previous transmit XON/XOFF
flow control setting
                                        return FALSE
                                }
                                break out of the loop
                        }
                        if (a character is available) {
                                switch (the character) {
                                        case NAK:
                                                send NAK message to the error
handler
                                                if (transfer aborted from keyboard) {
                                                        abort the transfer
                                                        close the file
                                                        restore the serial port's
previous data format
                                                        restore the serial port's
previous transmit XON/XOFF flow control setting
                                                        return FALSE
                                                }
                                                flag no CAN
                                                flag retransmit block
```

continued...

...from previous page

```
                    case ACK:
                        update the number of bytes sent
                        send ACK message to the error
handler
                        if (transfer aborted from the keyboard)
{
                            abort the transfer
                            close the file
                            restore the serial port's
previous data format
                        restore the serial port's previous
transmit XON/XOFF flow control setting
                            return FALSE
                        }
                        flag no CAN
                    case CAN:
                        if (second CAN) {
                            send message to the error
handler
                            close the file
                        restore the serial port's previous data
format
                            restore the serial port's
previous transmit XON/XOFF flow control setting
                            return FALSE
                        }
                        flag CAN received
                    default:
                        flag no CAN received
                        go wait for another character
                }
            }
            if (60 seconds has elapsed) {
                close the file
                restore the serial port's previous data format
                restore the serial port's previous transmit XON/XOFF
flow control setting
                return FALSE
            }
        }
```

continued...

...from previous page

```
                if (not retransmission)
                        bump the block number
        }
        close the file
        get the current system clock setting
        send an EOT
        while (TRUE) {
                if (loss of carrier detected) {
                        send message to the error handler
                        restore the serial port's previous data format
                        restore the serial port's previous transmit XON/XOFF flow
control setting
                        return FALSE
                }
                if (a character is available) {
                        if (ACK isn't received)
                                send an EOT
                }
                if (60 seconds has elapsed) {
                        restore the serial port's previous data format
                        restore the serial port's previous transmit XON/XOFF flow
control setting
                        return FALSE
                }
        }
        if (Xmodem or Xmodem-1K) {
                restore the serial port's previous data format
                restore the serial port's previous transmit XON/XOFF flow control
setting
                return TRUE
        }
        set the block size back to 1024
}
```

Function Description: getblock

The **getblock** function is used to get a data block from the transmitter. Its implementation is illustrated by the following pseudocode:

```
get a character
if (timed out)
        return timed out error
```

continued...

...from previous page

```
switch (the character) {
        case CAN:
                get a character
                if (CAN)
                        return CAN
                return timed out error
        case SOH:
                set block length to 128
        case STX:
                set block length to 1024
        case EOT:
                return EOT
        default
                return timed out error
}
get the block number
if (timed out)
        return timed out error
if (block number isn't what is expected)
        return bad block error
get complement of block number
if (timed out)
        return timed out error
if (complement of block number isn't what is expected)
        return bad block number
get the block's data bytes
if (timed out)
        return timed out error
if (checksum) {
        get character
        if (timed out)
                return timed out error
        calculate checksum for the received data bytes
}
else {
        get CRC
        if (timed out)
                return timed out error
        calculate the CRC for the received data bytes
}
if (received checksum or CRC doesn't match the calculated checksum or CRC)
        return CRC error
```

continued...

...from previous page

```
    if (block length is 128)
        return SOH
    return STX
```

Function Description: recv_file

The **recv_file** function is used to receive one or more files using either the Xmodem, Xmodem-1K, Ymodem, or Ymodem-G protocol. Its implementation is illustrated by the following pseudocode:

```
set the batch flag according to the protocol type
save the serial port's current data format
save the serial port's current transmit XON/XOFF flow control setting
set the serial port's data format to 8-N-1
turn off the serial port's transmit XON/XOFF flow control setting
while (TRUE) {
        flag use CRCs
        if (Ymodem-G)
                send a 'G'
        else
                send a 'C'
        if (batch transfer)
                block = 0
        else
                block = 1
        while (number of tries < 10) {
                get a block
                if (CAN or loss of carrier is detected) {
                        restore the serial port's previous data format
                restore the serial port's previous transmit XON/XOFF flow control
setting
                        return FALSE
                }
                if (a block or EOT wasn't received) {
                        switch (protocol) {
                                case Xmodem:
                                        if (less than three tries)
                                                send a 'C'
                                        else {
                                                send a NAK
                                                flag no CRCs
                                        }
```

continued...

...from previous page

```
                    case Xmodem-1K:
                    case Ymodem:
                         send a 'C'
                    case Ymodem-G:
                         send a 'G'
               }
          }
          else
               break out of the loop
     }
     if (transmitter didn't respond after 10 tries) {
          restore the serial port's previous data format
          restore the serial port's previous transmit XON/XOFF flow control
setting
          return FALSE
     }
     if (Xmodem or Xmodem 1K) {
          set the file name
          set the file's length and number of bytes received to 0
     }
     else {
          if (end of batch transfer) {
               restore the serial port's previous data format
          restore the serial port's previous transmit XON/XOFF flow control
setting
               return TRUE
          }
          get the file's name from the Block0
          get the file's length and modification date from the Block0
     }
     open the file
     if (couldn't open file) {
          abort the transfer
          restore the serial port's previous data format
          restore the serial port's previous transmit XON/XOFF flow control
setting
          return FALSE
     }
     send the file's name and length to the error handler
```

continued...

...from previous page

```
        if (transfer aborted by operator) {
                abort the transfer
                restore the serial port's previous data format
                restore the serial port's previous transmit XON/XOFF flow control
    setting
                return FALSE
        }
        if (Ymodem or Ymodem-G) {
                flag use CRCs
                send an ACK
                if (Ymodem-G)
                        send a 'G'
                else
                        send a 'C'
                set the block number to 1
                while (less than 10 tries) {
                        get a block
                        if (CAN or loss of carrier detected) {
                                restore the serial port's previous data format
                                restore the serial port's previous transmit XON/XOFF
    flow control setting
                                close the file
                                return FALSE
                        }
                        if (block wasn't received) {
                                if (Ymodem)
                                        send a 'C'
                                else
                                        send a 'G'
                        }
                        else
                                break out of the loop
                }
                if (block not received after 10 tries) {
                        abort the transfer
                        restore the serial port's previous data format
                        restore the serial port's previous transmit XON/XOFF flow
    control setting
                        close the file
                        return FALSE
                }
        }
```

continued...

...from previous page

```
        while (TRUE) {
                if (EOT) {
                        send end of transfer message to the error handler
                        break out of the loop
                }
                if (Xmodem or Xmodem-1K or a length wasn't specified) {
                        write the buffer to disk
                        update the number of bytes that have been received
                }
                else {
                        if (still more to go after this block) {
                                write the buffer to disk
                                update the number of bytes that have been received
                        }
                        else {
                                write the buffer to disk
                                update the number of bytes that have been received
                        }
                }
                send the number of bytes that have been received to the error handler
                if (transfer aborted by operator) {
                        abort the transfer
                        restore the serial port's previous data format
                        restore the serial port's previous transmit XON/XOFF flow
control setting
                        close the file
                        return FALSE
                }
                increment the block number
                if (not Ymodem-G)
                        send an ACK
                while (less than 10 tries) {
                        get a block
                        if (block received ok or EOT)
                                break out of loop
                        if (loss of carrier detected) {
                                send a message to the error handler
                                restore the serial port's previous data format
```

continued...

...from previous page

```
                    restore the serial port's previous transmit XON/XOFF flow
    control setting
                        close the file
                        return FALSE
                    }
                    switch (the getblock return code) {
                        case CAN:
                            send a message to the error handler
                            restore the serial port's previous data format
                            restore the serial port's previous XON/XOFF
    flow control setting
                            close the file
                            return FALSE
                        case timed out error:
                            send a short block message to the error
    handler
                            if (transfer aborted by operator) {
                                abort the transfer
                                restore the serial port's previous data
    format
                                restore the serial port's previous
    XON/XOFF flow control setting
                                close the file
                                return FALSE
                            }
                        case bad block number:
                            send a bad block number message to the error
    handler
                            if (transfer aborted by operator) {
                                abort the transfer
                                restore the serial port's previous data
    format
                                restore the serial port's previous
    XON/XOFF flow control setting
                                close the file
                                return FALSE
                            }
                        case CRC error:
                            send a CRC or checksum error message to the
    error handler
```

continued...

...from previous page

```
                                        if (transfer aborted by operator) {
                                             abort the transfer
                                             restore the serial port's previous data
format
                                             restore the serial port's previous
XON/XOFF flow control setting
                                             close the file
                                             return FALSE
                                        }
                              }
                              if (not Ymodem-G)
                                   send NAK
                    }
                    if (block not received after 10 tries) {
                              abort the transfer
                              restore the serial port's previous data format
                              restore the serial port's previous transmit XON/XOFF flow
control setting
                              return FALSE
                    }
          }
          send an ACK to acknowledge the EOT
          close the file
          if (Xmodem or Xmodem 1K)
               return TRUE
          if (a modification date was sent by the transmitter)
               set the file's modification date
}
```

Summary

In this chapter, you learned about the **Xmodem protocol** and how it evolved into the Xmodem-CRC, Xmodem-1K, Ymodem, and Ymodem-G protocols. Furthermore, this chapter presented the **source code** for the SERIAL toolbox's implementation of the Xmodem, Xmodem-1K, Ymodem, and Ymodem-G protocols.

Chapter 7

A C++ Protocol Object Class

Chapter 6 presented the SERIAL toolbox's routines for performing file transfers using the Xmodem, Xmodem-1K, Ymodem, and Ymodem-G protocols. This chapter presents a C++ object class that makes implementing these protocols into a C++ serial communications program a breeze. Essentially, this new object class is derived from the SERIALPORT object class that was presented in Chapter 5. As such, the new object class can be fully implemented by making a few simple changes to **sercpp.h**.

Header File: sercpp.h

Listing 7.1, **sercpp.h** is a revised version of the SERIAL toolbox C++ header file that was presented in Chapter 5. This updated version includes a new object class called **XFERPORT**. This object class is derived from the previously implemented SERIALPORT object class and basically just adds two member functions to perform file transfers.

Listing 7.1: sercpp.h

```
/****************************************************************
* sercpp.h - C++ Header File for Serial Comm Prog in C and C++    *
*              Copyright (c) 1992 By Mark D. Goodwin              *
****************************************************************/
#ifndef __SERCPPH__
#define __SERCPPH__

#include "serial.h"

class SERIALPORT {
    int port;
public:
    SERIALPORT(int n, int l) { open_port(n, l); }
    ~SERIALPORT(void) { close_port(); }
    int carrier(void) { return ::carrier(); }
    void fifo(int n) { ::fifo(n); }
    long get_baud(void) { return ::get_baud(); }
    int get_bits(void) { return ::get_bits(); }
    int get_parity(void) { return ::get_parity(); }
    int get_rx_dtr(void) { return ::get_rx_dtr(); }
    int get_rx_rts(void) { return ::get_rx_rts(); }
    int get_rx_xon(void) { return ::get_rx_xon(); }
    int get(void) { return get_serial(); }
    int get_stopbits(void) { return ::get_stopbits(); }
    int get_tx_dtr(void) { return ::get_tx_dtr(); }
    int get_tx_rts(void) { return ::get_tx_rts(); }
    int get_tx_xon(void) { return ::get_tx_xon(); }
    int in_ready(void) { return ::in_ready(); }
    void purge_in(void) { ::purge_in(); }
    int put(unsigned char n) { return put_serial(n); }
    void set_baud(long baud) { ::set_baud(baud); }
    void set_data_format(int bits = 8, int parity = NO_PARITY,
        int stopbit = 1) { ::set_data_format(bits, parity, stopbit); }
    void set_dtr(int n) { ::set_dtr(n); }
```

continued...

...from previous page (Listing 7.1)

```
    void set_port(long baud, int bits = 8, int parity = NO_PARITY,
        int stopbit = 1) { ::set_port(baud, bits, parity, stopbit); }
    void set_rx_dtr(int n) { ::set_rx_dtr(n); }
    void set_rx_rts(int n) { ::set_rx_rts(n); }
    void set_rx_xon(int n) { ::set_rx_xon(n); }
    void set_tx_dtr(int n) { ::set_tx_dtr(n); }
    void set_tx_rts(int n) { ::set_tx_rts(n); }
    void set_tx_xon(int n) { ::set_tx_xon(n); }
};

class XFERPORT : public SERIALPORT {
public:
    XFERPORT(int n, int l) : SERIALPORT(n, l)  { }
    int receive(int xtype, int(*error_handler)(int c, long p, char *s),
        char *path)    { return recv_file(xtype, error_handler, path); }
    int transmit(int xtype, int(*error_handler)(int c, long p, char *s),
        char *files[]) { return xmit_file(xtype, error_handler, files); }
};

#endif
```

Summary

This chapter presented a revised version of the **sercpp.h** header file. This latest version of the C++ header file features an object class for performing file transfers using the Xmodem, Xmodem-1K, Ymodem, and Ymodem-G protocols.

Chapter 8

ANSI Terminal Routines

Now that the low-level serial routines and file transfer protocols have been implemented, there is only one last piece to add to the SERIAL toolbox: a **terminal emulator**. To be able to correctly display the information it is receiving, both the receiving and transmitting serial devices must have an agreed upon way to handle the video display. Although there are many types of terminals that are in use today, ANSI is very much the dominant terminal type in the PC world. Accordingly, Chapter 8 presents all of the essential routines to emulate an **ANSI terminal** on an IBM PC or compatible.

The ANSI Escape Sequences

An **ANSI terminal** displays video information using a series of escape sequences. These escape sequences can be used to perform functions such as clearing the screen, moving the cursor, setting the text color, and more. These sequences are called *escape sequences* because they always start with an *ESC character (1BH)*. Additionally, the escape character is followed by a left bracket ([). Accordingly, all ANSI escape sequences start with the two characters **ESC[**. Following the **ESC[** characters are zero or more numeric or string parameters and a letter that indicates the video function to be performed by the escape sequence. Figures 8.1 through 8.14 illustrates the ANSI escape sequences that are commonly used on the IBM PC and compatibles. However, you should note that some of these differ from the actual ANSI standard; many of the ANSI escape sequences that are defined in the ANSI standard are not used on the PC.

Cursor Backward (CUB)

Syntax: `ESC[columnsD`

Description: The Cursor Backward (CUB) escape sequence moves the cursor to the left by a specified number of *columns*. If *columns* is not specified, the ANSI terminal will move the cursor left 1 column. If the cursor is already positioned at the display's left-most column, the remaining number of columns will be ignored.

Figure 8.1 *The ANSI Cursor Backward (CUB) Escape Sequence.*

Cursor Down (CUD)

Syntax: `ESC[linesB`

Description: The Cursor Down (CUD) escape sequence moves the cursor down by a specified number of *lines*. If *lines* is not specified, the ANSI terminal will move the cursor down 1 line. If the cursor is positioned at the display's bottom line the remaining number of lines will be ignored.

Figure 8.2 *The ANSI Cursor Down (CUD) Escape Sequence.*

Cursor Forward (CUF)

Syntax: `ESC[`*`columns`*`C`

Description: The Cursor Forward (CUF) escape sequence moves the cursor to the right by a specified number of *columns*. If *columns* is not specified, the ANSI terminal will move the cursor right 1 column. If the cursor is already positioned at the display's right-most column, the remaining number of columns will be ignored.

Figure 8.3 *The ANSI Cursor Forward (CUF) Escape Sequence.*

Cursor Position (CUP)

Syntax: `ESC[`*`line`*`;`*`column`*`H`

Description: The Cursor Position (CUP) escape sequence moves the cursor to the position specified by *line* and *column*. If *line* and *column* are omitted, the ANSI terminal will move the cursor to the upper-left corner of the video display.

Figure 8.4 *The ANSI Cursor Position (CUP) Escape Sequence.*

Cursor Up (CUU)

Syntax: `ESC[`*`lines`*`A`

Description: The Cursor Up (CUU) escape sequence moves the cursor up by a specified number of *lines*. If *lines* is not specified, the ANSI terminal will move the cursor up 1 line. If the cursor is positioned at the display's top line, the remaining number of lines will be ignored.

Figure 8.5 *The ANSI Cursor Up (CUU) Escape Sequence.*

Device Status Report (DSR)

Syntax: `ESC[6n`

Description: The Device Status Report (DSR) escape sequence tells the ANSI terminal to output an RCP sequence. Unfortunately, this is the method used by MS-DOS's ANSI.SYS and it is not correct. According to the ANSI standard, an **ESC[6n** escape sequence should generate an CPR escape sequence in response and ANSI.SYS does not support CPR escape sequences. Fortunately, a DSR is really only used in the PC world to detect if the remote terminal can support ANSI. To perform such a check, simply send a DSR and wait for an ESC in return. If an ESC is returned, it's pretty safe to assume that the terminal on the other end of the data link supports ANSI.

Figure 8.6 *The ANSI Device Status Report (DSR) Escape Sequence.*

Erase Display (ED)

Syntax: `ESC[2J`

Description: The Erase Display (ED) escape sequence erases the video display and moves the cursor to the display's upper-left corner.

Figure 8.7 *The ANSI Erase Display (ED) Escape Sequence.*

Erase Line (EL)

Syntax: `ESC[K`

Description: The Erase Line (EL) escape sequence erases the current display line starting at the current cursor position and ending with the line's rightmost column.

Figure 8.8 *The ANSI Erase Line (EL) Escape Sequence.*

Horizontal and Vertical Position (HVP)

Syntax: `ESC[line;columnF`

Description: The Horizontal and Vertical Position (HVP) escape sequence moves the cursor to the position specified by *line* and *column*. If *line* and *column* are omitted, the ANSI terminal will move the cursor to the upper-left corner of the video display.

Figure 8.9 *The ANSI Horizontal and Vertical Position (HVP) Escape Sequence.*

Restore Cursor Position (RCP)

Syntax: `ESC[u`

Description: The Restore Cursor Position (RCP) escape sequence restores the cursor to the position it held when the ANSI terminal last received a Save Cursor Position (SCP) escape sequence.

Figure 8.10 *The ANSI Restore Cursor Position (RCP) Escape Sequence.*

Reset Mode (RM)

Syntax: `ESC[=model`
`ESC[=l`
`ESC[=0l`
`ESC[=?7l`

Description: The Reset Mode (RM) escape sequence resets the ANSI terminal to one of the following modes:

Number	*Mode*
0	40 X 25 Black and White
1	40 x 25 Color
2	80 x 25 Black and White
3	80 x 25 Color
4	320 x 200 Color
5	320 x 200 Black and White
6	640 x 200 Black and White
7	Do not wrap at the end of each line
14	640 x 200 Color
15	640 x 350 Black and White
16	640 x 350 Color
17	640 x 480 Color
18	640 x 480 Color
19	320 x 200 Color

***Figure 8.11** The ANSI Reset Mode (RM) Escape Sequence.*

Save Cursor Position (SCP)

Syntax: `ESC[s`

Description: The Save Cursor Position (SCP) escape sequence tells the ANSI terminal to save the current cursor position. The cursor can be returned to this saved position at anytime with a Restore Cursor Position (RCP) escape sequence.

***Figure 8.12** The ANSI Save Cursor Position (SCP) Escape Sequence.*

Set Graphics Rendition (SGR)

Syntax: `ESC[`*`parameter`*`;...;`*`parameter`*`m`

Description: The Set Graphics Rendition (SGR) escape sequence is used to set display attributes and colors. These attributes are passed to the ANSI terminal by specifying one or more parameters separated by semicolons (`;`). The following is a list of attributes that the SGR escape sequence can set:

`parameter`	**Function**
0	Turn off all attributes
1	Turn bold on
4	Turn underscore on (monochrome displays only)
5	Turn blink on
7	Turn reverse video on
8	Turn concealed on

The following is a list of foreground colors that can be set by the SGR escape sequence:

`parameter`	**Foreground Color**
30	Black
31	Red
32	Green
33	Yellow
34	Blue
35	Magenta
36	Cyan
37	White

The following is a list of background colors that can be set by the SGR escape sequence:

`parameter`	**Background Color**
40	Black
41	Red
42	Green
43	Yellow
44	Blue
45	Magenta
46	Cyan
47	White

Figure 8.13 *The ANSI Set Graphics Rendition (SGR) Escape Sequence.*

Set Mode (SM)

Syntax:

```
ESC[=model
ESC[=l
ESC[=0l
ESC[=?7l
```

Description: The Set Mode (RM) escape sequence resets the ANSI terminal to one of the following modes:

Number	*Mode*
0	40 X 25 Black and White
1	40 x 25 Color
2	80 x 25 Black and White
3	80 x 25 Color
4	320 x 200 Color
5	320 x 200 Black and White
6	640 x 200 Black and White
7	Wrap at the end of each line
14	640 x 200 Color
15	640 x 350 Black and White
16	640 x 350 Color
17	640 x 480 Color
18	640 x 480 Color
19	320 x 200 Color

Figure 8.14 *The ANSI Set Mode (SM) Escape Sequence.*

Source Listing: ansi.c

Listing 8.1, **ansi.c**, contains the SERIAL toolbox routines that implement an ANSI terminal emulator. Additionally, this source code file presents a routine for converting IBM color attributes to ANSI escape sequences.

Listing 8.1: ansi.c

```
/*********************************************************************
* ansi.c - ANSI Terminal Driver                                      *
*          Copyright (c) 1992 By Mark D. Goodwin                     *
*********************************************************************/
#include <stdio.h>
#include <stdlib.h>
#include <string.h>
#include <conio.h>
#include <stdarg.h>
#ifndef __TURBOC__
#include <graph.h>
#endif
#include "serial.h"

static int cnt, crow = 1, ccol = 1;
static unsigned char buffer[256];
int ansi_dsr_flag = FALSE;
int (*ansi_dsr)(unsigned char n);

/* check for numeric digit */
static int bindigit(int c)
{
    return c >= '0' && c <= '9';
}

/* convert ASCII to binary */
static unsigned char *ascbin(unsigned char *s, int *n)
{
    *n = 0;
    while (TRUE) {
        if (bindigit(*s)) {
            *n *= 10;
            *n += (*s - '0');
            s++;
            continue;
        }
        return s;
    }
}
```

continued...

...from previous page (Listing 8.1)

```
/* convert IBM color attribute to ANSI text string */
char *ibmtoansi(int att, char *s)
{
    s[0] = 0;
    strcat(s, "\x1b[0");
    if (att & 0x80)
        strcat(s, ";5");
    if (att & 0x8)
        strcat(s, ";1");
    switch (att & 7) {
        case 0:
            strcat(s, ";30");
            break;
        case 1:
            strcat(s, ";34");
            break;
        case 2:
            strcat(s, ";32");
            break;
        case 3:
            strcat(s, ";36");
            break;
        case 4:
            strcat(s, ";31");
            break;
        case 5:
            strcat(s, ";35");
            break;
        case 6:
            strcat(s, ";33");
            break;
        case 7:
            strcat(s, ";37");
    }
```

continued...

...from previous page (Listing 8.1)

```
    switch ((att >> 4) & 7) {
        case 0:
            strcat(s, ";40");
            break;
        case 1:
            strcat(s, ";44");
            break;
        case 2:
            strcat(s, ";42");
            break;
        case 3:
            strcat(s, ";46");
            break;
        case 4:
            strcat(s, ";41");
            break;
        case 5:
            strcat(s, ";45");
            break;
        case 6:
            strcat(s, ";43");
            break;
        case 7:
            strcat(s, ";47");
    }
    strcat(s, "m");
    return s;
}

#ifndef __TURBOC__
void clreol(void)
{
    int i, r1, c1, r2, c2;
    struct rccoord cpos;

    _gettextwindow(&r1, &c1, &r2, &c2);
    cpos = _gettextposition();
    _settextwindow(cpos.row, cpos.col, cpos.row, c2);
    _clearscreen(_GWINDOW);
    _settextwindow(r1, c1, r2, c2);
    _settextposition(cpos.row, cpos.col);
}
#endif
```

continued...

...from previous page (Listing 8.1)

```
/* ANSI emulation routine */
void ansiout(int c)
{
    int n, row, col;
    #ifndef __TURBOC__
    int r1, c1, r2, c2;
    struct rccoord cpos;
    #endif
    unsigned char *bufptr;
    #ifdef __TURBOC__
    struct text_info tinfo;
    #endif

    if (!cnt) {
        if (c != 27)
            switch (c) {
                case 0:
                    break;
                case '\n':
                    #ifdef __TURBOC__
                    gettextinfo(&tinfo);
                    if (wherey() + 1 > tinfo.winbottom) {
                        movetext(1, 2, tinfo.winright,
                            tinfo.winbottom, 1, 1);
                        gotoxy(1, tinfo.winbottom);
                        clreol();
                    }
                    else
                        gotoxy(1, wherey() + 1);
                    #else
                    _gettextwindow(&r1, &c1, &r2, &c2);
                    cpos = _gettextposition();
                    if (cpos.row + 1 > r2) {
                        _scrolltextwindow(1);
                        _settextposition(r2, 1);
                        clreol();
                    }
```

continued...

...from previous page (Listing 8.1)

```
          else
              _settextposition(cpos.row + 1, 1);
          #endif
          break;
      case 8:
      case 127:
          #ifdef __TURBOC__
          if (wherex() != 1) {
              putch(8);
              putch(' ');
              putch(8);
          }
          #else
          cpos = _gettextposition();
          if (cpos.col != 1) {
              _settextposition(cpos.row, cpos.col - 1);
              _outmem(" ", 1);
              _settextposition(cpos.row, cpos.col - 1);
          }
          #endif
          break;
      case 13:
          #ifdef __TURBOC__
          gotoxy(1, wherey());
          #else
          cpos = _gettextposition();
          _settextposition(cpos.row, 1);
          #endif
          break;
      case '\t':
          do {
          #ifdef __TURBOC__
              putch(' ');
          } while (wherex() % 8 != 1);
          #else
              _outmem(" ", 1);
              cpos = _gettextposition();
          } while (cpos.row % 8 != 1);
          #endif
          break;
```

continued...

...from previous page (Listing 8.1)

```
                case 12:
                    #ifdef __TURBOC__
                    clrscr();
                    #else
                    _clearscreen(_GWINDOW);
                    #endif
                    break;
                default:
                    #ifdef __TURBOC__
                    putch(c);
                    #else
                    _outmem((char *)&c, 1);
                    #endif
            }
        else {
            buffer[cnt] = (unsigned char)c;
            cnt++;
        }
        return;
    }
    if (cnt == 1) {
        if (c == '[') {
            buffer[cnt] = (unsigned char)c;
            cnt++;
        }
        else {
            #ifdef __TURBOC__
            putch(27);
            #else
            _outmem("\x1b", 1);
            #endif
            if (c != 27) {
                #ifdef __TURBOC__
                putch(c);
                #else
                _outmem((char *)&c, 1);
                #endif
                cnt = 0;
            }
        }
        return;
    }
```

continued...

...from previous page (Listing 8.1)

```
    if (cnt == 2) {
        switch (c) {
            case 's':
                #ifdef __TURBOC__
                crow = wherey();
                ccol = wherex();
                #else
                cpos = _gettextposition();
                crow = cpos.row;
                ccol = cpos.col;
                #endif
                cnt = 0;
                return;
            case 'u':
                #ifdef __TURBOC__
                gotoxy(ccol, crow);
                #else
                _settextposition(crow, ccol);
                #endif
                cnt = 0;
                return;
            case 'K':
                clreol();
                cnt = 0;
                return;
            case 'H':
            case 'F':
                #ifdef __TURBOC__
                gotoxy(1, 1);
                #else
                _settextposition(1, 1);
                #endif
                cnt = 0;
                return;
            case 'A':
                #ifdef __TURBOC__
                gotoxy(wherex(), wherey() - 1);
                #else
                cpos = _gettextposition();
                _settextposition(cpos.row - 1, cpos.col);
                #endif
                cnt = 0;
                return;
```

continued...

...from previous page (Listing 8.1)

```
            case 'B':
                #ifdef __TURBOC__
                gotoxy(wherex(), wherey() + 1);
                #else
                cpos = _gettextposition();
                _settextposition(cpos.row + 1, cpos.col);
                #endif
                cnt = 0;
                return;
            case 'C':
                #ifdef __TURBOC__
                gotoxy(wherex() + 1, wherey());
                #else
                cpos = _gettextposition();
                _settextposition(cpos.row, cpos.col + 1);
                #endif
                cnt = 0;
                return;
            case 'D':
                #ifdef __TURBOC__
                gotoxy(wherex() - 1, wherey());
                #else
                cpos = _gettextposition();
                _settextposition(cpos.row, cpos.col - 1);
                #endif
                cnt = 0;
                return;
            default:
                if (bindigit(c)) {
                    buffer[cnt] = (unsigned char)c;
                    cnt++;
                    return;
                }
                cnt = 0;
                return;
        }
    }
```

continued...

...from previous page (Listing 8.1)

```
    if (bindigit(c) || c == ';') {
        buffer[cnt] = (unsigned char)c;
        cnt++;
        if (cnt > 256)
            cnt = 0;
        return;
    }
    bufptr = buffer + 2;
    buffer[cnt] = (unsigned char)c;
    switch (c) {
        case 'H':
        case 'F':
        case 'h':
        case 'f':
            bufptr = ascbin(bufptr, &row);
            if (*bufptr != ';') {
                #ifdef __TURBOC__
                gotoxy(1, row);
                #else
                _settextposition(row, 1);
                #endif
                cnt = 0;
                return;
            }
            bufptr++;
            if (!bindigit(*bufptr)) {
                cnt = 0;
                return;
            }
            ascbin(bufptr, &col);
            #ifdef __TURBOC__
            gotoxy(col, row);
            #else
            _settextposition(row, col);
            #endif
            cnt = 0;
            return;
```

continued...

...from previous page (Listing 8.1)

```
        case 'A':
            ascbin(bufptr, &n);
            #ifdef __TURBOC__
            gotoxy(wherex(), wherey() - n);
            #else
            cpos = _gettextposition();
            _settextposition(cpos.row - n, cpos.col);
            #endif
            cnt = 0;
            return;
        case 'B':
            ascbin(bufptr, &n);
            #ifdef __TURBOC__
            gotoxy(wherex(), wherey() + n);
            #else
            cpos = _gettextposition();
            _settextposition(cpos.row + n, cpos.col);
            #endif
            cnt = 0;
            return;
        case 'C':
            ascbin(bufptr, &n);
            #ifdef __TURBOC__
            gotoxy(wherex() + n, wherey());
            #else
            cpos = _gettextposition();
            _settextposition(cpos.row, cpos.col + n);
            #endif
            cnt = 0;
            return;
        case 'D':
            ascbin(bufptr, &n);
            #ifdef __TURBOC__
            gotoxy(wherex() - n, wherey());
            #else
            cpos = _gettextposition();
            _settextposition(cpos.row, cpos.col - n);
            #endif
            cnt = 0;
            return;
```

continued...

...from previous page (Listing 8.1)

```
        case 'n':
            ascbin(bufptr, &n);
            if (n == 6 && ansi_dsr_flag)
                (*ansi_dsr)('\x1b');
                (*ansi_dsr)('[');
                (*ansi_dsr)('u');
            cnt = 0;
            return;
        case 'J':
            ascbin(bufptr, &n);
            if (n == 2)
                #ifdef __TURBOC__
                clrscr();
                #else
                _clearscreen(_GWINDOW);
                #endif
            cnt = 0;
            return;
        case 'm':
            while (TRUE) {
                #ifdef __TURBOC__
                gettextinfo(&tinfo);
                #endif
                bufptr = ascbin(bufptr, &n);
                switch (n) {
                    case 0:
                        #ifdef __TURBOC__
                        textattr(7);
                        #else
                        _setbkcolor(0L);
                        _settextcolor(7);
                        #endif
                        break;
                    case 1:
                        #ifdef __TURBOC__
                        textattr(tinfo.attribute | 0x08);
                        #else
                        _settextcolor(_gettextcolor() | 0x08);
                        #endif
                        break;
```

continued...

...from previous page (Listing 8.1)

```
        case 5:
            #ifdef __TURBOC__
            textattr(tinfo.attribute | 0x80);
            #else
            _settextcolor(_gettextcolor() | 0x10);
            #endif
            break;
        case 30:
            #ifdef __TURBOC__
            textattr(tinfo.attribute & 0xf8);
            #else
            _settextcolor(_gettextcolor() & 0xf8);
            #endif
            break;
        case 31:
            #ifdef __TURBOC__
            textattr(tinfo.attribute & 0xf8 | 4);
            #else
            _settextcolor(_gettextcolor() & 0xf8 | 4);
            #endif
            break;
        case 32:
            #ifdef __TURBOC__
            textattr(tinfo.attribute & 0xf8 | 2);
            #else
            _settextcolor(_gettextcolor() & 0xf8 | 2);
            #endif
            break;
        case 33:
            #ifdef __TURBOC__
            textattr(tinfo.attribute & 0xf8 | 6);
            #else
            _settextcolor(_gettextcolor() & 0xf8 | 6);
            #endif
            break;
        case 34:
            #ifdef __TURBOC__
            textattr(tinfo.attribute & 0xf8 | 1);
            #else
            _settextcolor(_gettextcolor() & 0xf8 | 1);
            #endif
            break;
```

continued...

...from previous page (Listing 8.1)

```
case 35:
    #ifdef __TURBOC__
    textattr(tinfo.attribute & 0xf8 | 5);
    #else
    _settextcolor(_gettextcolor() & 0xf8 | 5);
    #endif
    break;
case 36:
    #ifdef __TURBOC__
    textattr(tinfo.attribute & 0xf8 | 3);
    #else
    _settextcolor(_gettextcolor() & 0xf8 | 3);
    #endif
    break;
case 37:
    #ifdef __TURBOC__
    textattr(tinfo.attribute & 0xf8 | 7);
    #else
    _settextcolor(_gettextcolor() & 0xf8 | 7);
    #endif
    break;
case 40:
    #ifdef __TURBOC__
    textattr(tinfo.attribute & 0x8f);
    #else
    _setbkcolor(0L);
    #endif
    break;
case 41:
    #ifdef __TURBOC__
    textattr(tinfo.attribute & 0x8f | 0x40);
    #else
    _setbkcolor(4L);
    #endif
    break;
case 42:
    #ifdef __TURBOC__
    textattr(tinfo.attribute & 0x8f | 0x20);
    #else
    _setbkcolor(2L);
    #endif
    break;
```

continued...

...from previous page (Listing 8.1)

```
                case 43:
                    #ifdef __TURBOC__
                    textattr(tinfo.attribute & 0x8f | 0x60);
                    #else
                    _setbkcolor(6L);
                    #endif
                    break;
                case 44:
                    #ifdef __TURBOC__
                    textattr(tinfo.attribute & 0x8f | 0x10);
                    #else
                    _setbkcolor(1L);
                    #endif
                    break;
                case 45:
                    #ifdef __TURBOC__
                    textattr(tinfo.attribute & 0x8f | 0x50);
                    #else
                    _setbkcolor(5L);
                    #endif
                    break;
                case 46:
                    #ifdef __TURBOC__
                    textattr(tinfo.attribute & 0x8f | 0x30);
                    #else
                    _setbkcolor(3L);
                    #endif
                    break;
                case 47:
                    #ifdef __TURBOC__
                    textattr(tinfo.attribute & 0x8f | 0x70);
                    #else
                    _setbkcolor(7L);
                    #endif
                    break;
            }
            if (*bufptr == ';') {
                bufptr++;
                continue;
            }
            cnt = 0;
            return;
        }
```

continued...

...from previous page (Listing 8.1)

```
        default:
            cnt = 0;
            return;
    }
}

void ansistring(char *s)
{
    while (*s)
        ansiout(*s++);
}

int ansiprintf(char *f, ...)
{
    int l;
    va_list m;
    char *b, *s;

    if ((b = (char *)malloc(1024)) == NULL)
        return -1;
    va_start(m, f);
    l = vsprintf(b, f, m);
    s = b;
    while (*s) {
        ansiout(*s);
        s++;
    }
    va_end(m);
    free(b);
    return l;
}
```

Function Description: bindigit

The **bindigit** function determines whether or not a character is a numeric digit. Its implementation is illustrated by the following pseudocode:

```
if (character is a numeric digit)
        return TRUE
else
        return FALSE
```

Function Description: ascbin

The **ascbin** function converts a numeric value's ASCII string representation to binary. Its implementation is illustrated by the following pseudocode:

```
set the numeric value to zero
while (TRUE) {
        if (character is a numeric digit) {
                multiply the current numeric value by 10
                add in the new one's place digit
                bump the string pointer
        }
        else
                return the numeric value
}
```

Function Description: ibmtoansi

The **ibmtoansi** function is used to convert an IBM PC color attribute to an ANSI escape sequence. Its implementation is illustrated by the following pseudocode:

```
set the initial escape sequence so that all text attributes are off
if (blink)
        add the blink code to the escape sequence
if (bold)
        add the bold code to the escape sequence
switch (foreground color) {
        case black:
                add the black foreground color code to the escape sequence
        case blue:
                add the blue foreground color code to the escape sequence
        case green:
                add the green foreground color code to the escape sequence
        case cyan:
                add the cyan foreground color code to the escape sequence
        case red:
                add the red foreground color code to the escape sequence
        case magenta:
                add the magenta foreground color code to the escape sequence
        case brown:
                add the brown foreground color code to the escape sequence
        case white:
                add the white foreground color code to the escape sequence
}
```

continued...

...from previous page

```
switch (background color) {
        case black:
                add the black background color code to the escape sequence
        case blue:
                add the blue background color code to the escape sequence
        case green:
                add the green background color code to the escape sequence
        case cyan:
                add the cyan background color code to the escape sequence
        case red:
                add the red background color code to the escape sequence
        case magenta:
                add the magenta background color code to the escape sequence
        case brown:
                add the brown background color code to the escape sequence
        case white:
                add the white background color code to the escape sequence
}
add an "m" to the end of the escape sequence to indicate an SGR escape sequence
return the ANSI escape sequence
```

Function Description: clreol

The **clreol** function clears the current display line starting at the current cursor position and ending with the display's rightmost column. It's implementation is illustrated by the following pseudocode:

```
get the current text window's coordinates
get the current cursor position
set the new text window for the remainder of the current line
clear the text window
restore the text window to its previous coordinates
restore the previous cursor position
```

Function Description: ansiout

The **ansiout** function displays a character on the video display using an ANSI terminal emulation. Its implementation is illustrated by the following pseudocode:

```
if (an ESC hasn't already been received) {
        if (the character isn't an ESC) {
                switch (the character) {
                        case null:
                                ignore nulls
                        case newline:
                        move the cursor to the start of the next line and scroll the text
window if necessary
                        case backspace:
                                backup and erase the previous character
                        case carriage return:
                                move the cursor to the start of the current line
                        case tab:
                                move the cursor to the next tab zone
                        case formfeed:
                                clear the screen
                        default:
                                display the character
                }
        }
        else {
                save the ESC character in the buffer
                increment the buffer count
        }
        return
}
if (this is the second character) {
        if (the character is a [) {
                save the [ character in the buffer
                increment the buffer count
        }
```

continued...

...from previous page

```
        else {
                display an ESC
                if (character isn't an ESC) {
                        display the character
                        flag the buffer as empty
                }
        }
        return
}
if (this is the third character) {
        switch (c) {
                case 's':
                        save the current cursor position
                        flag the buffer as empty
                        return
                case 'u':
                        restore the previously saved cursor position
                        flag the buffer as empty
                        return
                case 'K':
                        clear to the end of the current line
                        flag the buffer as empty
                        return
                case 'H':
                case 'F':
                        home the cursor
                        flag the buffer as empty
                        return
                case 'A':
                        move up a line
                        flag the buffer as empty
                        return
                case 'B':
                        move down a line
                        flag the buffer as empty
                        return
                case 'C':
                        move the cursor to the right one column
                        flag the buffer as empty
                        return
```

continued...

...from previous page

```
                case 'D':
                        move the cursor to the left one column
                        flag the buffer as empty
                        return
                default:
                        if (the character is a numeric digit) {
                                save the character in the buffer
                                bump the buffer count
                                return
                        }
                        flag the buffer as empty
        }
}
if (the character is a numeric digit or a semicolon) {
        save the character in the buffer
        bump the buffer count
        if (the buffer has overflowed)
                flag the buffer as empty
        return
}
switch (the character) {
        case 'H'
        case 'F':
        case 'h':
        case 'f':
                get the cursor's new row position
                if (the next character isn't a semicolon) {
                        set the cursor to the leftmost column of the indicated row
                        flag the buffer as empty
                        return
                }
                bump the buffer pointer
                get the cursor's new column position
                set the cursor's new position
                flag the buffer as empty
                return
        case 'A':
                get the number of lines
                move the cursor up by the specified number of lines
                flag the buffer as empty
                return
```

continued...

...from previous page

```
        case 'B':
                get the number of lines
                move the cursor down by the specified number of lines
                flag the buffer as empty
                return
        case 'C':
                get the number of columns
                move the cursor right by the specified number of columns
                flag the buffer as empty
                return
        case 'D':
                get the number of columns
                move the cursor left by the specified number of columns
                flag the buffer as empty
                return
        case 'n':
                if (valid DSR request and the DSR routine has been set)
                        send an RCP escape sequence to the DSR routine
                flag the buffer as empty
                return
        case 'J':
                if (valid erase display request)
                        clear the screen
                flag the buffer as empty
                return
        case 'm':
                while (TRUE) {
                        get the next code
                        switch (attribute code) {
                                case 0:
                                        turn off the attributes
                                case 1:
                                        turn on bold
                                case 5:
                                        turn on blink
                                case 30:
                                        set the foreground color to black
                                case 31:
                                        set the foreground color to red
                                case 32:
                                        set the foreground color to green
```

continued...

...from previous page

```
                    case 33:
                        set the foreground color to yellow
                    case 34:
                        set the foreground color to blue
                    case 35:
                        set the foreground color to magenta
                    case 36:
                        set the foreground color to cyan
                    case 37:
                        set the foreground color to white
                    case 40:
                        set the background color to black
                    case 41:
                        set the background color to red
                    case 42:
                        set the background color to green
                    case 43:
                        set the background color to yellow
                    case 44:
                        set the background color to blue
                    case 45:
                        set the background color to magenta
                    case 46:
                        set the background color to cyan
                    case 47:
                        set the background color to white
                }
                if (next character is a semicolon) {
                    bump the buffer pointer
                    loop again
                }
                flag the buffer as empty
                return
            }
        default:
            flag the buffer as empty
            return
    }
```

Function Description: ansistring

The ansistring function sends a string to the ANSI terminal emulator. Its implementation is illustrated by the following pseudocode:

```
while (not the end of the string) {
        send a character to the ANSI terminal emulator
        bump the string pointer
}
```

Function Description: ansiprintf

The **ansiprintf** function sends a formatted string to the ANSI terminal emulator. Its implementation is illustrated by the following pseudocode:

```
allocate buffer space
if (not enough memory)
        return -1
format the string
while (not the end of the string) {
        send a character to the ANSI terminal emulator
        bump the string pointer
}
free up the buffer space
return the number of characters that was sent to the ANSI terminal emulator
```

Summary

In this chapter you learned how the display of text information can be controlled on a remote serial device through the use of an **ANSI terminal emulator**. This chapter presented complete descriptions for the **ANSI escape sequences** that are commonly used on the IBM PC and compatibles, and it concluded with the **source code** for a complete ANSI terminal emulator.

Chapter 9

A C++ ANSI Terminal Object Class

Chapter 8 presented the SERIAL toolbox's routines for performing ANSI terminal emulation. This chapter presents a C++ object class, which greatly simplifies implementing an ANSI terminal emulator into a C++ serial communications program. For the most part, this new object class is defined in the **sercpp.h** header file using inlined function calls; however, the object class declares a formatted output routine, which must be defined in a separate source code file.

Header File: sercpp.h

Listing 9.1, **sercpp.h**, is a revised version of the SERIAL toolbox's C++ header file that was last presented in Chapter 7. This final version of the header file includes a new object called *ANSI*. This object class is used in a C++ program to implement an ANSI terminal emulator.

Listing 9.1: sercpp.h

```
/*****************************************************************
* sercpp.h - C++ Header File for Serial Comm Prog in C and C++    *
*                Copyright (c) 1992 By Mark D. Goodwin            *
*****************************************************************/
#ifndef __SERCPPH__
#define __SERCPPH__

#include "serial.h"

class SERIALPORT {
    int port;
public:
    SERIALPORT(int n, int l) { open_port(n, l); }
    ~SERIALPORT(void) { close_port(); }
    int carrier(void) { return ::carrier(); }
    void fifo(int n) { ::fifo(n); }
    long get_baud(void) { return ::get_baud(); }
    int get_bits(void) { return ::get_bits(); }
    int get_parity(void) { return ::get_parity(); }
    int get_rx_dtr(void) { return ::get_rx_dtr(); }
    int get_rx_rts(void) { return ::get_rx_rts(); }
    int get_rx_xon(void) { return ::get_rx_xon(); }
    int get(void) { return get_serial(); }
    int get_stopbits(void) { return ::get_stopbits(); }
    int get_tx_dtr(void) { return ::get_tx_dtr(); }
    int get_tx_rts(void) { return ::get_tx_rts(); }
    int get_tx_xon(void) { return ::get_tx_xon(); }
    int in_ready(void) { return ::in_ready(); }
    void purge_in(void) { ::purge_in(); }
    int put(unsigned char n) { return put_serial(n); }
    void set_baud(long baud) { ::set_baud(baud); }
    void set_data_format(int bits = 8, int parity = NO_PARITY,
        int stopbit = 1) { ::set_data_format(bits, parity, stopbit); }
    void set_dtr(int n) { ::set_dtr(n); }
    void set_port(long baud, int bits = 8, int parity = NO_PARITY,
        int stopbit = 1) { ::set_port(baud, bits, parity, stopbit); }
    void set_rx_dtr(int n) { ::set_rx_dtr(n); }
    void set_rx_rts(int n) { ::set_rx_rts(n); }
    void set_rx_xon(int n) { ::set_rx_xon(n); }
    void set_tx_dtr(int n) { ::set_tx_dtr(n); }
    void set_tx_rts(int n) { ::set_tx_rts(n); }
    void set_tx_xon(int n) { ::set_tx_xon(n); }
};
```

continued...

...from previous page (Listing 9.1)

```
class XFERPORT : public SERIALPORT {
public:
    XFERPORT(int n, int l) : SERIALPORT(n, l)  { }
    int receive(int xtype, int(*error_handler)(int c, long p, char *s),
        char *path)    { return recv_file(xtype, error_handler, path); }
    int transmit(int xtype, int(*error_handler)(int c, long p, char *s),
        char *files[]) { return xmit_file(xtype, error_handler, files); }
};

class ANSI {
public:
    ANSI(void) { ansi_dsr = put_serial; ansi_dsr_flag = TRUE; }
    void out(int c) { ansiout(c); }
    void string(char *s) { ansistring(s); }
    int printf(char *s, ... );
};

#endif
```

Source File: ansicpp.cpp

Listing 9.2, **ansicpp.cpp**, presents the source code for the ANSI object class's formatted output routine. Because of the function's size, it really isn't practical to define it as an inline function. Thus the necessity for a separate source code file.

Listing 9.2: ansicpp.cpp

```
/*********************************************************************
* ansicpp.cpp - ANSI C++ Routines                                    *
*              Copyright (c) 1992 By Mark D. Goodwin                 *
*********************************************************************/
#include <stdio.h>
#include <stdlib.h>
#include <stdarg.h>
#include "sercpp.h"

int ANSI::printf(char *f, ...)
{
    int l;
    va_list m;
    char *b, *s;
```

continued...

...from previous page (Listing 9.2)

```
    if ((b = (char *)malloc(1024)) == NULL)
        return -1;
    va_start(m, f);
    l = vsprintf(b, f, m);
    s = b;
    while (*s) {
        ansiout(*s);
        s++;
    }
    va_end(m);
    free(b);
    return l;
}
```

Function Description: ANSI::printf

The **ANSI::printf** function sends a formatted string to the ANSI terminal emulator. Its implementation is illustrated by the following pseudocode:

```
allocate buffer space
if (not enough memory)
        return -1
format the string
while (not the end of the string) {
        send a character to the ANSI terminal emulator
        bump the string pointer
}
free up the buffer space
return the number of characters that was sent to the ANSI terminal emulator
```

Summary

This chapter presented the final version of the **sercpp.h** header file. This latest version of the C++ header file features an object class for performing ANSI terminal emulation. Additionally, the chapter presented a **source code file** for the ANSI object class's formatted output routine.

Chapter 10

A Simple Communications Program

Chapters 1 through 9 have been devoted to constructing the **SERIAL toolbox**. To demonstrate how the SERIAL toolbox is used in an actual application program's implementation, this chapter presents both a C and a C++ version of a sample SERIAL application program called *Simple Comm*. As its name implies, Simple Comm is a very rudimentary serial communications program; however, it is fully functional and can serve as a basis for a much more sophisticated serial communications program.

Using Simple Comm

Simple Comm is very easily operated through the use of seven function keys. Figure 10.1 illustrates these seven function keys and the task that they perform. As Figure 10.1 shows, Simple Comm really is pretty simple to use.

Function Key	*Purpose*
Alt-C	Configure Simple Comm
Alt-D	Dial a number
Alt-H	Hang up
Alt-X	Exit Simple Comm
F1	Display a help screen
Pg Up	Upload a file
Pg Dn	Download a file

Figure 10.1 *The Simple Comm Function Keys.*

Source File: simple.c

Listing 10.1, **simple.c**, is the C source code version of Simple Comm. This demonstration program illustrates many of the functions found in the SERIAL toolbox: low-level serial input/output; file transfers using the Xmodem, Xmodem-1K, Ymodem, and Ymodem-G protocols; ANSI terminal emulation; data flow control; and more.

Listing 10.1: simple.c

```
/*******************************************************************
* simple.c - Simple Comm 1.0 - A Simple Communications Program    *
*            Copyright (c) 1992 By Mark D. Goodwin                 *
*******************************************************************/
#include <stdio.h>
#include <stdlib.h>
#include <string.h>
#include <conio.h>
#include <dos.h>
#include <ctype.h>
#ifndef __TURBOC__
#include <graph.h>
#include <direct.h>
#else
#include <dir.h>
#endif
#include "serial.h"

/* data format constants */
#define P8N1 1
#define P7E1 0

/* configuration file record structure */
typedef struct {
    int port;
    long baud_rate;
    int parity;
    int lock_port;
    char initialization_string[81];
    char hangup_string[41];
    char dial_prefix[41];
} CONFIG;

/* function prototypes */
void config_program(void);
void dial(void);
void download(void);
void exit_program(void);
char *get_modem_string(char *s, char *d);
void help(void);
void hangup(void);
void modem_control_string(char *s);
void read_config(void);
void save_config(void);
void upload(void);
```

continued...

...from previous page (Listing 10.1)

```
char *files[10];
CONFIG config;

void main(void)
{
    int c;

    read_config();                          /* read in the config file */
    ansi_dsr = put_serial;                  /* set ANSI routine */
    ansi_dsr_flag = TRUE;
    ansiout(12);
    ansiprintf("Simple Comm v1.0\n");
    ansiprintf("Copyright (c) 1992 By Mark D. Goodwin\n\n");
    ansiprintf("Initializing Modem.....\n\n");
    open_port(config.port, 4096);           /* open the comm port */
    /* configure the port if no carrier */
    if (carrier())
        ansiprintf("Already connected at %ld baud!\n\n", get_baud());
    else {
        set_port(config.baud_rate, config.parity ? 8 : 7,
            config.parity ? NO_PARITY : EVEN_PARITY, 1);
    }
    set_tx_rts(TRUE);                       /* set XON/XOFF and RTS/CTS */
    set_tx_xon(TRUE);                       /* flow control */
    set_rx_rts(TRUE);
    set_rx_xon(TRUE);
    /* reset the modem and send initialization string if no carrier */
    if (!carrier()) {
        modem_control_string("ATZ^M");
        delay(1500);
        modem_control_string(config.initialization_string);
        delay(500);
    }
    /* main program loop */
    while (TRUE) {
        if (kbhit()) {
            c = getch();                    /* get the key */
            if (!c) {
                switch(getch()) {
                    case 32:                /* Alt-D - Dials */
                        dial();
                        break;
                    case 35:                /* Alt-H - Hangs Up */
                        hangup();
                        break;
                    case 45:                /* Alt-X - Exits the Program */
                        exit_program();
                        break;
```

continued...

...from previous page (Listing 10.1)

```
                    case 46:            /* Alt-C - Configure Program */
                        config_program();
                        break;
                    case 59:            /* F1 - Displays Help Screen */
                        help();
                        break;
                    case 73:            /* Pg Up - Upload a File */
                        upload();
                        break;
                    case 81:            /* Pg Dn - Download a File */
                        download();
                        break;
                }
                continue;
            }
            put_serial((unsigned char)c); /* send the key out the port */
        }
        if (in_ready()) {               /* get and display incoming */
            c = get_serial();           /*  characters */
            ansiout(c);
        }
    }
}

/* file transfer error handler */
int e_handler(int c, long p, char *s)
{
    int k;

    switch (c) {
        case SENDING:                   /* file is being sent */
            ansiprintf("Sending: %s\n", strupr(s));
            ansiprintf("Length : %ld\n", p);
            break;
        case RECEIVING:                 /* file is being received */
            ansiprintf("Receiving: %s\n", strupr(s));
            ansiprintf("Length : %ld\n", p);
            break;
        case SENT:                      /* block was sent */
            ansiprintf("%ld bytes sent.\r", p);
            break;
        case RECEIVED:                  /* block was received */
            ansiprintf("%ld bytes received.\r", p);
            break;
        case ERROR:                     /* an error occurred */
            ansiprintf("\nError: %s in block %ld\n", s, p);
            break;
```

continued...

...from previous page (Listing 10.1)

```
        case COMPLETE:                      /* file transfer complete */
            ansiprintf("\n%s\n", s);
            break;
    }
    if (kbhit()) {                          /* check for key pressed */
        if (!(k = getch())) {               /*  abort if ESC pressed */
            getch();
            return TRUE;
        }
        if (k == 27)
            return FALSE;
    }
    return TRUE;
}

/* download file routine */
void download(void)
{
    int c;
    char cdir[81], line[81];

    getcwd(cdir, 81);                       /* get the current directory */
    ansiprintf("\n");                           /* display the menu */
    ansiprintf("<X> - Xmodem\n");
    ansiprintf("<K> - Xmodem-1K\n");
    ansiprintf("<Y> - Ymodem\n");
    ansiprintf("<G> - Ymodem-G\n");
    ansiprintf("<Q> - Quit\n");
    ansiprintf("\nPlease make a selection: ");
    while (TRUE) {
        while (!kbhit()) ;
        switch (toupper(getch())) {
            case 0:                         /* handle extended keys */
                getch();
                break;
            case 'X':                       /* Xmodem or Xmodem-1K */
            case 'K':
                /* prompt the user for the filename */
                ansiprintf("X\n\nPlease enter the filename: ");
                gets(line);
                ansiprintf("\n");
                if (!*line)
                    return;
                recv_file(XMODEM, e_handler, line); /* get the file */
                return;
```

continued...

...from previous page (Listing 10.1)

```
            case 'Y':
                ansiprintf("Y\n\n");
                recv_file(YMODEM, e_handler, cdir); /* get the file */
                return;
            case 'G':
                ansiprintf("G\n\n");
                recv_file(YMODEMG, e_handler, cdir); /* get the file */
                return;
            case 'Q':                        /* quit */
                ansiprintf("Q\n\n");
                return;
        }
    }
}

/* upload a file */
void upload(void)
{
    int c;
    char line[81];

    ansiprintf("\n");                        /* display the menu */
    ansiprintf("<X> - Xmodem\n");
    ansiprintf("<K> - Xmodem-1K\n");
    ansiprintf("<Y> - Ymodem\n");
    ansiprintf("<G> - Ymodem-G\n");
    ansiprintf("<Q> - Quit\n");
    ansiprintf("\nPlease make a selection: ");
    while (TRUE) {
        while (!kbhit()) ;
        switch (toupper(getch())) {
            case 0:                          /* handle extended keys */
                getch();
                break;
            case 'X':
                /* prompt the user for the filename */
                ansiprintf("X\n\nPlease enter the filename: ");
                gets(line);
                ansiprintf("\n");
                if (!*line)
                    return;
                files[0] = line;
                files[1] = NULL;
                xmit_file(XMODEM, e_handler, files); /* send the file */
                return;
```

continued...

...from previous page (Listing 10.1)

```
            case 'K':
                /* prompt the user for the filename */
                ansiprintf("K\n\nPlease enter the filename: ");
                gets(line);
                ansiprintf("\n");
                if (!*line)
                    return;
                files[0] = line;
                files[1] = NULL;
                xmit_file(XMODEM1K, e_handler, files); /* send the file */
                return;
            case 'Y':
                /* prompt the user for the filename */
                ansiprintf("Y\n\nPlease enter the filename: ");
                gets(line);
                ansiprintf("\n");
                if (!*line)
                    return;
                files[0] = line;
                files[1] = NULL;
                xmit_file(YMODEM, e_handler, files); /* send the file */
                return;
            case 'G':
                /* prompt the user for the filename */
                ansiprintf("G\n\nPlease enter the filename: ");
                gets(line);
                ansiprintf("\n");
                if (!*line)
                    return;
                files[0] = line;
                files[1] = NULL;
                xmit_file(YMODEMG, e_handler, files); /* send the file */
                return;
            case 'Q':
                ansiprintf("Q\n\n");        /* quit */
                return;
        }
    }
}
```

continued...

...from previous page (Listing 10.1)

```
/* Help Routine */
void help(void)
{
    ansiprintf("\n");                           /* display the special keys */
    ansiprintf("Alt-C - Configure Program\n");
    ansiprintf("Alt-D - Dial Phone\n");
    ansiprintf("Alt-H - Hang Up Modem\n");
    ansiprintf("Pg Up - Upload a File\n");
    ansiprintf("Pg Dn - Download a File\n");
    ansiprintf("Alt-X - Exit Program\n");
    ansiprintf("\n");
    ansiprintf("Press any key to continue.....\n");
    ansiprintf("\n");
    while (!kbhit()) {                      /* wait for a key */
        if (!getch())
            getch();
        return;
    }
}

/* Exit Program Routine */
void exit_program(void)
{
    /* if carrier, ask whether to D/C or not */
    if (carrier()) {
        ansiprintf("\nStill connected.....Hang Up (Y/n)? ");
        while (TRUE) {
            if (kbhit()) {
                switch (toupper(getch())) {
                    case 0:             /* handle extended keys */
                        getch();
                        continue;
                    case 13:
                    case 'Y':
                        ansiprintf("Y\n\n"); /* hangup */
                        hangup();
                        break;
                    case 'N':
                        ansiprintf("N\n\n"); /* don't hangup */
                        break;
                    default:
                        continue;
                }
                break;
            }
        }
    }
    close_port();                           /* close the serial port */
    exit(0);                                /* exit the program */
}
```

continued...

...from previous page (Listing 10.1)

```
/* dial routine */
void dial(void)
{
    int br;
    char line[81], dstring[81], number[81];

    /* prompt user for the number to be dialed */
    ansiprintf("\nEnter the number you wish to dial: ");
    gets(number);
    if (!*number)
        return;
    sprintf(dstring, "%s%s", config.dial_prefix, number);
    while (TRUE) {
        ansiprintf("\nDailing %s\n", number);
        delay(2000);
        ansiprintf("Seconds Remaining: ");
        sprintf(line, "%s^M", dstring);
        modem_control_string(line);     /* dial the number */
        get_modem_string(line, dstring); /* get a response */
        /* dial interrupted by user */
        if (!strcmp(line, "INTERRUPTED")) {
            ansiprintf("\n");
            return;
        }
        /* user wants to repeat the dial immediately */
        if (!strcmp(line, "RECYCLE")) {
            ansiprintf("\n");
            continue;
        }
        /* connection was made */
        if (strstr(line, "CONNECT") != NULL) {
            ansiprintf("\n%s\n", line);
            /* set DTE rate to match the connection rate if port */
            /*  isn't locked */
            if (!config.lock_port) {
                br = atoi(line + 7);
                if (br)
                    set_baud(br);
                else
                    set_baud(300);
            }
            return;
        }
        ansiprintf("\n%s\n", line);         /* display the result string */
    }
}
```

continued...

...from previous page (Listing 10.1)

```
/* get response string */
char *get_modem_string(char *s, char *d)
{
    int i, c;
    unsigned last;

    last = mpeek(0, 0x46c);
    i = 1092;
    *s = 0;
    ansiprintf("%-2d", (i * 10) / 182);      /* display time remaining */
    while (TRUE) {
        /* check for user intervention */
        if (kbhit()) {
            switch (c = getch()) {
                case 0:                  /* handle extended keys */
                    getch();
                    break;
                case 27:                 /* ESC - abort dial */
                    put_serial(13);
                    sprintf(s, "INTERRUPTED");
                    return s;
                case ' ':                /* SPACE - redial */
                    put_serial(13);
                    sprintf(s, "RECYCLE");
                    return s;
            }
            continue;
        }
        /* get a character from the port if one's there */
        if (in_ready()) {
            switch (c = get_serial()) {
                case 13:                 /* CR - return the result string */
                    if (*s)
                        return s;
                    continue;
                default:
                    if (c != 10) {       /* add char to end of string */
                        s[strlen(s) + 1] = 0;
                        s[strlen(s)] = (char)c;
                        /* ignore RINGING and the dial string */
                        if (!strcmp(s, "RINGING") || !strcmp(s, d))
                            *s = 0;
                    }
            }
        }
```

continued...

...from previous page (Listing 10.1)

```
        /* check for timeout and display time remaining */
        if (last != mpeek(0, 0x46c)) {
            last = mpeek(0, 0x46c);
            i--;
            ansiprintf("\b \b\b \b%-2d", (i * 10) / 182);
            if (!i) {
                *s = 0;
                put_serial(13);
                return s;
            }
        }
    }
}

/* Hang Up Modem Routine */
void hangup(void)
{
    int i;
    unsigned last;

    ansiprintf("\nHanging Up");
    last = mpeek(0, 0x46c);                 /* get current system clock */
    i = 180;                                /* try for about 10 seconds */
    set_dtr(FALSE);                         /* drop DTR */
    while (carrier() && i) {                /* loop till loss of carrier */
        if (last != mpeek(0, 0x46c)) {      /*  or time out */
            i--;
            last = mpeek(0, 0x46c);
            ansiprintf(".");
        }
    }
    set_dtr(TRUE);                          /* raise DTR */
    if (!carrier()) {                       /* return if disconnect */
        ansiprintf("\n");
        purge_in();
        return;
    }
    modem_control_string(config.hangup_string); /* send software command */
    i = 180;                                /* try for about 10 seconds */
    while (carrier() && i) {                /* loop till loss of carrier */
        if (last != mpeek(0, 0x46c)) {       /*  or time out */
            i--;
            last = mpeek(0, 0x46c);
            ansiprintf(".");
        }
    }
    purge_in();
    ansiprintf("\n");
}
```

continued...

...from previous page (Listing 10.1)

```
/* Send Control String to Modem */
void modem_control_string(char *s)
{
    while (*s) {                        /* loop for the entire string */
        switch (*s) {
            case '~':                   /* if ~, wait a half second */
                delay(500);
                break;
            default:
                switch (*s) {
                    case '^':           /* if ^, it's a control code */
                        if (s[1]) {     /* send the control code */
                            s++;
                            put_serial((unsigned char)(*s - 64));
                        }
                        break;
                    default:
                        put_serial(*s); /* send the character */
                }
                delay(50);              /* wait 50 ms. for slow modems */
        }
        s++;                            /* bump the string pointer */
    }
}

/* read program configuration file */
void read_config(void)
{
    FILE *f;

    /* open the file, create default if it doesn't exist */
    if ((f = fopen("SIMPLE.CFG", "rb")) == NULL) {
        if ((f = fopen("SIMPLE.CFG", "wb")) != NULL) {
            config.port = 2;
            config.baud_rate = 2400;
            config.parity = P8N1;
            config.lock_port = FALSE;
            sprintf(config.initialization_string, "ATS0=0V1X4^M");
            sprintf(config.hangup_string, "~~~+++~~~ATH0^M");
            sprintf(config.dial_prefix, "ATDT");
            fwrite(&config, sizeof(CONFIG), 1, f);
            return;
        }
        return;
    }
    fread(&config, sizeof(CONFIG), 1, f); /* read in config info */
}
```

continued...

...from previous page (Listing 10.1)

```
/* write program configuration file */
void write_config(void)
{
    FILE *f;

    /* write the config info */
    if ((f = fopen("SIMPLE.CFG", "w+b")) != NULL) {
        fwrite(&config, sizeof(CONFIG), 1, f);
        fclose(f);
    }
}

/* program configuration routine */
void config_program(void)
{
    int t;
    long tl;
    char line[81];

    while (TRUE) {
        /* display the menu */
        ansiprintf("\n");
        ansiprintf("<1> Serial Port      : %d\n", config.port);
        ansiprintf("<2> Baud Rate        : %ld\n", config.baud_rate);
        ansiprintf("<3> Parity           : %s\n",
            config.parity == P8N1 ? "8N1" : "7E1");
        ansiprintf("<4> Lock Serial Port: %s\n",
            config.lock_port ? "Yes" : "No");
        ansiprintf("<5> Init. String     : %s\n", config.initialization_string);
        ansiprintf("<6> Hangup String    : %s\n", config.hangup_string);
        ansiprintf("<7> Dial Prefix      : %s\n", config.dial_prefix);
        ansiprintf("<S> Save and Quit\n");
        ansiprintf("<Q> Quit\n");
        ansiprintf("\nPlease make a selection: ");
        while (TRUE) {
            while (!kbhit()) ;
            switch (toupper(getch())) {
                case 0:                 /* handle extended keys */
                    getch();
                    continue;
                case '1':               /* get new port */
                    ansiprintf("1\n\n");
                    ansiprintf("Please select the new serial port: ");
                    gets(line);
                    ansiprintf("\n");
                    if (!(t = atoi(line)))
                        break;
```

continued...

...from previous page (Listing 10.1)

```
        /* make sure it's a valid port */
        if (t > 4 || !port_exist(t))
            ansiprintf("That port doesn't exist!\n");
        else {
            close_port();
            config.port = t;
            open_port(config.port, 4096);
        }
        break;
    case '2':                /* get new baud rate */
        ansiprintf("2\n\n");
        ansiprintf("Please enter the new baud rate: ");
        gets(line);
        ansiprintf("\n");
        if ((tl = atol(line))) {
            config.baud_rate = tl;
            set_baud(config.baud_rate);
        }
        break;
    case '3':                /* toggle data format */
        ansiprintf("3\n\n");
        config.parity = (config.parity == P8N1 ? P7E1 : P8N1);
        set_data_format(config.parity ? 8 : 7,
            config.parity ? NO_PARITY : EVEN_PARITY, 1);
        break;
    case '4':                /* toggle locked port flag */
        ansiprintf("4\n\n");
        config.lock_port = !config.lock_port;
        break;
    case '5':                /* get new init string */
        ansiprintf("5\n\n");
        ansiprintf("Please enter the new initialization string: ");
        gets(line);
        ansiprintf("\n");
        if (*line)
            sprintf(config.initialization_string, strupr(line));
        break;
    case '6':                /* get new hangup string */
        ansiprintf("6\n\n");
        ansiprintf("Please enter the new hangup string: ");
        gets(line);
        ansiprintf("\n");
        if (*line)
            sprintf(config.hangup_string, strupr(line));
        break;
```

continued...

...from previous page (Listing 10.1)

```
            case '7':                   /* get new dial prefix */
                ansiprintf("7\n\n");
                ansiprintf("Please enter the new dial prefix: ");
                gets(line);
                ansiprintf("\n");
                if (*line)
                    sprintf(config.dial_prefix, strupr(line));
                break;
            case 'S':                   /* save config and return */
                ansiprintf("S\n\n");
                write_config();
                return;
            case 'Q':                   /* quit */
                ansiprintf("Q\n\n");
                return;
            default:
                continue;
        }
        break;
    }
  }
}
```

Function Description: main

As with all C programs, the **main** function is the program's main program loop. Its implementation is illustrated by the following pseudocode:

```
read the configuration file
set the ANSI DSR routine
clear the screen
display the sign on message
open the serial port
if (carrier already exists)
        display an "Already connected message"
else
        set the serial port's baud rate and data format
turn on XON/XOFF and RTS/CTS flow control
if (no carrier) {
        reset the modem
        send the initialization string
}
```

continued...

...from previous page

```
while (TRUE) {
        if (key pressed) {
                get the key
                if (extended key) {
                        switch (scan code) {
                                Alt-D:
                                        dial a number
                                Alt-H:
                                        hang up
                                Alt-X:
                                        exit the program
                                Alt-C:
                                        configure the program
                                F1:
                                        display the help screen
                                PG UP:
                                        upload a file
                                PG DN:
                                        download a file
                        }
                        continue looping
                }
                send the character out the serial port
        }
        if (a character is available) {
                get the character
                display the character
        }
}
```

Function Description: e_handler

The **e_handler** function is the file transfer error handler. Its implementation is illustrated by the following pseudocode:

```
switch (error code) {
        case SENDING:
                display the file's name
                display the file's length
```

continued...

...from previous page

```
		case RECEIVING:
			display the file's name
			display the file's length
		case SENT:
			display the new number of bytes sent
		case RECEIVED:
			display the new number of bytes received
		case ERROR:
			display the error message
		case COMPLETE:
			clean up the display
	}
	if (key pressed) {
		if (extended key) {
			get scan code
			return TRUE
		}
		if (ESC pressed)
			return FALSE
	}
	return TRUE
```

Function Description: download

The **download** function is used to download a file. Its implementation is illustrated by the following pseudocode:

```
	get the current work directory
	display the protocol menu
	while (TRUE) {
		wait for a key to be pressed
		switch (the key that was pressed) {
			case extended key:
				ignore it
			case 'X':
			case 'K':
				get the file name
				if (null string)
					return
				download the file
				return
```

continued...

...from previous page

```
                case 'Y':
                        download the file
                        return
                case 'G':
                        download the file
                        return
                case 'Q':
                        return
        }
}
```

Function Description: upload

The **upload** function is used to upload a file. Its implementation is illustrated by the following pseudocode:

```
display the protocol menu
while (TRUE) {
        wait till a key is pressed
        switch (the key that was pressed) {
                case extended key:
                        ignore it
                case 'X':
                        get the file name
                        if (null string)
                                return
                        upload the file
                        return
                case 'K':
                        get the file name
                        if (null string)
                                return
                        upload the file
                        return
                case 'Y':
                        get the file name
                        if (null string)
                                return
                        upload the file
```

continued...

...from previous page

```
                case 'G':
                        get the file name
                        if (null string)
                                return
                        upload the file
                case 'Q':
                        return
        }
}
```

Function Description: help

The **help** function displays a help screen. Its implementation is illustrated by the following pseudocode:

```
display the help screen
wait for a key to be pressed
```

Function Description: exit_program

The **exit_program** function exits the program. Its implementation is illustrated by the following pseudocode:

```
if (carrier) {
        ask if the user wants to hang up
        while (TRUE) {
                if (key pressed) {
                        switch (the key that was pressed) {
                                case extended key:
                                        ignore it
                                case 13:
                                case 'Y':
                                        hang up
                                        break out of the loop
                                case 'N':
                                        break out of the loop
                        }
                }
        }
}
close the serial port
exit the program
```

Function Description: dial

The **dial** function dials a telephone number. Its implementation is illustrated by the following pseudocode:

```
get the telephone number
if (null string)
        return
add on the dial prefix
while (TRUE) {
        delay 2 seconds
        send the dial command to the modem
        get the result string
        if (interrupted by the operator)
                return
        if (operator wants to redial)
                loop
        if (CONNECT result string) {
                if (the port isn't locked)
                        adjust the baud rate to the CONNECT rate
                return
        }
        display the result string
}
```

Function Description: get_modem_string

The **get_modem_string** function gets a result string from the modem. Its implementation is illustrated by the following pseudocode:

```
get the current system clock count
set time out delay for sixty seconds
display the number of seconds remaining
while (TRUE) {
        if (key pressed) {
                switch (the key that was pressed) {
                        case extended key:
                                ignore it
                        case ESC:
                                abort the call
                                return an INTERRUPTED message
```

continued...

...from previous page

```
                case SPACE:
                    abort the call
                    return a RECYCLE message
            }
        }
        if (a character is available through the serial port) {
            switch (the serial port's character) {
                case carriage return:
                    if (there is a result string)
                        return
                default:
                    if (character isn't a line feed) {
                        add the character to the result string
                        if (the result string is a RINGING or the dial
    string)
                            ignore it
                    }
        }
        if (system clock has ticked) {
            update the counter
            display the number of seconds remaining
            if (timeout) {
                abort the transfer
                return a null string
            }
        }
    }
```

Function Description: hangup

The **hangup** function hangs up the phone. Its implementation is illustrated by the following pseudocode:

```
    drop DTR
    while (carrier and 10 seconds hasn't elapsed) ;
    assert DTR
    if (carrier not present) {
        purge the input buffer
        return
    }
    send the software hangup command
    while (carrier and 10 seconds hasn't elapsed) ;
    purge the input buffer
```

Function Description: modem_control_string

The **modem_control_string** function sends an AT command string to the modem. Its implementation is illustrated by the following pseudocode:

```
while (not the end of the string) {
        switch (next character) {
                case '~':
                        delay for ½ of a second
                default:
                        switch (the character) {
                                case '^':
                                        if (there's another character) {
                                                bump the string pointer
                                                send the next character as a control
code
                                        }
                                default:
                                        send the character out the serial port
                        }
                        delay slightly for slow modems
        }
        bump the string pointer
}
```

Function Description: read_config

The **read_config** function reads the Simple Comm configuration file. Its implementation is illustrated by the following pseudocode:

```
open the file
if (open failed) {
        create a new file
        set the Simple Comm configuration to its default settings
        save the default settings as the configuration file
        return
}
read the configuration
```

Function Description: write_config

The **write_config** function saves the current Simple Comm configuration to disk. Its implementation is illustrated by the follow pseudocode:

```
open the configuration file
save the current configuration to disk
close the configuration file
```

Function Description: config_program

The **config_program** function allows the user to configure Simple Comm. Its implementation is illustrated by the following pseudocode:

```
display the configuration menu
while (TRUE) {
        wait till a key is pressed
        switch (the key that was pressed) {
                case extended key:
                        ignore it
                case '1':
                        set the serial port
                case '2':
                        set the baud rate
                case '3':
                        set the data format
                case '4':
                        toggle the locked serial port flag
                case '5':
                        set the modem's initialization string
                case '6':
                        set the modem's hang up string
                case '7':
                        set the modem's dial prefix
                case 'S':
                        save the new configuration
                        return
                case 'Q':
                        return
        }
}
```

Source File: simcpp.cpp

Listing 10.2, **simcpp.cpp**, is the C++ source code version of Simple Comm. Like its C counterpart, this demonstration program illustrates many of the functions found in the SERIAL toolbox; however, the C++ version uses the XFERPORT object classes to implement the program.

Listing 10.2: simcpp.cpp

```
/*********************************************************************
* simcpp.cpp - Simple Comm 1.0 - A Simple Communications Program    *
*              Copyright (c) 1992 By Mark D. Goodwin                *
*********************************************************************/
#include <stdio.h>
#include <stdlib.h>
#include <string.h>
#include <conio.h>
#include <dos.h>
#include <ctype.h>
#ifndef __TURBOC__
#include <graph.h>
#include <direct.h>
#else
#include <dir.h>
#endif
#include "sercpp.h"

/* data format constants */
#define P8N1 1
#define P7E1 0

/* configuration file record structure */
typedef struct {
    int port;
    long baud_rate;
    int parity;
    int lock_port;
    char initialization_string[81];
    char hangup_string[41];
    char dial_prefix[41];
} CONFIG;
```

continued...

...from previous page (Listing 10.2)

```
/* function prototypes */
void config_program(void);
void dial(void);
void download(void);
void exit_program(void);
char *get_modem_string(char *s, char *d);
void help(void);
void hangup(void);
void modem_control_string(char *s);
void read_config(void);
void save_config(void);
void upload(void);

char *files[10];
CONFIG config;
XFERPORT *port;
ANSI ansi;

void main(void)
{
    int c;

    read_config();                      /* read in the config file */
    ansi.out(12);
    ansi.printf("Simple Comm v1.0\n");
    ansi.printf("Copyright (c) 1992 By Mark D. Goodwin\n\n");
    ansi.printf("Initializing Modem.....\n\n");
    port = new XFERPORT(config.port, 4096);
    /* configure the port if no carrier */
    if (carrier())
        ansi.printf("Already connected at %ld baud!\n\n", get_baud());
    else {
        port->set_port(config.baud_rate, config.parity ? 8 : 7,
            config.parity ? NO_PARITY : EVEN_PARITY, 1);
    }
    port->set_tx_rts(TRUE);                 /* set XON/XOFF and RTS/CTS */
    port->set_tx_xon(TRUE);                 /* flow control */
    port->set_rx_rts(TRUE);
    port->set_rx_xon(TRUE);
    /* reset the modem and send initialization string if no carrier */
    if (!carrier()) {
        modem_control_string("ATZ^M");
        delay(1500);
        modem_control_string(config.initialization_string);
        delay(500);
    }
```

continued...

...from previous page (Listing 10.2)

```
    /* main program loop */
    while (TRUE) {
        if (kbhit()) {
            c = getch();                /* get the key */
            if (!c) {
                switch(getch()) {
                    case 32:            /* Alt-D - Dials */
                        dial();
                        break;
                    case 35:            /* Alt-H - Hangs Up */
                        hangup();
                        break;
                    case 45:            /* Alt-X - Exits the Program */
                        exit_program();
                        break;
                    case 46:            /* Alt-C - Configure Program */
                        config_program();
                        break;
                    case 59:            /* F1 - Displays Help Screen */
                        help();
                        break;
                    case 73:            /* Pg Up - Upload a File */
                        upload();
                        break;
                    case 81:            /* Pg Dn - Download a File */
                        download();
                        break;
                }
                continue;
            }
            port->put((unsigned char)c); /* send the key out the port */
        }
        if (in_ready()) {               /* get and display incoming */
            c = port->get();            /*  characters */
            ansi.out(c);
        }
    }
}

/* file transfer error handler */
int e_handler(int c, long p, char *s)
{
    int k;

    switch (c) {
        case SENDING:                   /* file is being sent */
            ansi.printf("Sending: %s\n", strupr(s));
            ansi.printf("Length : %ld\n", p);
            break;
```

continued...

...from previous page (Listing 10.2)

```
        case RECEIVING:                 /* file is being received */
            ansi.printf("Receiving: %s\n", strupr(s));
            ansi.printf("Length : %ld\n", p);
            break;
        case SENT:                      /* block was sent */
            ansi.printf("%ld bytes sent.\r", p);
            break;
        case RECEIVED:                  /* block was received */
            ansi.printf("%ld bytes received.\r", p);
            break;
        case ERROR:                     /* an error occurred */
            ansi.printf("\nError: %s in block %ld\n", s, p);
            break;
        case COMPLETE:                    /* file transfer complete */
            ansi.printf("\n%s\n", s);
            break;
    }
    if (kbhit()) {                      /* check for key pressed */
        if (!(k = getch())) {           /*  abort if ESC pressed */
            getch();
            return TRUE;
        }
        if (k == 27)
            return FALSE;
    }
    return TRUE;
}

/* download file routine */
void download(void)
{
    int c;
    char cdir[81], line[81];

    getcwd(cdir, 81);                   /* get the current directory */
    ansi.printf("\n");                      /* display the menu */
    ansi.printf("<X> - Xmodem\n");
    ansi.printf("<K> - Xmodem-1K\n");
    ansi.printf("<Y> - Ymodem\n");
    ansi.printf("<G> - Ymodem-G\n");
    ansi.printf("<Q> - Quit\n");
    ansi.printf("\nPlease make a selection: ");
    while (TRUE) {
        while (!kbhit()) ;
        switch (toupper(getch())) {
            case 0:                     /* handle extended keys */
                getch();
                break;
            case 'X':                   /* Xmodem or Xmodem-1K */
```

continued...

...from previous page (Listing 10.2)

```
            case 'K':
                /* prompt the user for the filename */
                ansi.printf("X\n\nPlease enter the filename: ");
                gets(line);
                ansi.printf("\n");
                if (!*line)
                    return;
                port->receive(XMODEM, e_handler, line);    /* get the file */
                return;
            case 'Y':
                ansi.printf("Y\n\n");
                port->receive(YMODEM, e_handler, cdir);    /* get the file */
                return;
            case 'G':
                ansi.printf("G\n\n");
                port->receive(YMODEMG, e_handler, cdir); /* get the file */
                return;
            case 'Q':                         /* quit */
                ansi.printf("Q\n\n");
                return;
        }
    }
}

/* upload a file */
void upload(void)
{
    int c;
    char line[81];

    ansi.printf("\n");                          /* display the menu */
    ansi.printf("<X> - Xmodem\n");
    ansi.printf("<K> - Xmodem-1K\n");
    ansi.printf("<Y> - Ymodem\n");
    ansi.printf("<G> - Ymodem-G\n");
    ansi.printf("<Q> - Quit\n");
    ansi.printf("\nPlease make a selection: ");
    while (TRUE) {
        while (!kbhit()) ;
        switch (toupper(getch())) {
            case 0:                           /* handle extended keys */
                getch();
                break;
```

continued...

...from previous page (Listing 10.2)

```
          case 'X':
              /* prompt the user for the filename */
              ansi.printf("X\n\nPlease enter the filename: ");
              gets(line);
              ansi.printf("\n");
              if (!*line)
                  return;
              files[0] = line;
              files[1] = NULL;
              port->transmit(XMODEM, e_handler, files); /* send the file */
              return;
          case 'K':
              /* prompt the user for the filename */
              ansi.printf("K\n\nPlease enter the filename: ");
              gets(line);
              ansi.printf("\n");
              if (!*line)
                  return;
              files[0] = line;
              files[1] = NULL;
              port->transmit(XMODEM1K, e_handler, files); /* send the file */
              return;
          case 'Y':
              /* prompt the user for the filename */
              ansi.printf("Y\n\nPlease enter the filename: ");
              gets(line);
              ansi.printf("\n");
              if (!*line)
                  return;
              files[0] = line;
              files[1] = NULL;
              port->transmit(YMODEM, e_handler, files); /* send the file */
              return;
          case 'G':
              /* prompt the user for the filename */
              ansi.printf("G\n\nPlease enter the filename: ");
              gets(line);
              ansi.printf("\n");
              if (!*line)
                  return;
              files[0] = line;
              files[1] = NULL;
              port->transmit(YMODEMG, e_handler, files); /* send the file */
              return;
          case 'Q':
              ansi.printf("Q\n\n");          /* quit */
              return;
      }
    }
}
```

continued...

...from previous page (Listing 10.2)

```
/* Help Routine */
void help(void)
{
    ansi.printf("\n");                          /* display the special keys */
    ansi.printf("Alt-C - Configure Program\n");
    ansi.printf("Alt-D - Dial Phone\n");
    ansi.printf("Alt-H - Hang Up Modem\n");
    ansi.printf("Pg Up - Upload a File\n");
    ansi.printf("Pg Dn - Download a File\n");
    ansi.printf("Alt-X - Exit Program\n");
    ansi.printf("\n");
    ansi.printf("Press any key to continue.....\n");
    ansi.printf("\n");
    while (!kbhit()) {                      /* wait for a key */
        if (!getch())
            getch();
        return;
    }
}

/* Exit Program Routine */
void exit_program(void)
{
    /* if carrier, ask whether to D/C or not */
    if (port->carrier()) {
        ansi.printf("\nStill connected.....Hang Up (Y/n)? ");
        while (TRUE) {
            if (kbhit()) {
                switch (toupper(getch())) {
                    case 0:             /* handle extended keys */
                        getch();
                        continue;
                    case 13:
                    case 'Y':
                        ansi.printf("Y\n\n"); /* hangup */
                        hangup();
                        break;
                    case 'N':
                        ansi.printf("N\n\n"); /* don't hangup */
                        break;
                    default:
                        continue;
                }
                break;
            }
        }
    }
    delete port;                            /* close the serial port */
    exit(0);                                /* exit the program */
}
```

continued...

...from previous page (Listing 10.2)

```
/* dial routine */
void dial(void)
{
    int br;
    char line[81], dstring[81], number[81];

    /* prompt user for the number to be dialed */
    ansi.printf("\nEnter the number you wish to dial: ");
    gets(number);
    if (!*number)
        return;
    sprintf(dstring, "%s%s", config.dial_prefix, number);
    while (TRUE) {
        ansi.printf("\nDailing %s\n", number);
        delay(2000);
        ansi.printf("Seconds Remaining: ");
        sprintf(line, "%s^M", dstring);
        modem_control_string(line);         /* dial the number */
        get_modem_string(line, dstring); /* get a response */
        /* dial interrupted by user */
        if (!strcmp(line, "INTERRUPTED")) {
            ansi.printf("\n");
            return;
        }
        /* user wants to repeat the dial immediately */
        if (!strcmp(line, "RECYCLE")) {
            ansi.printf("\n");
            continue;
        }
        /* connection was made */
        if (strstr(line, "CONNECT") != NULL) {
            ansi.printf("\n%s\n", line);
            /* set DTE rate to match the connection rate if port */
            /*  isn't locked */
            if (!config.lock_port) {
                br = atoi(line + 7);
                if (br)
                    set_baud(br);
                else
                    set_baud(300);
            }
            return;
        }
        ansi.printf("\n%s\n", line);             /* display the result string */
    }
}
```

continued...

...from previous page (Listing 10.2)

```
/* get response string */
char *get_modem_string(char *s, char *d)
{
    int i, c;
    unsigned last;
    last = mpeek(0, 0x46c);
    i = 1092;
    *s = 0;
    ansi.printf("%-2d", (i * 10) / 182);        /* display time remaining */
    while (TRUE) {
        /* check for user intervention */
        if (kbhit()) {
            switch (c = getch()) {
                case 0:                 /* handle extended keys */
                    getch();
                    break;
                case 27:                /* ESC - abort dial */
                    port->put(13);
                    sprintf(s, "INTERRUPTED");
                    return s;
                case ' ':               /* SPACE - redial */
                    port->put(13);
                    sprintf(s, "RECYCLE");
                    return s;
            }
            continue;
        }
        /* get a character from the port if one's there */
        if (port->in_ready()) {
            switch (c = port->get()) {
                case 13:                /* CR - return the result string */
                    if (*s)
                        return s;
                    continue;
                default:
                    if (c != 10) {      /* add char to end of string */
                        s[strlen(s) + 1] = 0;
                        s[strlen(s)] = (char)c;
                        /* ignore RINGING and the dial string */
                        if (!strcmp(s, "RINGING") || !strcmp(s, d))
                            *s = 0;
                    }
            }
        }
```

continued...

...from previous page (Listing 10.2)

```
        /* check for timeout and display time remaining */
        if (last != mpeek(0, 0x46c)) {
            last = mpeek(0, 0x46c);
            i--;
            ansi.printf("\b \b\b \b%-2d", (i * 10) / 182);
            if (!i) {
                *s = 0;
                port->put(13);
                return s;
            }
        }
    }
}

/* Hang Up Modem Routine */
void hangup(void)
{
    int i;
    unsigned last;

    ansi.printf("\nHanging Up");
    last = mpeek(0, 0x46c);                /* get current system clock */
    i = 180;                               /* try for about 10 seconds */
    port->set_dtr(FALSE);                          /* drop DTR */
    while (port->carrier() && i) {             /* loop till loss of carrier */
        if (last != mpeek(0, 0x46c)) {   /*  or time out */
            i--;
            last = mpeek(0, 0x46c);
            ansi.printf(".");
        }
    }
    port->set_dtr(TRUE);                           /* raise DTR */
    if (!port->carrier()) {                    /* return if disconnect */
        ansi.printf("\n");
        port->purge_in();
        return;
    }
    modem_control_string(config.hangup_string); /* send software command */
    i = 180;                               /* try for about 10 seconds */
    while (port->carrier() && i) {               /* loop till loss of carrier */
        if (last != mpeek(0, 0x46c)) {    /*  or time out */
            i--;
            last = mpeek(0, 0x46c);
            ansi.printf(".");
        }
    }
    port->purge_in();
    ansi.printf("\n");
}
```

continued...

...from previous page (Listing 10.2)

```
/* Send Control String to Modem */
void modem_control_string(char *s)
{
    while (*s) {                        /* loop for the entire string */
        switch (*s) {
            case '~':                   /* if ~, wait a half second */
                delay(500);
                break;
            default:
                switch (*s) {
                    case '^':           /* if ^, it's a control code */
                        if (s[1]) {     /* send the control code */
                            s++;
                            port->put((unsigned char)(*s - 64));
                        }
                        break;
                    default:
                        port->put(*s);  /* send the character */
                }
                delay(50);              /* wait 50 ms. for slow modems */
        }
        s++;                            /* bump the string pointer */
    }
}

/* read program configuration file */
void read_config(void)
{
    FILE *f;

    /* open the file, create default if it doesn't exist */
    if ((f = fopen("SIMPLE.CFG", "rb")) == NULL) {
        if ((f = fopen("SIMPLE.CFG", "wb")) != NULL) {
            config.port = 2;
            config.baud_rate = 2400;
            config.parity = P8N1;
            config.lock_port = FALSE;
            sprintf(config.initialization_string, "ATS0=0V1X4^M");
            sprintf(config.hangup_string, "~~~+++~~~ATH0^M");
            sprintf(config.dial_prefix, "ATDT");
            fwrite(&config, sizeof(CONFIG), 1, f);
            return;
        }
        return;
    }
    fread(&config, sizeof(CONFIG), 1, f); /* read in config info */
}
```

continued...

...from previous page (Listing 10.2)

```
/* write program configuration file */
void write_config(void)
{
    FILE *f;

    /* write the config info */
    if ((f = fopen("SIMPLE.CFG", "w+b")) != NULL) {
        fwrite(&config, sizeof(CONFIG), 1, f);
        fclose(f);
    }
}

/* program configuration routine */
void config_program(void)
{
    int t;
    long tl;
    char line[81];

    while (TRUE) {
        /* display the menu */
        ansi.printf("\n");
        ansi.printf("<1> Serial Port      : %d\n", config.port);
        ansi.printf("<2> Baud Rate        : %ld\n", config.baud_rate);
        ansi.printf("<3> Parity           : %s\n",
            config.parity == P8N1 ? "8N1" : "7E1");
        ansi.printf("<4> Lock Serial Port: %s\n",
            config.lock_port ? "Yes" : "No");
        ansi.printf("<5> Init. String     : %s\n", config.initialization_string);
        ansi.printf("<6> Hangup String    : %s\n", config.hangup_string);
        ansi.printf("<7> Dial Prefix      : %s\n", config.dial_prefix);
        ansi.printf("<S> Save and Quit\n");
        ansi.printf("<Q> Quit\n");
        ansi.printf("\nPlease make a selection: ");
        while (TRUE) {
            while (!kbhit()) ;
            switch (toupper(getch())) {
                case 0:                 /* handle extended keys */
                    getch();
                    continue;
                case '1':               /* get new port */
                    ansi.printf("1\n\n");
                    ansi.printf("Please select the new serial port: ");
                    gets(line);
                    ansi.printf("\n");
                    if (!(t = atoi(line)))
                        break;
```

continued...

...from previous page (Listing 10.2)

```
            /* make sure it's a valid port */
            if (t > 4 || !port_exist(t))
                ansi.printf("That port doesn't exist!\n");
            else {
                delete port;
                config.port = t;
                port = new XFERPORT(config.port, 4096);
            }
            break;
        case '2':               /* get new baud rate */
            ansi.printf("2\n\n");
            ansi.printf("Please enter the new baud rate: ");
            gets(line);
            ansi.printf("\n");
            if ((tl = atol(line))) {
                config.baud_rate = tl;
                port->set_baud(config.baud_rate);
            }
            break;
        case '3':               /* toggle data format */
            ansi.printf("3\n\n");
            config.parity = (config.parity == P8N1 ? P7E1 : P8N1);
            port->set_data_format(config.parity ? 8 : 7,
                config.parity ? NO_PARITY : EVEN_PARITY, 1);
            break;
        case '4':               /* toggle locked port flag */
            ansi.printf("4\n\n");
            config.lock_port = !config.lock_port;
            break;
        case '5':               /* get new init string */
            ansi.printf("5\n\n");
            ansi.printf("Please enter the new initialization string: ");
            gets(line);
            ansi.printf("\n");
            if (*line)
                sprintf(config.initialization_string, strupr(line));
            break;
        case '6':               /* get new hangup string */
            ansi.printf("6\n\n");
            ansi.printf("Please enter the new hangup string: ");
            gets(line);
            ansi.printf("\n");
            if (*line)
                sprintf(config.hangup_string, strupr(line));
            break;
```

continued...

...from previous page (Listing 10.2)

```
                case '7':               /* get new dial prefix */
                    ansi.printf("7\n\n");
                    ansi.printf("Please enter the new dial prefix: ");
                    gets(line);
                    ansi.printf("\n");
                    if (*line)
                        sprintf(config.dial_prefix, strupr(line));
                    break;
                case 'S':               /* save config and return */
                    ansi.printf("S\n\n");
                    write_config();
                    return;
                case 'Q':               /* quit */
                    ansi.printf("Q\n\n");
                    return;
                default:
                    continue;
            }
            break;
        }
    }
}
```

Function Description: main

As with all C++ programs, the **main** function is the program's main program loop. Its implementation is illustrated by the following pseudocode:

```
read the configuration file
set the ANSI DSR routine
clear the screen
display the sign on message
open the serial port
if (carrier already exists)
        display an "Already connected message"
else
        set the serial port's baud rate and data format
turn on XON/XOFF and RTS/CTS flow control
if (no carrier) {
        reset the modem
        send the initialization string
}
```

continued...

...from previous page

```
while (TRUE) {
        if (key pressed) {
                get the key
                if (extended key) {
                        switch (scan code) {
                                Alt-D:
                                        dial a number
                                Alt-H:
                                        hang up
                                Alt-X:
                                        exit the program
                                Alt-C:
                                        configure the program
                                F1:
                                        display the help screen
                                PG UP:
                                        upload a file
                                PG DN:
                                        download a file
                        }
                        continue looping
                }
                send the character out the serial port
        }
        if (a character is available) {
                get the character
                display the character
        }
}
```

Function Description: e_handler

The **e_handler** function is the file transfer error handler. Its implementation is illustrated by the following pseudocode:

```
switch (error code) {
        case SENDING:
                display the file's name
                display the file's length
```

continued...

...from previous page

```
        case RECEIVING:
            display the file's name
            display the file's length
        case SENT:
            display the new number of bytes sent
        case RECEIVED:
            display the new number of bytes received
        case ERROR:
            display the error message
        case COMPLETE:
            clean up the display
    }
    if (key pressed) {
        if (extended key) {
            get scan code
            return TRUE
        }
        if (ESC pressed)
            return FALSE
    }
    return TRUE
```

Function Description: download

The **download** function is used to download a file. Its implementation is illustrated by the following pseudocode:

```
    get the current work directory
    display the protocol menu
    while (TRUE) {
        wait for a key to be pressed
        switch (the key that was pressed) {
            case extended key:
                ignore it
            case 'X':
            case 'K':
                get the file name
                if (null string)
                    return
                download the file
                return
```

continued...

...from previous page

```
                case 'Y':
                        download the file
                        return
                case 'G':
                        download the file
                        return
                case 'Q':
                        return
        }
}
```

Function Description: upload

The **upload** function is used to upload a file. Its implementation is illustrated by the following pseudocode:

```
display the protocol menu
while (TRUE) {
        wait till a key is pressed
        switch (the key that was pressed) {
                case extended key:
                        ignore it
                case 'X':
                        get the file name
                        if (null string)
                                return
                        upload the file
                        return
                case 'K':
                        get the file name
                        if (null string)
                                return
                        upload the file
                        return
                case 'Y':
                        get the file name
                        if (null string)
                                return
                        upload the file
```

continued...

...from previous page

```
                case 'G':
                        get the file name
                        if (null string)
                                return
                        upload the file
                case 'Q':
                        return
        }
}
```

Function Description: help

The **help** function displays a help screen. Its implementation is illustrated by the following pseudocode:

```
display the help screen
wait for a key to be pressed
```

Function Description: exit_program

The **exit_program** function exits the program. Its implementation is illustrated by the following pseudocode:

```
if (carrier) {
        ask if the user wants to hang up
        while (TRUE) {
                if (key pressed) {
                        switch (the key that was pressed) {
                                case extended key:
                                        ignore it
                                case 13:
                                case 'Y':
                                        hang up
                                        break out of the loop
                                case 'N':
                                        break out of the loop
                        }
                }
        }
}
close the serial port
exit the program
```

Function Description: dial

The **dial** function dials a telephone number. Its implementation is illustrated by the following pseudocode:

```
get the telephone number
if (null string)
        return
add on the dial prefix
while (TRUE) {
        delay 2 seconds
        send the dial command to the modem
        get the result string
        if (interrupted by operator)
                return
        if (operator wants to redial)
                loop
        if (CONNECT result string) {
                if (the port isn't locked)
                        adjust the baud rate to the CONNECT rate
                return
        }
        display the result string
}
```

Function Description: get_modem_string

The **get_modem_string** function gets a result string from the modem. Its implementation is illustrated by the following pseudocode:

```
get the current system clock count
set time out delay for sixty seconds
display the number of seconds remaining
while (TRUE) {
        if (key pressed) {
                switch (the key that was pressed) {
                        case extended key:
                                ignore it
                        case ESC:
                                abort the call
                                return an INTERRUPTED message
```

continued...

...from previous page

```
                case SPACE:
                        abort the call
                        return a RECYCLE message
        }
}
if (a character is available through the serial port) {
        switch (the serial port's character) {
                case carriage return:
                        if (there is a result string)
                                return
                default:
                        if (character isn't a line feed) {
                                add the character to the result string
                                if (the result string is a RINGING or the dial
string)
                                        ignore it
                        }
}
if (system clock has ticked) {
        update the counter
        display the number of seconds remaining
        if (timeout) {
                abort the transfer
                return a null string
        }
}
}
```

Function Description: hangup

The **hangup** function hangs up the phone. Its implementation is illustrated by the following pseudocode:

```
drop DTR
while (carrier and 10 seconds hasn't elapsed) ;
assert DTR
if (carrier not present) {
        purge the input buffer
        return
}
send the software hangup command
while (carrier and 10 seconds hasn't elapsed) ;
purge the input buffer
```

Function Description: modem_control_string

The **modem_control_string** function sends an AT command string to the modem. Its implementation is illustrated by the following pseudocode:

```
while (not the end of the string) {
        switch (next character) {
                case '~':
                        delay for ½ of a second
                default:
                        switch (the character) {
                                case '^':
                                        if (there's another character) {
                                                bump the string pointer
                                                send the next character as a control code
                                        }
                                default:
                                        send the character out the serial port
                        }
                        delay slightly for slow modems
        }
        bump the string pointer
}
```

Function Description: read_config

The **read_config** function reads the Simple Comm configuration file. Its implementation is illustrated by the following pseudocode:

```
open the file
if (open failed) {
        create a new file
        set the Simple Comm configuration to its default settings
        save the default settings as the configuration file
        return
}
read the configuration
```

Function Description: write_config

The **write_config** function saves the current Simple Comm configuration to disk. Its implementation is illustrated by the follow pseudocode:

```
open the configuration file
save the current configuration to disk
close the configuration file
```

Function Description: config_program

The **config_program** function allows the user to configure Simple Comm. Its implementation is illustrated by the following pseudocode:

```
display the configuration menu
while (TRUE) {
    wait till a key is pressed
    switch (the key that was pressed) {
        case extended key:
            ignore it
        case '1':
            set the serial port
        case '2':
            set the baud rate
        case '3':
            set the data format
        case '4':
            toggle the locked serial port flag
        case '5':
            set the modem's initialization string
        case '6':
            set the modem's hang up string
        case '7':
            set the modem's dial prefix
        case 'S':
            save the new configuration
            return
        case 'Q':
            return
    }
}
```

Summary

This chapter presented a serial communications program called *Simple Comm*. Although Simple Comm is indeed rather simple, it clearly demonstrates how the SERIAL toolbox is used in an actual application program. Besides presenting Simple Comm's C implementation, the chapter featured a **C++ implementation** of Simple Comm as well.

Appendix A

The Serial Toolbox Reference Guide

Global Variables

As mentioned in Chapter 8, the SERIAL toolbox defines two global variables for configuring the SERIAL toolbox's ANSI terminal emulator. The following describes these two global variables.

ansi_dsr

Summary: int (*ansi_dsr)(unsigned char n);

Description: The **ansi_dsr** variable is used by the ANSI terminal emulator to hold the address of the function the emulator is to call when it needs to send the RCP escape sequence in response to a DSR escape sequence. **Note**: This function pointer should normally be set to the SERIAL toolbox's **put_serial** function. Additionally, the **ansi_dsr_flag** must be set to TRUE (1).

ansi_dsr_flag

Summary: int ansi_dsr_flag;

Description: The **ansi_dsr_flag** is used to enable the sending of an ANSI RCP escape sequence in response to a DSR escape sequence. If **ansi_dsr_flag** is set to TRUE (1), the ANSI terminal emulator will send a RCP escape sequence via the routine pointed to by the **ansi_dsr** function pointer. If **ansi_dsr_flag** is set to FALSE (0), the ANSI terminal emulator will not send a RCP escape sequence in response to a DSR escape sequence. **Note**: The **ansi_dsr_flag** is initially set to FALSE and should not be set to TRUE until an appropriate function has been set with the **ansi_dsr** function pointer.

The C Functions

The SERIAL toolbox contains numerous C functions. To facilitate their use in application programs, this section describes the SERIAL toolbox's C functions as follows:

Summary: Presents an exact syntactic model for each of the SERIAL C functions.

Description: Describes the function's purpose and how it is used in an application program.

Return Value: Explains any of the possible return values for a SERIAL C function.

See Also: Lists any similar or related SERIAL C functions.

Example: Illustrates how a SERIAL C function could actually be used in an application program.

ansiout

Summary: #include “serial.h”

void ansiout(int *character*);

int *character*; (character to be displayed)

Description: The **ansiout** function displays a specified character on the display screen using the ANSI terminal emulator.

Return Value: No value is returned.

See Also: **ansiprintf** and **ansistring**

Example: The following program demonstrates how the **ansiout** function is used by displaying a variety of characters:

```
#include <stdio.h>
#include "serial.h"

void main(void)
{
      int i;

      ansiout('*');
      ansiout('\n');
      for (i = 0; i < 70; i++)
            ansiout('-');
      ansiout('\n');
      while (!kbhit()) ;
      if (!getch())
            getch();
}
```

ansiprintf

Summary: #include "serial.h"

int ansiprintf(char **format*, ...);

char **format*; (is the format string)

Description: As the C run time library printf function is used to display formatted output to the video display, the **ansiprintf** function is used to display formatted output to the ANSI terminal emulator. The format of the output is specified by *format* and zero or more additional parameters are used to specify the format string's required values. If you are unfamiliar with the use of the C printf function, you should consult your C run time library manual for details about this very useful function's use.

Return Value: The **ansiprintf** function returns the number of characters that were sent to the ANSI terminal emulator.

See Also: **ansiout** and **ansistring**

Example: The following program demonstrates how the **ansiprintf** function is used by displaying a variety of formatted strings:

```
#include <stdio.h>
#include "serial.h"

void main(void)
{
      int i;

      ansiprintf("%s %s %s\n", "Ryan", "Matthew", "Crystal");
      for (i = 0; i < 10; i++)
            ansiprintf("%d\n", i);
      while (!kbhit()) ;
      if (!getch())
            getch();
}
```

ansistring

Summary: #include "serial.h"

void ansistring(char **string*);

char **string*; (is the string to be displayed)

Description: The **ansistring** function displays a specified *string* on the display screen using the ANSI terminal emulator. Although the **ansiprintf** function is more versatile, the **ansistring** function is faster. Therefore, the **ansistring** function should be used when only one string needs to be displayed.

Return Value: No value is returned.

See Also: **ansiout** and **ansiprintf**.

Example: The following program demonstrates the **ansistring** function by displaying a variety of strings:

```
#include <stdio.h>
#include "serial.h"

void main(void)
{
        ansistring("Ryan\n");
        ansistring("Matthew\n");
        ansistring("Crystal\n");
        while (!kbhit()) ;
        if (!getch())
              getch();
}
```

carrier

Summary: #include "serial.h"

int carrier(void);

Description: The **carrier** function checks the serial port to see if carrier is present.

Return Value: The **carrier** function returns **TRUE** if carrier is present. Otherwise, the **carrier** function returns **FALSE** to indicate that carrier isn't present.

Example: The following program demonstrates the **carrier** function by displaying whether or not carrier is present on COM2:

```
#include <stdio.h>
#include "serial.h"

void main(void)
{
      open_port(2, 4096);
      if (carrier())
            printf("Carrier detected on COM2\n");
      else
            printf("No carrier detected on COM2\n");
      close_port();
}
```

close_port

Summary: #include "serial.h"

void close_port(void);

Description: The **close_port** function closes a previously opened serial port.

Return Value: No value is returned.

See Also: **open_port**

Example: The following program demonstrates the **close_port** function by closing a previously opened serial port:

```
#include <stdio.h>
#include "serial.h"

void main(void)
{
      open_port(2, 4096);
      set_port(38400L, 8, NO_PARITY, 1);
      close_port();
}
```

delay

Summary: #include <time.h>

#include "serial.h"

void delay(clock_t *n*);

clock_t *n*; (milliseconds delay)

Description: The **delay** function halts program execution for a specified length of time. The length of time is specified by *n* and is the number of milliseconds the program is to halt for. **Note**: This function is already a part of the Turbo C++ run time library and is only compiled in the SERIAL toolbox with either Microsoft C or Microsoft Quick C.

Return Value: No value is returned.

Example: The following program demonstrates the **delay** function by halting program execution for five seconds:

```
#include <stdio.h>
#include <time.h>
#include "serial.h"

void main(void)
{
      printf("Pausing five seconds.....\n");
      delay(5000);
}
```

fifo

Summary: #include "serial.h"

void fifo(int *n*);

int *n*; (the receive FIFO buffer threshold)

Description: The **fifo** function enables and disables a 16550 UARTs FIFO buffer. The receive FIFO buffer's threshold is specified by *n* and can be any one of the following values:

n	**Receive FIFO Buffer Threshold**
1	1 byte
4	4 bytes
8	8 bytes
14	14 bytes

You should note that any other value than the four values mentioned previously will disable the FIFO buffers. Additionally, the SERIAL toolbox will enable full FIFO buffering whenever a port is opened and a 16550 UART is present.

Return Value: No value is returned.

See Also: **open_port**

Example: The following program demonstrates the **fifo** function by disabling and then re-enabling a 16550 UART's FIFO buffers:

```
#include <stdio.h>
#include "serial.h"

void main(void)
{
      open_port(2, 4096);
      set_port(38400L, 8, NO_PARITY, 1);
      printf("Press a key to disable the FIFO buffer.....\n");
      while (!kbhit()) ;
      if (!getch())
            getch();
      fifo(0);
      printf("Press a key to re-enable the FIFO buffer.....\n");
      while (!kbhit()) ;
      if (!getch())
            getch();
      fifo(14);
      close_port();
}
```

get_baud

Summary: #include "serial.h"

long get_baud(void);

Description: The **get_baud** function examines a serial port to determine what baud rate it is set for.

Return Value: The **get_baud** function returns the serial port's current baud rate setting.

See Also: **set_baud** and **set_port**

Example: The following program demonstrates the **get_baud** function by displaying a serial port's current baud rate:

```
#include <stdio.h>
#include "serial.h"

void main(void)
{
      open_port(2, 4096);
      set_port(2400L, 8, NO_PARITY, 1);
      printf("COM2 is set for %ld baud\n", get_baud());
      close_port();
}
```

get_bits

Summary: #include "serial.h"

int get_bits(void);

Description: The **get_bits** function examines a serial port to determine the number of data bits it is set for.

Return Value: The **get_bits** function returns the serial port's current number of data bits.

See Also: **set_data_format** and **set_port**

Example: The following program demonstrates the **get_bits** function by displaying a serial port's current number of data bits:

```
#include <stdio.h>
#include "serial.h"

void main(void)
{
      open_port(2, 4096);
      set_port(2400L, 8, NO_PARITY, 1);
      printf("COM2 is set for %d data bits\n", get_bits());
      close_port();
}
```

get_parity

Summary: #include "serial.h"

int get_parity(void);

Description: The **get_parity** function examines a serial port to determine its current parity setting.

Return Value: The **get_parity** function returns **NO_PARITY** if the serial port is set for no parity, **EVEN_PARITY** if the serial port is set for even parity, or **ODD_PARITY** if the serial port is set for odd parity. **NO_PARITY**, **EVEN_PARITY**, and **ODD_PARITY** are manifest constants that are defined in the **serial.h** header file.

See Also: **set_data_format** and **set_port**

Example: The following program demonstrates the **get_parity** function by displaying a serial port's current parity setting:

```
#include <stdio.h>
#include "serial.h"

void main(void)
{
      open_port(2, 4096);
      set_port(2400L, 8, NO_PARITY, 1);
      printf("COM2 is set for %s parity\n", get_parity() == NO_PARITY ?
            "no" : (get_parity() == EVEN_PARITY ? "even" : "odd"));
      close_port();
}
```

get_rx_dtr

Summary: #include “serial.h”

int get_rx_dtr(void);

Description: The **get_rx_dtr** function returns the current setting for the receiver's DTR/DSR flow control.

Return Value: The **get_rx_dtr** function returns TRUE if DTR/DSR flow control is enabled for the receiver or FALSE if DTR/DSR flow control is disabled for the receiver.

See Also: **set_rx_dtr**

Example: The following program demonstrates the **get_rx_dtr** function by displaying the current state of the receiver's DTR/DSR flow control:

```
#include <stdio.h>
#include "serial.h"

void main(void)
{
      open_port(2, 4096);
      set_port(2400L, 8, NO_PARITY, 1);
      printf("Receiver DTR/DSR flow control is %s.\n",
            get_rx_dtr() ? "on" : "off");
      close_port();
}
```

get_rx_rts

Summary: #include "serial.h"

int get_rx_rts(void);

Description: The **get_rx_rts** function returns the current setting for the receiver's RTS/CTS flow control.

Return Value: The **get_rx_rts** function returns TRUE if RTS/CTS flow control is enabled for the receiver or FALSE if RTS/CTS flow control is disabled for the receiver.

See Also: **set_rx_rts**

Example: The following program demonstrates the **get_rx_rts** function by displaying the current state of the receiver's RTS/CTS flow control:

```
#include <stdio.h>
#include "serial.h"

void main(void)
{
      open_port(2, 4096);
      set_port(2400L, 8, NO_PARITY, 1);
      printf("Receiver RTS/CTS flow control is %s.\n",
            get_rx_rts() ? "on" : "off");
      close_port();
}
```

get_rx_xon

Summary: #include "serial.h"

int get_rx_xon(void);

Description: The **get_rx_xon** function returns the current setting for the receiver's XON/XOFF flow control.

Return Value: The **get_rx_xon** function returns TRUE if XON/XOFF flow control is enabled for the receiver or FALSE if XON/XOFF flow control is disabled for the receiver.

See Also: **set_rx_xon**

Example: The following program demonstrates the **get_rx_xon** function by displaying the current state of the receiver's XON/XOFF flow control:

```
#include <stdio.h>
#include "serial.h"

void main(void)
{
      open_port(2, 4096);
      set_port(2400L, 8, NO_PARITY, 1);
      printf("Receiver XON/XOFF flow control is %s.\n",
            get_rx_xon() ? "on" : "off");
      close_port();
}
```

get_serial

Summary: #include "serial.h"

int get_serial(void);

Description: The **get_serial** function gets a character, if any, from the receiver's input buffer.

Return Value: If a character is available, the **get_serial** function returns the character's appropriate value. Otherwise, the **get_serial** function returns **-1** to indicate that the input buffer is empty.

See Also: **in_ready**

Example: The following program demonstrates the **get_serial** function by returning a variety of values from the serial port's buffer:

```
#include <stdio.h>
#include <stdlib.h>
#include "serial.h"

void main(void)
{
      int c;

      open_port(2, 4096);
      set_port(2400L, 8, NO_PARITY, 1);
      while (TRUE) {
            if (kbhit()) {
                  c = getch();
                  switch (c) {
                        case 0:
                              if (getch() == 45) { /* Alt-X to exit*/
                                    close_port();
                                    exit(0);
                              }
                              break;
                        default:
                              put_serial(c);
                  }
            }
            if (in_ready()) {
                  c = get_serial();
                  putch(c);
            }
      }
}
```

get_stopbits

Summary: #include "serial.h"

int get_stopbits(void);

Description: The **get_stopbits** function examines a serial port to determine the number of stop bits it is set for.

Return Value: The **get_stopbits** function returns the serial port's current number of stop bits.

See Also: **set_data_format** and **set_port**

Example: The following program demonstrates the **get_stopbits** function by displaying a serial port's current number of stop bits:

```
#include <stdio.h>
#include "serial.h"

void main(void)
{
	open_port(2, 4096);
	set_port(2400L, 8, NO_PARITY, 1);
	printf("COM2 is set for %d stop bits.\n", get_stopbits());
	close_port();
}
```

get_tx_dtr

Summary: #include "serial.h"

int get_tx_dtr(void);

Description: The **get_tx_dtr** function returns the current setting for the transmitter's DTR/DSR flow control.

Return Value: The **get_tx_dtr** function returns TRUE if DTR/DSR flow control is enabled for the transmitter or FALSE if DTR/DSR flow control is disabled for the transmitter.

See Also: **set_tx_dtr**

Example: The following program demonstrates the **get_tx_dtr** function by displaying the current state of the transmitter's DTR/DSR flow control:

```
#include <stdio.h>
#include "serial.h"

void main(void)
{
	open_port(2, 4096);
	set_port(2400L, 8, NO_PARITY, 1);
	printf("Transmitter DTR/DSR flow control is %s.\n",
		get_tx_dtr() ? "on" : "off");
	close_port();
}
```

get_tx_rts

Summary: #include "serial.h"

int get_tx_rts(void);

Description: The **get_tx_rts** function returns the current setting for the transmitter's RTS/CTS flow control.

Return Value: The **get_tx_rts** function returns TRUE if RTS/CTS flow control is enabled for the transmitter or FALSE if RTS/CTS flow control is disabled for the transmitter.

See Also: **set_tx_rts**

Example: The following program demonstrates the **get_tx_rts** function by displaying the current state of the transmitter's RTS/CTS flow control:

```
#include <stdio.h>
#include "serial.h"

void main(void)
{
      open_port(2, 4096);
      set_port(2400L, 8, NO_PARITY, 1);
      printf("Transmitter RTS/CTS flow control is %s.\n",
            get_tx_rts() ? "on" : "off");
      close_port();
}
```

get_tx_xon

Summary: #include "serial.h"

int get_tx_xon(void);

Description: The **get_tx_xon** function returns the current setting for the transmitter's XON/XOFF flow control.

Return Value: The **get_tx_xon** function returns TRUE if XON/XOFF flow control is enabled for the transmitter or FALSE if XON/XOFF flow control is disabled for the transmitter.

See Also: **set_tx_xon**

Example: The following program demonstrates the **get_tx_xon** function by displaying the current state of the transmitter's XON/XOFF flow control:

```
#include <stdio.h>
#include "serial.h"

void main(void)
{
      open_port(2, 4096);
      set_port(2400L, 8, NO_PARITY, 1);
      printf("Transmitter XON/XOFF flow control is %s.\n",
            get_tx_xon() ? "on" : "off");
      close_port();
}
```

ibmtoansi

Summary: #include "serial.h"

char *ibmtoansi(int *att*, char **s*);

int *att*;	(is the color attribute)
char **s*;	(is the string pointer)

Description: The **ibmtoansi** converts an IBM display attribute specified by *att* into an ANSI escape sequence. The ANSI escape sequence is built in the string buffer pointed to by *s*.

Return Value: The **ibmtoansi** function returns a pointer to the ANSI escape sequence string.

Example: The following program demonstrates the **ibmtoansi** function by displaying the ANSI escape sequences for a variety of IBM display attributes:

```
#include <stdio.h>
#include "serial.h"

void main(void)
{
      char line[81];

      printf("%s\n", ibmtoansi(7, line));
      printf("%s\n", ibmtoansi(0x17, line));
      printf("%s\n", ibmtoansi(0x3e, line));
}
```

in_ready

Summary: #include "serial.h"

int in_ready(void);

Description: The **in_ready** function checks the serial port's receive buffer to see if there is a character available.

Return Value: The **in_ready** function returns TRUE if there's a character in the receive buffer. Otherwise, FALSE is returned to indicate that the receive buffer is empty.

See Also: **get_serial**

Example: The following program demonstrates how the **in_ready** function is used to monitor for incoming characters:

```
#include <stdio.h>
#include <stdlib.h>
#include "serial.h"

void main(void)
{
      int c;

      open_port(2, 4096);
      set_port(2400L, 8, NO_PARITY, 1);
      while (TRUE) {
            if (kbhit()) {
                  c = getch();
                  switch (c) {
                        case 0:
                              if (getch() == 45) { /* Alt-X to exit*/
                                    close_port();
                                    exit(0);
                              }
                              break;
                        default:
                              put_serial(c);
                  }
            }
            if (in_ready()) {
                  c = get_serial();
                  putch(c);
            }
      }
}
```

mpeek

Summary: #include "serial.h"

unsigned mpeek(unsigned *seg*, unsigned *off*);

unsigned *seg*;	(is the address's segment)
unsigned *off*;	(is the address's offset)

Description: The **mpeek** function retrieves a word of memory stored at the memory address whose segment is specified by *seg* and whose offset is specified by *off*.

Return Value: The **mpeek** function returns the memory address's word value.

Example: The following program demonstrates the **mpeek** function by displaying the words that are stored at a variety of memory locations:

```
#include <stdio.h>
#include "serial.h"

void main(void)
{
      int i;

      for (i = 0; i < 16; i++)
            printf("0000:%04X %04X\n", i * 2, mpeek(0, i * 2));
}
```

open_port

Summary: #include "serial.h"

void open_port(int *port*, int *blength*);

int *port*;	(is the port number)
int *blength*;	(is the input buffer's length)

Description: The **open_port** function opens a serial port specified by *port*. Additionally, the receiver's buffer size is specified by *blength*.

Return Value: No value is returned.

See Also: **close_port**

Example: The following program demonstrates the **open_port** function by opening a port for use by a dumb terminal program:

```
#include <stdio.h>
#include <stdlib.h>
#include "serial.h"

void main(void)
{
	int c;

	open_port(2, 4096);
	set_port(2400L, 8, NO_PARITY, 1);
	while (TRUE) {
		if (kbhit()) {
			c = getch();
			switch (c) {
				case 0:
					if (getch() == 45) { /* Alt-X to exit*/
						close_port();
						exit(0);
					}
					break;
				default:
					put_serial(c);
			}
		}
		if (in_ready()) {
			c = get_serial();
			putch(c);
		}
	}
}
```

port_exist

Summary: #include “serial.h”

int port_exist(int *port*);

int *port*; (is the port to be checked)

Description: The **port_exist** function checks to see if a serial port exists. The port to be checked for is specified by *port*. **Note**: This function may not correctly recognize an existing port with all ROM BIOSes.

Return Value: The **port_exist** function returns TRUE if the port exists. Otherwise, FALSE is returned to indicate a nonexistent port.

Example: The following program demonstrates the **port_exist** function by checking for the existence of COM1 through COM4:

```
#include <stdio.h>
#include "serial.h"

void main(void)
{
	printf("COM1: %s\n", port_exist(1) ? "Yes" : "No");
	printf("COM2: %s\n", port_exist(2) ? "Yes" : "No");
	printf("COM3: %s\n", port_exist(3) ? "Yes" : "No");
	printf("COM4: %s\n", port_exist(4) ? "Yes" : "No");
}
```

purge_in

Summary: #include "serial.h"

void purge_in(void);

Description: The **purge_in** function deletes any characters that are waiting in the serial port's receive buffer.

Return Value: No value is returned.

See Also: **get_serial** and **in_ready**

Example: The following program demonstrates the **purge_in** function by deleting all incoming characters in the serial port's receive buffer:

```
#include <stdio.h>
#include <stdlib.h>
#include "serial.h"

void main(void)
{
	int c;

	open_port(2, 4096);
	set_port(2400L, 8, NO_PARITY, 1);
	while (TRUE) {
		if (kbhit()) {
			c = getch();
			switch (c) {
				case 0:
					if (getch() == 45) { /* Alt-X to exit*/
						close_port();
						exit(0);
					}
```

continued...

...from previous page

```
                        break;
                    default:
                        put_serial(c);
                }
            }
            purge_in();
            if (in_ready()) {
                c = get_serial();
                putch(c);
            }
        }
}
```

put_serial

Summary: #include "serial.h"

void put_serial(unsigned char *c*);

unsigned char *c*; (is the character to send)

Description: The **put_serial** function sends a character specified by *c* out the serial port.

Return Value: No value is returned.

See Also: **get_serial**

Example: The following program demonstrates the **put_serial** function by sending a variety of key presses out the serial port:

```
#include <stdio.h>
#include <stdlib.h>
#include "serial.h"

void main(void)
{
    int c;

    open_port(2, 4096);
    set_port(2400L, 8, NO_PARITY, 1);
    while (TRUE) {
        if (kbhit()) {
            c = getch();
            switch (c) {
                case 0:
                    if (getch() == 45) { /* Alt-X to exit*/
                        close_port();
                        exit(0);
                    }
```

continued...

...from previous page

```
                                break;
                        default:
                                put_serial(c);
                }
        }
        if (in_ready()) {
                c = get_serial();
                putch(c);
        }
    }
}
```

recv_file

Summary: #include "serial.h"

int recv_file(int *xtype*, int(**handler*)(int *code*, long *position*,
char **message*), char **path*);

int *xtype*; (is the protocol to be used)

int (**handler*)(int, long, char *) (is the error handler)

char **path*; (is the file name or directory)

Description: The **recv_file** function is used to download a file. The type of file transfer is specified by *xtype* and can be one of the following manifest constants (defined in **serial.h**):

Constant	**Type of Transfer**
XMODEM	Receive the file using Xmodem.
XMODEM1K	Receive the file using Xmodem-1K.
YMODEM	Receive the file using Ymodem.
YMODEMG	Receive the file using Ymodem-G.

During the file transfer, the **recv_file** function will make one or more calls to an error handler specified by the function pointer *handler*. Whenever the **recv_file** function calls the error handler, it will pass three arguments to the error handler as follows:

Code	Position	Message
RECEIVING	File size.	The name of the file being received.
RECEIVED	Current position.	N/A
ERROR	N/A	Error message.
COMPLETE	N/A	N/A

The error handler routine can return a value of FALSE to abort the transfer or a value of TRUE to continue with the transfer. **Note**: Transfers are automatically aborted for a variety of reasons by the **recv_file** function.

The file name for the file to be received is specified by *path* for Xmodem and Xmodem-1K transfers and the directory for the file or files to be downloaded is specified by *path* for Ymodem and Ymodem-G transfers.

Return Value: The **recv_file** function returns TRUE if the file transfer was successful. Otherwise, FALSE is returned to indicate an unsuccessful file transfer.

See Also: **xmit_file**

Example: The following program demonstrates the **recv_file** function by downloading a file using the Xmodem protocol.

Note: Due to the physical constraints of this book, some lines in the following listing are shown wrapped. These should be entered as single lines.

```
#include <stdio.h>
#include <stdlib.h>
#include <string.h>
#include <conio.h>
#include "serial.h"

int e_handler(int c, long p, char *s);
```

continued...

...from previous page

```
void main(void)
{
	int c;

	open_port(2, 4096);
	set_port(2400L, 8, NO_PARITY, 1);
	while (TRUE) {
		if (kbhit()) {
			c = getch();
			switch (c) {
				case 0:
					switch (getch()) {
						case 32:	/* Alt-D to
download */

							recv_file(XMODEM, e_handler,
"C:\DOWNLOAD.FIL");

							continue;
						case 45:	/* Alt-X to exit */
							close_port();
							exit(0);
					}
					break;
				default:
					put_serial(c);
			}
		}
		if (in_ready()) {
			c = get_serial();
			putch(c);
		}
	}
}


int e_handler(int c, long p, char *s)
{
	int k;
	switch (c) {
		case SENDING:
			printf("Sending: %s\n", strupr(s));
			printf("Length : %ld\n", p);
			break;
		case RECEIVING:
			printf("Receiving: %s\n", strupr(s));
			printf("Length : %ld\n", p);
			break;
		case SENT:
			printf("%ld bytes sent.\r", p);
			break;
		case RECEIVED:
			printf("%ld bytes received.\r", p);
			break;
```

continued...

...from previous page

```
            case ERROR:
                  printf("\nError: %s in block %ld\n", s, p);
                  break;
            case COMPLETE:
                  printf("\n%s\n", s);
                  break;
      }
      if (kbhit()) {
            if (!(k = getch())) {
                  getch();
                  return TRUE;
            }
            if (k == 27)
                  return FALSE;
      }
      return TRUE;
}
```

set_baud

Summary: #include "serial.h"

void set_baud(long *baud*);

long *baud*; (is the new baud rate)

Description: The **set_baud** function sets a serial port's baud rate to the value specified by *baud*.

Return Value: No value is returned.

See Also: **set_port**

Example: The following program demonstrates the **set_baud** function by setting a serial port's baud rate to 38,400 baud:

```
#include <stdio.h>
#include "serial.h"

void main(void)
{
      open_port(2, 4096);
      set_baud(38400L);
      printf("The baud rate is %ld baud.\n", get_baud());
      close_port();
}
```

set_data_format

Summary: #include "serial.h"

void set_data_format(int *bits*, int *parity*, int *stopbits*);

int *bits*;	(is the number of data bits)
int *parity*;	(is the parity setting)
int *stopbits*;	(is the number of stop bits)

Description: The **set_data_format** function sets a serial port's number of data bits, parity setting, and number of stop bits. The number of data bits is specified by *bits* and can be 5, 6, 7, or 8. The parity setting is specified by *parity* and can be one of the following manifest constants (defined in **serial.h**):

Constant	Parity Setting
NO_PARITY	No parity.
EVEN_PARITY	Even parity.
ODD_PARITY	Odd parity.

The number of stop bits is specified by *stopbits* and can be 1 or 2. **Note**: If 2 stop bits is specified and the number of data bits is set to 5, the UART will actually use 1½ stop bits.

Return Value: No value is returned.

See Also: **set_port**

Example: The following program demonstrates the **set_data_format** function by setting a serial port for 8 data bits, no parity, and 1 stop bit:

```
#include <stdio.h>
#include "serial.h"

void main(void)
{
      open_port(2, 4096);
      set_data_format(8, NO_PARITY, 1);
      printf("COM2 is set for %d data bits\n", get_bits());
      printf("COM2 is set for %s parity\n", get_parity() == NO_PARITY ?
            "no" : (get_parity() == EVEN_PARITY ? "even" : "odd"));
      printf("COM2 is set for %d stop bits\n", get_stopbits());
      close_port();
}
```

set_dtr

Summary: #include "serial.h"

void set_dtr(int *n*);

int *n*; (is the new DTR setting)

Description: The **set_dtr** function is used to set the UART's DTR line. If *n* is equal to TRUE, DTR is asserted. If *n* is equal to FALSE, DTR is unasserted and will break the connection after a certain length of time for most modems.

Return Value: No value is returned.

See Also: **carrier**

Example: The following program demonstrates the **set_dtr** function by lowering DTR on COM2:

```
#include <stdio.h>
#include "serial.h"

void main(void)
{
        open_port(2, 4096);
        set_dtr(FALSE);
        printf("DTR has been lowered on COM2:\n");
        close_port();
}
```

set_port

Summary: #include "serial.h"

void set_port(long *baud*, int *bits*, int *parity*, int *stopbits*);

long *baud*; (is the baud rate)

int *bits*; (is the number of data bits)

int *parity*; (is the parity setting)

int *stopbits*; (is the number of stop bits)

Description: The **set_port** function sets a serial port's baud rate, number of data bits, parity setting, and number of stop bits. The baud rate is specified by *baud*. The number of data bits is specified by *bits* and can be 5, 6, 7, or 8. The parity setting is specified by *parity* and can be one of the following manifest constants (defined in **serial.h**):

Constant	Parity Setting
NO_PARITY	No parity.
EVEN_PARITY	Even parity.
ODD_PARITY	Odd parity.

The number of stop bits is specified by *stopbits* and can be 1 or 2. **Note**: If 2 stop bits are specified and the number of data bits is set to 5, the UART will actually use 1½ stop bits.

Return Value: No value is returned.

See Also: **set_baud** and **set_data_format**

Example: The following program demonstrates the **set_port** function by setting a serial port for 38,400 baud, 8 data bits, no parity, and 1 stop bit:

```
#include <stdio.h>
#include "serial.h"

void main(void)
{
      open_port(2, 4096);
      set_port(38400L, 8, NO_PARITY, 1);
      printf("COM2 is set for %ld baud\n", get_baud());
      printf("COM2 is set for %d data bits\n", get_bits());
      printf("COM2 is set for %s parity\n", get_parity() == NO_PARITY ?
            "no" : (get_parity() == EVEN_PARITY ? "even" : "odd"));
      printf("COM2 is set for %d stop bits\n", get_stopbits());
      close_port();
}
```

set_rx_dtr

Summary: #include "serial.h"

void set_rx_dtr(int *n*);

int *n*; (is the new setting)

Description: The **set_rx_dtr** function enables or disables the receiver's DTR/DSR flow control. If *n* is TRUE, the receiver's DTR/DSR flow control will be enabled. If *n* is FALSE, the receiver's DTR/DSR flow control will be disabled.

Return Value: No value is returned.

See Also: **get_rx_dtr**

Example: The following program demonstrates the **set_rx_dtr** function by enabling the receiver's DTR/DSR flow control:

```
#include <stdio.h>
#include "serial.h"

void main(void)
{
      open_port(2, 4096);
      set_rx_dtr(TRUE);
      printf("The receiver's DTR/DSR flow control is %s\n",
            get_rx_dtr() ? "On" : "Off");
      close_port();
}
```

set_rx_rts

Summary: #include "serial.h"

void set_rx_rts(int *n*);

int *n*; (is the new setting)

Description: The **set_rx_rts** function enables or disables the receiver's RTS/CTS flow control. If *n* is TRUE, the receiver's RTS/CTS flow control will be enabled. If *n* is FALSE, the receiver's RTS/CTS flow control will be disabled.

Return Value: No value is returned.

See Also: **get_rx_rts**

Example: The following program demonstrates the **set_rx_rts** function by enabling the receiver's RTS/CTS flow control:

```
#include <stdio.h>
#include "serial.h"

void main(void)
{
	open_port(2, 4096);
	set_rx_rts(TRUE);
	printf("The receiver's RTS/CTS flow control is %s\n",
		get_rx_rts() ? "On" : "Off");
	close_port();
}
```

set_rx_xon

Summary: #include "serial.h"

void set_rx_xon(int *n*);

int *n*; (is the new setting)

Description: The **set_rx_xon** function enables or disables the receiver's XON/XOFF flow control. If *n* is TRUE, the receiver's XON/XOFF flow control will be enabled. If *n* is FALSE, the receiver's XON/XOFF flow control will be disabled.

Return Value: No value is returned.

See Also: **get_rx_xon**

Example: The following program demonstrates the **set_rx_xon** function by enabling the receiver's XON/XOFF flow control:

```
#include <stdio.h>
#include "serial.h"

void main(void)
{
	open_port(2, 4096);
	set_rx_xon(TRUE);
	printf("The receiver's XON/XOFF flow control is %s\n",
		get_rx_xon() ? "On" : "Off");
	close_port();
}
```

set_tx_dtr

Summary: #include "serial.h"

void set_tx_dtr(int *n*);

int *n*; (is the new setting)

Description: The **set_tx_dtr** function enables or disables the transmitter's DTR/DSR flow control. If *n* is TRUE, the transmitter's DTR/DSR flow control will be enabled. If *n* is FALSE, the transmitter's DTR/DSR flow control will be disabled.

Return Value: No value is returned.

See Also: **get_tx_dtr**

Example: The following program demonstrates the **set_tx_dtr** function by enabling the transmitter's DTR/DSR flow control:

```
#include <stdio.h>
#include "serial.h"

void main(void)
{
	open_port(2, 4096);
	set_tx_dtr(TRUE);
	printf("The transmitter's DTR/DSR flow control is %s\n",
		get_tx_dtr() ? "On" : "Off");
	close_port();
}
```

set_tx_rts

Summary: #include "serial.h"

void set_tx_rts(int *n*);

int *n*; (is the new setting)

Description: The **set_tx_rts** function enables or disables the transmitter's RTS/CTS flow control. If *n* is TRUE, the transmitter's RTS/CTS flow control will be enabled. If *n* is FALSE, the transmitter's RTS/CTS flow control will be disabled.

Return Value: No value is returned.

See Also: **get_tx_rts**

Example: The following program demonstrates the **set_tx_rts** function by enabling the transmitter's RTS/CTS flow control:

```
#include <stdio.h>
#include "serial.h"

void main(void)
{
      open_port(2, 4096);
      set_tx_rts(TRUE);
      printf("The transmitter's RTS/CTS flow control is %s\n",
            get_tx_rts() ? "On" : "Off");
      close_port();
}
```

set_tx_xon

Summary: #include <stdio.h>

void set_tx_xon(int *n*);

int *n*; (is the new setting)

Description: The **set_tx_xon** function enables or disables the transmitter's XON/XOFF flow control. If *n* is TRUE, the transmitter's XON/XOFF flow control will be enabled. If *n* is FALSE, the transmitter's XON/XOFF flow control will be disabled.

Return Value: No value is returned.

See Also: **get_tx_xon**

Example: The following program demonstrates the **set_tx_xon** function by enabling the receiver's DTR/DSR flow control:

```
#include <stdio.h>
#include "serial.h"

void main(void)
{
      open_port(2, 4096);
      set_tx_xon(TRUE);
      printf("The transmitter's XON/XOFF flow control is %s\n",
            get_tx_xon() ? "On" : "Off");
      close_port();
}
```

xmit_file

Summary:

#include "serial.h"

int xmit_file(int *xtype*, int(**handler*)(int *code*, long *position*,

char **message*), char **files*[]);

int *xtype*;	(is the protocol to be used)
int (**handler*)(int, long, char *)	(is the error handler)
char **files*[];	(is the files to be sent)

Description:

The **xmit_file** function is used to upload one or more files. The type of file transfer is specified by *xtype* and can be one of the following manifest constants (defined in **serial.h**):

Constant	Type of Transfer
XMODEM	Transmit the file using Xmodem.
XMODEM1K	Transmit the file using Xmodem-1K.
YMODEM	Transmit the file(s) using Ymodem.
YMODEMG	Transmit the file(s) using Ymodem-G.

During the file transfer, the **xmit_file** function will make one or more calls to an error handler specified by the function pointer *handler*. Whenever the **xmit_file** function calls the error handler, it will pass three arguments to the error handler as follows:

Code	Position	Message
SENDING	File size.	The name of the file being sent.
SENT	Current position.	N/A
ERROR	N/A	Error message.
COMPLETE	N/A	N/A

The error handler routine can return a value of FALSE to abort the transfer or a value of TRUE to continue with the transfer. **Note**: Transfers are automatically aborted for a variety of reasons by the **xmit_file** function.

The file names for the files to be transmitted is specified by *files*, which is a pointer to an array of string pointers. For Xmodem and Xmodem-1K file transfers, the file name is specified by the array's first string pointer. For Ymodem and Ymodem-G file transfers, the array specifies the names of one or more files to be transmitted and the pointer following the last file name is set to NULL.

Return Value: The **xmit_file** function returns TRUE if the file transfer was successful. Otherwise, FALSE will be returned to indicate an unsuccessful file transfer.

See Also: **recv_file**

Example: The following program demonstrates the **xmit_file** function by uploading a file using the Xmodem protocol.

Note: Due to the physical constraints of this book, some lines in the following listing are shown wrapped. These should be entered as single lines.

```
#include <stdio.h>
#include <stdlib.h>
#include <string.h>
#include <conio.h>
#include "serial.h"

int e_handler(int c, long p, char *s);

char *files[10];

void main(void)
{
	int c;

	open_port(2, 4096);
	set_port(2400L, 8, NO_PARITY, 1);
	while (TRUE) {
		if (kbhit()) {
			c = getch();
			switch (c) {
				case 0:
					switch (getch()) {
						case 22:	/* Alt-U to upload
*/
							files[0] = "serial.h";
							xmit_file(XMODEM, e_handler,
files);
							continue;
						case 45:	/* Alt-X to exit */
							close_port();
							exit(0);
					}
					break;
				default:
					put_serial(c);
			}
		}
```

continued...

...from previous page

```
            if (in_ready()) {
                c = get_serial();
                putch(c);
            }
        }
}


int e_handler(int c, long p, char *s)
{
        int k;

        switch (c) {
            case SENDING:
                printf("Sending: %s\n", strupr(s));
                printf("Length : %ld\n", p);
                break;
            case RECEIVING:
                printf("Receiving: %s\n", strupr(s));
                printf("Length : %ld\n", p);
                break;
            case SENT:
                printf("%ld bytes sent.\r", p);
                break;
            case RECEIVED:
                printf("%ld bytes received.\r", p);
                break;
            case ERROR:
                printf("\nError: %s in block %ld\n", s, p);
                break;
            case COMPLETE:
                printf("\n%s\n", s);
                break;
        }
        if (kbhit()) {
            if (!(k = getch())) {
                getch();
                return TRUE;
            }
            if (k == 27)
                return FALSE;
        }
        return TRUE;
}
```

The SERIALPORT Object

The Turbo C++ implementation of the SERIAL toolbox defines a **SERIALPORT** object class for dealing with a serial communications port. To facilitate the use of a **SERIALPORT** object in application programs, this section describes the **SERIALPORT** object class's constructor and member functions as follows:

Summary: Presents an exact syntactic model for the **SERIALPORT** constructor and member functions.

Description: Describes the constructor or member function's purpose and how it is used in an application program.

Return Value: Explains any of the possible return values for the member functions.

See Also: List any similar or related **SERIALPORT** functions.

Example: Illustrates how a **SERIALPORT** constructor or member function is used in an application program.

SERIALPORT

Summary: #include "sercpp.h"

SERIALPORT(int *port*, int *blength*);

int *port*; (is the port number)

int *blength*; (is the input buffer's length)

Description: The **SERIALPORT** constructor creates a serial communications port object and opens the port specified by *port*. Additionally, the receiver's buffer size is specified by *blength*. **Note**: Because of the way Turbo C++ calls destructors, you may want to dynamically allocate a **SERIALPORT** object with the **new** operator and then dispose of it with the **delete** operator. Failure to due this may mean that the serial port is left in an open state by the program on exit.

Example: The following program demonstrates the **SERIALPORT** constructor by creating an object for use by a dumb terminal program:

```
#include <stdio.h>
#include <stdlib.h>
#include <conio.h>
#include "sercpp.h"

void main(void)
{
      int c;
      SERIALPORT *port;

      port = new SERIALPORT(2, 4096);
      port->set_port(2400L, 8, NO_PARITY, 1);
      while (TRUE) {
            if (kbhit()) {
                  c = getch();
                  switch (c) {
                        case 0:
                              if (getch() == 45) { /* Alt-X to exit*/
                                    delete port;
                                    exit(0);
                              }
                              break;
                        default:
                              port->put(c);
                  }
            }
            if (port->in_ready()) {
                  c = port->get();
                  putch(c);
            }
      }
}
```

carrier

Summary: #include "sercpp.h"

int *object*.carrier(void);

SERIALPORT *object*; (is the serial port object)

Description: The **carrier** function checks an *object*'s serial port to see if carrier is present.

Return Value: The **carrier** function returns TRUE if carrier is present. Otherwise, the **carrier** function returns FALSE to indicate that carrier isn't present.

Example: The following program demonstrates the **carrier** function by displaying whether or not carrier is present on COM2:

```
#include <stdio.h>
#include "sercpp.h"

void main(void)
{
      SERIALPORT port(2, 4096);

      if (port.carrier())
            printf("Carrier detected on COM2\n");
      else
            printf("No carrier detected on COM2\n");
}
```

fifo

Summary: #include "sercpp.h"

void *object*.fifo(int *n*);

SERIALPORT *object*	(is the serial port object)
int *n*;	(the receive FIFO buffer's threshold)

Description: The **fifo** function enables and disables a 16550 UART's FIFO buffer. The serial port object is specified by *object*. The receive FIFO buffer's threshold is specified by *n* and can be any one of the following values:

n	**Receive FIFO Buffer's Threshold**
1	1 byte
4	4 bytes
8	8 bytes
14	14 bytes

You should note that any value other than the four values mentioned previously will disable the FIFO buffers. Additionally, the SERIALPORT constructor will enable full FIFO buffering whenever a port is opened and a 16550 UART is present.

Return Value: No value is returned.

Example: The following program demonstrates the **fifo** function by disabling and then re-enabling a 16550 UART's FIFO buffers:

```
#include <stdio.h>
#include <conio.h>
#include "sercpp.h"

void main(void)
{
      SERIALPORT port(2, 4096);

      port.set_port(38400L, 8, NO_PARITY, 1);
      printf("Press a key to disable the FIFO buffer.....\n");
      while (!kbhit()) ;
      if (!getch())
            getch();
      port.fifo(0);
      printf("Press a key to re-enable the FIFO buffer.....\n");
      while (!kbhit()) ;
      if (!getch())
            getch();
      port.fifo(14);
}
```

get_baud

Summary: #include “sercpp.h”

long *object*.get_baud(void);

SERIALPORT *object*; (is the serial port object)

Description: The **get_baud** function examines an *object*'s serial port to determine what baud rate it is set for.

Return Value: The **get_baud** function returns the serial port's current baud rate setting.

See Also: **set_baud** and **set_port**

Example: The following program demonstrates the **get_baud** function by displaying a serial port's current baud rate:

```
#include <stdio.h>
#include <conio.h>
#include "sercpp.h"

void main(void)
{
      SERIALPORT port(2, 4096);

      port.set_port(2400L, 8, NO_PARITY, 1);
      printf("COM2 is set for %ld baud\n", port.get_baud());
}
```

get_bits

Summary: #include "sercpp.h"

int *object*.get_bits(void);

SERIALPORT *object*; (is the serial port object)

Description: The **get_bits** function examines an *object*'s serial port to determine the number of data bits it is set for.

Return Value: The **get_bits** function returns the serial port's current number of data bits.

See Also: **set_data_format** and **set_port**

Example: The following program demonstrates the **get_bits** function by displaying a serial port's current number of data bits:

```
#include <stdio.h>
#include <conio.h>
#include "sercpp.h"

void main(void)
{
      SERIALPORT port(2, 4096);

      port.set_port(2400L, 8, NO_PARITY, 1);
      printf("COM2 is set for %d data bits\n", port.get_bits());
}
```

get_parity

Summary: #include "sercpp.h"

int *object*.get_parity(void);

SERIALPORT *object*; (is the serial port object)

Description: The **get_parity** function examines an *object*'s serial port to determine its current parity setting.

Return Value: The **get_parity** function returns **NO_PARITY** if the serial port is set for no parity, **EVEN_PARITY** if the serial port is set for even parity, or **ODD_PARITY** if the serial port is set for odd parity. **NO_PARITY**, **EVEN_PARITY**, and **ODD_PARITY** are manifest constants that are defined in the **sercpp.h** header file.

See Also: **set_data_format** and **set_port**

Example: The following program demonstrates the **get_parity** function by displaying a serial port's current parity setting.

Note: Due to the physical constraints of this book, some lines in the following listing are shown wrapped. These should be entered as single lines.

```
#include <stdio.h>
#include <conio.h>
#include "sercpp.h"

void main(void)
{
      SERIALPORT port(2, 4096);

      port.set_port(2400L, 8, NO_PARITY, 1);
      printf("COM2 is set for %s parity\n", port.get_parity() ==
NO_PARITY ?
             "no" : (port.get_parity() == EVEN_PARITY ? "even" :
"odd"));
}
```

get_rx_dtr

Summary: #include "sercpp.h"

int *object*.get_rx_dtr(void);

SERIALPORT *object*; (is the serial port's object)

Description: The **get_rx_dtr** function returns the current setting for the receiver's DTR/DSR flow control. The serial port object is specified by *object*.

Return Value: The **get_rx_dtr** function returns TRUE if DTR/DSR flow control is enabled for the receiver or FALSE if DTR/DSR flow control is disabled for the receiver.

See Also: **set_rx_dtr**

Example: The following program demonstrates the **get_rx_dtr** function by displaying the current state of the receiver's DTR/DSR flow control:

```
#include <stdio.h>
#include <conio.h>
#include "sercpp.h"

void main(void)
{
      SERIALPORT port(2, 4096);

      port.set_port(2400L, 8, NO_PARITY, 1);
      printf("Receiver DTR/DSR flow control is %s\n",
            port.get_rx_dtr() ? "on" : "off");
}
```

get_rx_rts

Summary: #include "sercpp.h"

int *object*.get_rx_rts(void);

SERIALPORT *object*; (is the serial port object)

Description: The **get_rx_rts** function returns the current setting for the receiver's RTS/CTS flow control. The serial port's object is specified by *object*.

Return Value: The **get_rx_rts** function returns TRUE if RTS/CTS flow control is enabled for the receiver or FALSE if RTS/CTS flow control is disabled for the receiver.

See Also: **set_rx_rts**

Example: The following program demonstrates the **get_rx_rts** function by displaying the current state of the receiver's RTS/CTS flow control:

```
#include <stdio.h>
#include <conio.h>
#include "sercpp.h"

void main(void)
{
      SERIALPORT port(2, 4096);

      port.set_port(2400L, 8, NO_PARITY, 1);
      printf("Receiver RTS/CTS flow control is %s\n",
            port.get_rx_rts() ? "on" : "off");
}
```

get_rx_xon

Summary: #include "sercpp.h"

int *object*.get_rx_xon(void);

SERIALPORT *object*; (is the serial port's object)

Description: The **get_rx_xon** function returns the current setting for the receiver's XON/XOFF flow control. The serial port's object is specified by *object*.

Return Value: The **get_rx_xon** function returns TRUE if XON/XOFF flow control is enabled for the receiver or FALSE if XON/XOFF flow control is disabled for the receiver.

See Also: **set_rx_xon**

Example: The following program demonstrates the **get_rx_xon** function by displaying the current state of the receiver's XON/XOFF flow control:

```
#include <stdio.h>
#include <conio.h>
#include "sercpp.h"

void main(void)
{
      SERIALPORT port(2, 4096);

      port.set_port(2400L, 8, NO_PARITY, 1);
      printf("Receiver XON/XOFF flow control is %s\n",
            port.get_rx_xon() ? "on" : "off");
}
```

get

Summary: #include "sercpp.h"

int *object*.get(void);

SERIALPORT *object*; (is the serial port's object)

Description: The **get** function gets a character, if any, from the receiver's input buffer. The serial port object is specified by *object*.

Return Value: If a character is available, the **get** function returns the character's appropriate value. Otherwise, the **get** function returns **-1** to indicate that the input buffer is empty.

See Also: **in_ready**

Example: The following program demonstrates the **get** function by returning a variety of values from the serial port's buffer:

```
#include <stdio.h>
#include <stdlib.h>
#include <conio.h>
#include "sercpp.h"

void main(void)
{
      int c;
      SERIALPORT *port;

      port = new SERIALPORT(2, 4096);
      port->set_port(2400L, 8, NO_PARITY, 1);
      while (TRUE) {
            if (kbhit()) {
                  c = getch();
                  switch (c) {
                        case 0:
                              if (getch() == 45) { /* Alt-X to exit*/
                                    delete port;
                                    exit(0);
                              }
                              break;
                        default:
                              port->put(c);
                  }
            }
            if (port->in_ready()) {
                  c = port->get();
                  putch(c);
            }
      }
}
```

get_stopbits

Summary: #include "sercpp.h"

int *object*.get_stopbits(void);

SERIALPORT *object*; (is the serial port's object)

Description: The **get_stopbits** function examines a serial port to determine the number of stop bits it is set for. The serial port's object is specified by *object*.

Return Value: The **get_stopbits** function returns the serial port's current number of stop bits.

Set Also: **set_data_format** and **set_port**

Example: The following program demonstrates the **get_stopbits** function by displaying a serial port's current number of stop bits:

Note: Due to the physical constraints of this book, some lines in the following listing are shown wrapped. These should be entered as single lines.

```
#include <stdio.h>
#include <conio.h>
#include "sercpp.h"

void main(void)
{
      SERIALPORT port(2, 4096);

      port.set_port(2400L, 8, NO_PARITY, 1);
      printf("COM2 is set for %d stop bits\n",
port.get_stopbits());
}
```

get_tx_dtr

Summary: #include "sercpp.h"

int *object*.get_tx_dtr(void);

SERIALPORT *object*; (is the serial port's object)

Description: The **get_tx_dtr** function returns the current setting for the transmitter's DTR/DSR flow control. The serial port's object is specified by *object*.

Return Value: The **get_tx_dtr** function returns TRUE if DTR/DSR flow control is enabled for the transmitter or FALSE if DTR/DSR flow control is disabled for the transmitter.

See Also: **set_tx_dtr**

Example: The following program demonstrates the **get_tx_dtr** function by displaying the current state of the transmitter's DTR/DSR flow control:

```
#include <stdio.h>
#include <conio.h>
#include "sercpp.h"

void main(void)
{
       SERIALPORT port(2, 4096);

       port.set_port(2400L, 8, NO_PARITY, 1);
       printf("Transmitter DTR/DSR flow control is %s\n",
              port.get_tx_dtr() ? "on" : "off");
}
```

get_tx_rts

Summary: #include "sercpp.h"

int *object*.get_tx_rts(void);

SERIALPORT *object*; (is the serial port's object)

Description: The **get_tx_rts** function returns the current setting for the transmitter's RTS/CTS flow control. The serial port's object is specified by *object*.

Return Value: The **get_tx_rts** function returns TRUE if RTS/CTS flow control is enabled for the transmitter or FALSE if RTS/CTS flow control is disabled for the transmitter.

See Also: **set_tx_rts**

Example: The following program demonstrates the **get_tx_rts** function by displaying the current state of the transmitter's RTS/CTS flow control:

```
#include <stdio.h>
#include <conio.h>
#include "sercpp.h"

void main(void)
{
      SERIALPORT port(2, 4096);

      port.set_port(2400L, 8, NO_PARITY, 1);
      printf("Transmitter RTS/CTS flow control is %s\n",
            port.get_tx_rts() ? "on" : "off");
}
```

get_tx_xon

Summary: #include "sercpp.h"

int *object*.get_tx_xon(void);

SERIALPORT objcct; (is thc scrial port's object)

Description: The **get_tx_xon** function returns the current setting for the transmitter's XON/XOFF flow control. The serial port's object is specified by *object*.

Return Value: The **get_tx_xon** function returns TRUE if XON/XOFF flow control is enabled for the transmitter or FALSE if XON/XOFF flow control is disabled for the transmitter.

See Also: **set_tx_xon**

Example: The following program demonstrates the **get_tx_xon** function by displaying the current state of the transmitter's XON/XOFF flow control:

```
#include <stdio.h>
#include <conio.h>
#include "sercpp.h"

void main(void)
{
      SERIALPORT port(2, 4096);

      port.set_port(2400L, 8, NO_PARITY, 1);
      printf("Transmitter XON/XOFF flow control is %s\n",
            port.get_tx_xon() ? "on" : "off");
}
```

in_ready

Summary: #include "sercpp.h"

int *object*.in_ready(void);

SERIALPORT *object*; (is the serial port's object)

Description: The **in_ready** function checks the serial port's receive buffer to see if there is a character available. The serial port's object is specified by *object*.

Return Value: The **in_ready** function returns TRUE if there's a character in the receive buffer. Otherwise, FALSE is returned to indicate that the receive buffer is empty.

See Also: **get**

Example: The following program demonstrates how the **in_ready** function is used to monitor for incoming characters:

```
#include <stdio.h>
#include <stdlib.h>
#include <conio.h>
#include "sercpp.h"

void main(void)
{
	int c;
	SERIALPORT *port;

	port = new SERIALPORT(2, 4096);
	port->set_port(2400L, 8, NO_PARITY, 1);
	while (TRUE) {
		if (kbhit()) {
			c = getch();
			switch (c) {
				case 0:
					if (getch() == 45) { /* Alt-X to exit*/
						delete port;
						exit(0);
					}
					break;
				default:
					port->put(c);
			}
		}
		if (port->in_ready()) {
			c = port->get();
			putch(c);
		}
	}
}
```

purge_in

Summary: #include "sercpp.h"

void *object*.purge_in(void);

SERIALPORT *object*; (is the serial port's object)

Description: The **purge_in** function deletes any characters that are waiting in the serial port's receive buffer. The serial port's object is specified by *object*.

Return Value: No value is returned.

See Also: **get** and **in_ready**

Example: The following program demonstrates the **purge_in** function by deleting all incoming characters in the serial port's receive buffer:

```
#include <stdio.h>
#include <stdlib.h>
#include <conio.h>
#include "sercpp.h"

void main(void)
{
	int c;
	SERIALPORT *port;

	port = new SERIALPORT(2, 4096);
	port->set_port(2400L, 8, NO_PARITY, 1);
	while (TRUE) {
		if (kbhit()) {
			c = getch();
			switch (c) {
				case 0:
					if (getch() == 45) { /* Alt-X to exit*/
						delete port;
						exit(0);
					}
					break;
				default:
					port->put(c);
			}
		}
		port->purge_in();
		if (port->in_ready()) {
			c = port->get();
			putch(c);
		}
	}
}
```

put

Summary: #include "sercpp.h"

void *object*.put(unsigned char *c*);

SERIALPORT *object*;	(is the serial port's object)
unsigned char *c*;	(is the character to send)

Description: The **put** function sends a character specified by *c* out the serial port. The serial port's object is specified by *object*.

Return Value: No value is returned.

See Also: **get**

Example: The following program demonstrates the **put** function by sending a variety of key presses out the serial port:

```
#include <stdio.h>
#include <stdlib.h>
#include <conio.h>
#include "sercpp.h"

void main(void)
{
	int c;
	SERIALPORT *port;

	port = new SERIALPORT(2, 4096);
	port->set_port(2400L, 8, NO_PARITY, 1);
	while (TRUE) {
		if (kbhit()) {
			c = getch();
			switch (c) {
				case 0:
					if (getch() == 45) { /* Alt-X to exit*/
						delete port;
						exit(0);
					}
					break;
				default:
					port->put(c);
			}
		}
		if (port->in_ready()) {
			c = port->get();
			putch(c);
		}
	}
}
```

set_baud

Summary: #include "sercpp.h"

void *object*.set_baud(long *baud*);

SERIALPORT *object*;	(is the serial port's object)
long *baud*;	(is the new baud rate)

Description: The **set_baud** function sets a serial port's baud rate to the value specified by *baud*. The serial port's object is specified by *baud*.

Return Value: No value is returned.

See Also: **set_port**

Example: The following program demonstrates the **set_baud** function by setting a serial port's baud rate to 38,400 baud:

```
#include <stdio.h>
#include "sercpp.h"

void main(void)
{
      SERIALPORT port(2, 4096);

      port.set_baud(38400L);
      printf("The baud rate is %ld baud.\n", port.get_baud());
}
```

set_data_format

Summary: #include "sercpp.h"

void *object*.set_data_format(int *bits*, int *parity*, int *stopbits*);

SERIALPORT *object*;	(is the serial port's object)
int *bits*;	(is the number of data bits)
int *parity*;	(is the parity setting)
int *stopbits*;	(is the number of stop bits)

Description: The **set_data_format** function sets a serial port's number of data bits, parity setting, and number of stop bits. The serial port's object is specified by *object*. The number of data bits is specified by *bits* and can be 5, 6, 7, or 8. The parity setting is specified by *parity* and can be one of the following manifest constants (defined in **serial.h**):

Constant	Parity Setting
NO_PARITY	No parity.
EVEN_PARITY	Even parity.
ODD_PARITY	Odd parity.

The number of stop bits is specified by *stopbits* and can be 1 or 2. **Note**: If 2 stop bits are specified and the number of data bits is set to 5, the UART will actually use 1½ stop bits.

Return Value: No value is returned.

See Also: **set_port**

Example: The following program demonstrates the **set_data_format** function by setting a serial port for 8 data bits, no parity, and 1 stop bit:

Note: Due to the physical constraints of this book, some lines in the following listing are shown wrapped. These should be entered as single lines.

```
#include <stdio.h>
#include "sercpp.h"

void main(void)
{
      SERIALPORT port(2, 4096);

      port.set_data_format(8, NO_PARITY, 1);
      printf("COM2 is set for %d data bits\n", port.get_bits());
      printf("COM2 is set for %s parity\n", port.get_parity() ==
NO_PARITY ?
            "no" : (port.get_parity() == EVEN_PARITY ? "even" :
"odd"));
      printf("COM2 is set for %d stop bits\n", port.get_stopbits());
}
```

set_dtr

Summary: #include "sercpp.h"

void *object*.set_dtr(int *n*);

SERIALPORT *object*;	(is the serial port's object)
int *n*;	(is the new DTR setting)

Description: The **set_dtr** function is used to set the UART's DTR line. The serial port's object is specified by *object*. If *n* is equal to TRUE, DTR is asserted. If *n* is equal to FALSE, DTR is unasserted and will break the connection after a certain length of time for most modems.

Return Value: No value is returned.

See Also: **carrier**

Example: The following program demonstrates the **set_dtr** function by lowering DTR on COM2:

```
#include <stdio.h>
#include "sercpp.h"

void main(void)
{
      SERIALPORT port(2, 4096);

      port.set_dtr(FALSE);
      printf("DTR has been lowered on COM2:\n");
}
```

set_port

Summary: #include "sercpp.h"

void *object*.set_port(long *baud*, int *bits*, int *parity*, int *stopbits*);

SERIALPORT *object*;	(is the serial port's object)
long *baud*;	(is the baud rate)
int *bits*;	(is the number of data bits)
int *parity*;	(is the parity setting)
int *stopbits*;	(is the number of stop bits)

Description: The **set_port** function sets a serial port's baud rate, number of data bits, parity setting, and number of stop bits. The serial port's object is specified by *object*. The baud rate is specified by *baud*. The number of data bits is specified by *bits* and can be 5, 6, 7, or 8. The parity setting is specified by *parity* and can be one of the following manifest constants (defined in **serial.h**):

Constant	Parity Setting
NO_PARITY	No parity.
EVEN_PARITY	Even parity.
ODD_PARITY	Odd parity.

The number of stop bits is specified by *stopbits* and can be 1 or 2. **Note**: If 2 stop bits are specified and the number of data bits is set to 5, the UART will actually use 1½ stop bits.

Return Value: No value is returned.

See Also: **set_baud** and **set_data_format**

Example: The following program demonstrates the **set_port** function by setting a serial port for 38,400 baud, 8 data bits, no parity, and 1 stop bit:

Note: Due to the physical constraints of this book, some lines in the following listing are shown wrapped. These should be entered as single lines.

```
#include <stdio.h>
#include "sercpp.h"

void main(void)
{
      SERIALPORT port(2, 4096);

      port.set_port(38400L, 8, NO_PARITY, 1);
      printf("COM2 is set for %ld baud\n", port.get_baud());
      printf("COM2 is set for %d data bits\n", port.get_bits());
      printf("COM2 is set for %s parity\n", port.get_parity() ==
NO_PARITY ?
            "no" : (port.get_parity() == EVEN_PARITY ? "even" :
"odd"));
      printf("COM2 is set for %d stop bits\n", port.get_stopbits());
}
```

set_rx_dtr

Summary: #include "sercpp.h"

void *object*.set_rx_dtr(int *n*);

SERIALPORT *object*;	(is the serial port's object)
int *n*;	(is the new setting)

Description: The **set_rx_dtr** function enables or disables the receiver's DTR/DSR flow control. The serial port's object is specified by *object*. If *n* is TRUE, the receiver's DTR/DSR flow control will be enabled. If *n* is FALSE, the receiver's DTR/DSR flow control will be disabled.

Return Value: No value is returned.

See Also: **get_rx_dtr**

Example: The following program demonstrates the **set_rx_dtr** function by enabling the receiver's DTR/DSR flow control:

```
#include <stdio.h>
#include "sercpp.h"

void main(void)
{
      SERIALPORT port(2, 4096);

      port.set_rx_dtr(TRUE);
      printf("The receiver's DTR/DSR flow control is %s\n",
            port.get_rx_dtr() ? "On" : "Off");
}
```

set_rx_rts

Summary: #include "sercpp.h"

void *object*.set_rx_rts(int *n*);

SERIALPORT *object*;	(is the serial port's object)
int *n*;	(is the new setting)

Description: The **set_rx_rts** function enables or disables the receiver's RTS/CTS flow control. The serial port's object is specified by *object*. If *n* is TRUE, the receiver's RTS/CTS flow control will be enabled. If *n* is FALSE, the receiver's RTS/CTS flow control will be disabled.

Return Value: No value is returned.

See Also: **get_rx_rts**

Example: The following program demonstrates the **set_rx_rts** function by enabling the receiver's RTS/CTS flow control:

```
#include <stdio.h>
#include "sercpp.h"

void main(void)
{
      SERIALPORT port(2, 4096);

      port.set_rx_rts(TRUE);
      printf("The receiver's RTS/CTS flow control is %s\n",
            port.get_rx_rts() ? "On" : "Off");
}
```

set_rx_xon

Summary: #include “sercpp.h”

void *object*.set_rx_xon(int *n*);

SERIALPORT *object*; (is the serial port's object)

int *n*; (is the new setting)

Description: The **set_rx_xon** function enables or disables the receiver's XON/XOFF flow control. The serial port's object is specified by *object*. If *n* is TRUE, the receiver's XON/XOFF flow control will be enabled. If *n* is FALSE, the receiver's XON/XOFF flow control will be disabled.

Return Value: No value is returned.

See Also: **get_rx_xon**

Example: The following program demonstrates the **set_rx_xon** function by enabling the receiver's XON/XOFF flow control:

```
#include <stdio.h>
#include "sercpp.h"

void main(void)
{
      SERIALPORT port(2, 4096);

      port.set_rx_xon(TRUE);
      printf("The receiver's XON/XOFF flow control is %s\n",
            port.get_rx_xon() ? "On" : "Off");
}
```

set_tx_dtr

Summary: #include "sercpp.h"

void *object*.set_tx_dtr(int *n*);

SERIALPORT *object*; (is the serial port's object)

int *n*; (is the new setting)

Description: The **set_tx_dtr** function enables or disables the transmitter's DTR/DSR flow control. The serial port's object is specified by *object*. If *n* is TRUE, the transmitter's DTR/DSR flow control will be enabled. If *n* is FALSE, the transmitter's DTR/DSR flow control will be disabled.

Return Value: No value is returned.

See Also: **get_tx_dtr**

Example: The following program demonstrates the **set_tx_dtr** function by enabling the transmitter's DTR/DSR flow control:

```
#include <stdio.h>
#include "sercpp.h"

void main(void)
{
      SERIALPORT port(2, 4096);

      port.set_tx_dtr(TRUE);
      printf("The transmitter's DTR/DSR flow control is %s\n",
            port.get_tx_dtr() ? "On" : "Off");
}
```

set_tx_rts

Summary: #include "sercpp.h"

void *object*.set_tx_rts(int *n*);

SERIALPORT *object*; (is the serial port's object)

int *n*; (is the new setting)

Description: The **set_tx_rts** function enables or disables the transmitter's RTS/CTS flow control. The serial port's object is specified by *object*. If *n* is TRUE, the transmitter's RTS/CTS flow control will be enabled. If *n* is FALSE, the transmitter's RTS/CTS flow control will be disabled.

Return Value: No value is returned.

See Also: **get_tx_rts**

Example: The following program demonstrates the **set_tx_rts** function by enabling the transmitter's RTS/CTS flow control:

```
#include <stdio.h>
#include "sercpp.h"

void main(void)
{
      SERIALPORT port(2, 4096);

      port.set_tx_rts(TRUE);
      printf("The transmitter's RTS/CTS flow control is %s\n",
            port.get_tx_rts() ? "On" : "Off");
}
```

set_tx_xon

Summary: #include "sercpp.h"

void *object*.set_tx_xon(int *n*);

SERIALPORT *object*; (is the serial port's object)

int *n*; (is the new setting)

Description: The **set_tx_xon** function enables or disables the transmitter's XON/XOFF flow control. The serial port's object is specified by *object*. If *n* is TRUE, the transmitter's XON/XOFF flow control will be enabled. If *n* is FALSE, the transmitter's XON/XOFF flow control will be disabled.

Return Value: No value is returned.

See Also: **get_tx_xon**

Example: The following program demonstrates the **set_tx_xon** function by enabling the receiver's DTR/DSR flow control:

```
#include <stdio.h>
#include "sercpp.h"

void main(void)
{
      SERIALPORT port(2, 4096);

      port.set_tx_xon(TRUE);
      printf("The transmitter's XON/XOFF flow control is %s\n",
            port.get_tx_xon() ? "On" : "Off");
}
```

The XFERPORT Object

In addition to the **SERIALPORT** object class, the Turbo C++ implementation of the SERIAL toolbox defines an **XFERPORT** object class for file transfers. The **XFERPORT** object class is derived from the **SERIALPORT** object class and features all of the functions that the **SERIALPORT** object class contains and a few new ones of its own. To facilitate the use of a **XFERPORT** object in application programs, this section describes the **XFERPORT** object class's constructor and functions that are unique to this derived class as follows:

Summary: Presents an exact syntactic model for the **XFERPORT** constructor and member functions.

Description: Describes the constructor or member function's purpose and how it is used in an application program.

Return Value: Explains any of the possible return values for the member functions.

See Also: Lists any similar or related **XFERPORT** functions.

Example: Illustrates how a **XFERPORT** constructor or member function is used in an application program.

XFERPORT

Summary: #include "sercpp.h"

XFERPORT(int *port*, int *blength*);

int *port*; (is the serial port)

int *blength*; (is the input buffer's length)

Description: The **XFERPORT** constructor creates the serial communications port object and opens the port specified by *port*. Additionally, the receiver's buffer size is specified to *blength*. **Note**: Because of the way Turbo C++ calls destructors, you may want to dynamically allocate a **XFERPORT** object with the **new** operator and then dispose of it with the **delete** operator. Failure to due this may mean that the serial port is left in an open state by the program on exit.

Example: The following program demonstrates the **XFERPORT** constructor by creating an object for use by a dumb terminal program:

```
#include <stdio.h>
#include <stdlib.h>
#include <conio.h>
#include "sercpp.h"

void main(void)
{
      int c;
      XFERPORT *port;

      port = new XFERPORT(2, 4096);
      port->set_port(2400L, 8, NO_PARITY, 1);
      while (TRUE) {
            if (kbhit()) {
                  c = getch();
                  switch (c) {
                        case 0:
                              if (getch() == 45) { /* Alt-X to exit*/
                                    delete port;
                                    exit(0);
                              }
                              break;
                        default:
                              port->put(c);
                  }
            }
            if (port->in_ready()) {
                  c = port->get();
                  putch(c);
            }
      }
}
```

receive

Summary: #include "sercpp.h"

int *object*.receive(int *xtype*, int (**handler*)(int *code*, long *position*,
    char **message*), char **path*);

XFERPORT *object*; (is the serial port's object)

int *xtype*; (is the protocol to be used)

int (**handler*)(int, long, char *) (is the error handler)

char **path*; (is the file name or directory)

Description: The **receive** function is used to download a file. The serial port's object is specified by *object*. The type of file transfer is specified by *xtype* and can be one of the following manifest constants (defined in **serial.h**):

Constant	Type of Transfer
XMODEM	Receive the file using Xmodem.
XMODEM1K	Receive the file using Xmodem-1K.
YMODEM	Receive the file using Ymodem.
YMODEMG	Receive the file using Ymodem-G.

During the file transfer, the **receive** function will make one or more calls to an error handler specified by the function pointer *handler*. Whenever, the **receive** function calls the error handler, it will pass three arguments to the error handler as follows:

Code	Position	Message
RECEIVING	File size.	The name of the file being received.
RECEIVED	Current position.	N/A
ERROR	N/A	Error message.
COMPLETE	N/A	N/A

The error handler routine can return a value of FALSE to abort the transfer or a value of TRUE to continue with the transfer. **Note**: Transfers are automatically aborted for a variety of reasons by the **receive** function.

The file name for the file to be received is specified by *path* for Xmodem and Xmodem-1K transfers and the directory for the file or files to be downloaded is specified by *path* for Ymodem and Ymodem-G transfers.

Return Value: The **receive** function returns TRUE if the file transfer was successful. Otherwise, FALSE is returned to indicate an unsuccessful file transfer.

See Also: **transmit**

Example: The following program demonstrates the **receive** function by downloading a file using the Xmodem protocol:

Note: Due to the physical constraints of this book, some lines in the following listing are shown wrapped. These should be entered as single lines.

```
#include <stdio.h>
#include <stdlib.h>
#include <string.h>
#include <conio.h>
#include "sercpp.h"

int e_handler(int c, long p, char *s);

void main(void)
{
	int c;
	XFERPORT *port;

	port = new XFERPORT(2, 4096);
	port->set_port(2400L, 8, NO_PARITY, 1);
	while (TRUE) {
		if (kbhit()) {
			c = getch();
			switch (c) {
				case 0:
					switch (getch()) {
						case 32:		/* Alt-D to
download */
							port->receive(XMODEM,
e_handler, "C:\DOWNLOAD.FIL");
							continue;
						case 45:		/* Alt-X to exit */
							delete port;
							exit(0);
					}
					break;
				default:
					port->put(c);
			}
		}
		if (port->in_ready()) {
			c = port->get();
			putch(c);
		}
	}
}
```

continued...

...from previous page

```
int e_handler(int c, long p, char *s)
{
      int k;

      switch (c) {
            case SENDING:
                  printf("Sending: %s\n", strupr(s));
                  printf("Length : %ld\n", p);
                  break;
            case RECEIVING:
                  printf("Receiving: %s\n", strupr(s));
                  printf("Length : %ld\n", p);
                  break;
            case SENT:
                  printf("%ld bytes sent.\r", p);
                  break;
            case RECEIVED:
                  printf("%ld bytes received.\r", p);
                  break;
            case ERROR:
                  printf("\nError: %s in block %ld\n", s, p);
                  break;
            case COMPLETE:
                  printf("\n%s\n", s);
                  break;
      }
      if (kbhit()) {
            if (!(k = getch())) {
                  getch();
                  return TRUE;
            }
            if (k == 27)
                  return FALSE;
      }
      return TRUE;
}
```

transmit

Summary: #include “sercpp.h”

int *object*.transmit(int *xtype*, int (**handler*)(int *code*, long *position*, char **message*), char **files*[]);

XFERPORT *object*; (is the serial port's object)

int *xtype*; (is the protocol to be used)

int (**handler*)(int, long, char *) (is the error handler)

char **files*[]; (is the files to be sent)

Description: The **transmit** function is used to upload one or more files. The serial port's object is specified by *object*. The type of file transfer is specified by *xtype* and can be one of the following manifest constants (defined in **serial.h**):

Constant	Type of Transfer
XMODEM	Transmit the file using Xmodem.
XMODEM1K	Transmit the file using Xmodem-1K.
YMODEM	Transmit the file(s) using Ymodem.
YMODEMG	Transmit the file(s) using Ymodem-G.

During the file transfer, the **transmit** function will make one or more calls to an error handler specified by the function pointer *handler*. Whenever the **transmit** function calls the error handler, it will pass three arguments to the error handler as follows:

Code	Position	Message
SENDING	File size.	The name of the file being sent.
SENT	Current position.	N/A
ERROR	N/A	Error message.
COMPLETE	N/A	N/A

The error handler routine can return a value of FALSE to abort the transfer or a value of TRUE to continue with the transfer. **Note**: Transfers are automatically aborted for a variety of reasons by the **transmit** function.

The file names for the files to be transmitted is specified by *files*, which is a pointer to an array of string pointers. For Xmodem and Xmodem-1K file transfers, the file name is specified by the array's first string pointer. For Ymodem and Ymodem-G file transfers, the array specifies the names of one or more files to be transmitted and the pointer following the last file name is set to **NULL**.

Return Value: The **transmit** function returns TRUE if the file transfer was successful. Otherwise, FALSE will be returned to indicate an unsuccessful file transfer.

See Also: **receive**

Example: The following program demonstrates the **transmit** function by uploading a file using the Xmodem protocol:

Note: Due to the physical constraints of this book, some lines in the following listing are shown wrapped. These should be entered as single lines.

```
#include <stdio.h>
#include <stdlib.h>
#include <string.h>
#include <conio.h>
#include "sercpp.h"

int e_handler(int c, long p, char *s);

char *files[10];

void main(void)
{
      int c;
      XFERPORT *port;

      port = new XFERPORT(2, 4096);
      port->set_port(2400L, 8, NO_PARITY, 1);
      while (TRUE) {
            if (kbhit()) {
                  c = getch();
                  switch (c) {
                        case 0:
                              switch (getch()) {
                                    case 22:       /* Alt-U to upload
*/
                                          files[0] = "serial.h";
                                          port->transmit(XMODEM,
e_handler, files);
                                          continue;
                                    case 45:       /* Alt-X to exit */
                                          delete port;
                                          exit(0);
                              }
                              break;
                        default:
                              port->put(c);
                  }
            }
            if (port->in_ready()) {
                  c = port->get();
                  putch(c);
            }
      }
}
```

continued...

...from previous page

```
int e_handler(int c, long p, char *s)
{
      int k;

      switch (c) {
            case SENDING:
                  printf("Sending: %s\n", strupr(s));
                  printf("Length : %ld\n", p);
                  break;
            case RECEIVING:
                  printf("Receiving: %s\n", strupr(s));
                  printf("Length : %ld\n", p);
                  break;
            case SENT:
                  printf("%ld bytes sent.\r", p);
                  break;
            case RECEIVED:
                  printf("%ld bytes received.\r", p);
                  break;
            case ERROR:
                  printf("\nError: %s in block %ld\n", s, p);
                  break;
            case COMPLETE:
                  printf("\n%s\n", s);
                  break;
      }
      if (kbhit()) {
            if (!(k = getch())) {
                  getch();
                  return TRUE;
            }
            if (k == 27)
                  return FALSE;
      }
      return TRUE;
}
```

The ANSI Object

The Turbo C++ implementation of the SERIAL toolbox defines an **ANSI** object class for ANSI terminal emulation. To facilitate the use of an **ANSI** object in application programs, this section describes the **ANSI** object class's constructor and functions as follows:

Summary: Presents an exact syntactic model for the **ANSI** constructor and member functions.

Description: Describes the constructor or member function's purpose and how it is used in an application program.

Return Value: Explains any of the possible return values for the member functions.

See Also: Lists any similar or related **ANSI** functions.

Example: Illustrates how an **ANSI** constructor or member function is used in an application program.

ANSI

Summary: #include "sercpp.h"

ANSI(void);

Description: The **ANSI** constructor initializes the ANSI terminal emulator object by setting the **ansi_dsr** function pointer to **put_serial** and enabling the function by setting **ansi_dsr_flag** to TRUE.

See Also: **ansi_dsr**, **ansi_dsr_flag**, and **put_serial**

Example: The following program demonstrates the **ANSI** constructor by creating an object and sending a few strings to the ANSI terminal emulator:

```
#include <stdio.h>
#include "sercpp.h"

void main(void)
{
      ANSI ansi;

      ansi.string("This is a string\n");
      ansi.string("This is a string too\n");
}
```

out

Summary: #include "sercpp.h"

void *object*.out(int *character*);

ANSI *object*;	(the ANSI terminal object)
int *character*;	(the character to be displayed)

Description: The **out** function displays a specified *character* on the display screen using the ANSI terminal emulator object that is specified by *object*.

Return Value: No value is returned.

See Also: **printf** and **string**

Example: The following program demonstrates how the **out** function is used by displaying a variety of characters:

```
#include <stdio.h>
#include <conio.h>
#include "sercpp.h"

void main(void)
{
        int i;
        ANSI ansi;

        ansi.out('*');
        ansi.out('\n');
        for (i = 0; i < 70; i++)
              ansi.out('-');
        ansi.out('\n');
        while (!kbhit()) ;
        if (!getch())
              getch();
}
```

printf

Summary: #include "sercpp.h"

int *object*.printf(char **format*, ...);

ANSI *object*;	(is the ANSI terminal object)
char **format*;	(is the format string)

Description: As the C run time library printf function is used to display formatted output to the video display, the ANSI **printf** member function is used to display formatted output to the ANSI terminal emulator object specified by *object*. The format of the output is specified by *format* and zero or more additional parameters are used to specify the format string's required values. If you are unfamiliar with the use of the printf function, you should consult your C run time library manual for details about this very practical function's use.

Return Value: The **printf** function returns the number of characters that was sent to the ANSI terminal emulator.

See Also: **out** and **string**

Example: The following program demonstrates how the **printf** function is used by displaying a variety of formatted strings:

```
#include <stdio.h>
#include <conio.h>
#include "sercpp.h"

void main(void)
{
      int i;
      ANSI ansi;

      ansi.printf("%s %s %s\n", "Ryan", "Matthew", "Crystal");
      for (i = 0; i < 10; i++)
            ansi.printf("%d\n", i);
      while (!kbhit()) ;
      if (!getch())
            getch();
}
```

string

Summary: #include "sercpp.h"

void *object*.string(char **string*);

ANSI *object*;	(is the ANSI terminal object)
char **string*;	(is the string to be displayed)

Description: The **string** function displays a specified *string* on the display screen via the ANSI terminal emulator object specified by *object*. Although the **printf** function is more versatile, the **string** function is faster. Therefore, the **string** function should be used when only one string needs to be displayed.

Return Value: No value is returned.

See Also: **out** and **printf**

Example: The following program demonstrates the **string** function by displaying a variety of strings:

```
#include <stdio.h>
#include <conio.h>
#include "sercpp.h"

void main(void)
{
      ANSI ansi;

      ansi.string("Ryan\n");
      ansi.string("Matthew\n");
      ansi.string("Crystal\n");
      while (!kbhit()) ;
      if (!getch())
            getch();
}
```

Appendix B

The AT Command Set

As mentioned in Chapter 2, the **AT** command set was originally developed by Hayes Microcomputer Products, Inc. for their line of modems and is used to instruct a modem what operation it is to performed. The **AT** command set gets its name because each command is preceded by the letters *AT*. This appendix presents the **AT** command set for a typical Hayes-compatible modem; however, you should note that your modem's **AT** command set may differ somewhat from what is described here. You should consult your modem's manual if have a question as to how it responds to a specific **AT** command.

Command: A

Sending an **ATA** to the modem will instruct it to answer an incoming call.

Command: A/

Sending an **A/** to the modem will tell the modem to repeat the last command it received. You should note that the **A/** command is not preceded by **AT** and you do not have to press ENTER.

Command: AT

The **AT** command means attention and is usually used to send a command to the modem.

Command: B

The **ATB** command sets the modem's compatibility modem. The command **ATB0** is typically used to set CCITT V.22 and V.22bis compatibility and the command **ATB1** is typically used to set Bell 103 and 212A compatibility.

Command: D

The **ATD** command tells the modem to dial the number that follows using one or more of the following characters:

Character	**Function**
0 through 9, # and *	Dial the indicated digit.
P	Use pulse dialing.
R	This character is used at the end of the dial string and tells the modem to send out answer tones instead of originate tones.
T	Use touch-tone dialing.
W	Wait for a second dial tone.
@	Wait for one or more rings and five seconds of silence.
,	Pause.
!	Flash.
;	Return to command mode after dialing.

Command: DS=n

The **ATDS=n** command dials one of four telephone numbers that have been stored in the modem's NRAM. Where **n** is the number to be dialed.

Command: E

The **ATE** command tells the modem whether or not it is to echo commands back to the terminal. The **ATE0** command tells the modem not to echo commands and the **ATE1** command tells the modem to echo commands.

Command: Escape

The escape sequence tells the modem to switch from online mode to the command mode. The escape sequence is sent to the modem by pausing for one second, sending three escape characters, and then pausing for another second. The escape character for most modem's is + and is usually configured with the modem's S2 register. Therefore, waiting one second, sending +++, and then waiting one second more will instruct the modem to switch from the online mode to the command mode.

Command: H

The **ATH** command is used to tell the modem whether it is to go on or off the hook. Sending an **ATH0** command will cause the modem to go on hook (or hang up) and sending an **ATH1** command will cause the modem to go off hook.

Command: I

The **ATI** command is used to test the modem. Sending an **ATI0** command to the modem will return the modem's product-identification code and sending an **ATI1** command to the modem will return a ROM checksum.

Command: L

The **ATL** command is used to adjust the modem's speaker volume as follows:

Command	Function
ATL0	Low volume setting.
ATL1	Medium volume setting.
ATL3	High volume setting.

Command: M

The **ATM** command controls the modem's speaker as follows:

Command	Function
ATM0	Speaker is always off
ATM1	Speaker is on until carrier is detected
ATM2	Speaker is always on
ATM3	Speaker is turned on after dialing is complete and is turned off again once carrier is detected

Command: O

The **ATO** command is used to return the modem back to the online mode from the command mode after an escape sequence has been issued.

Command: Q

The **ATQ** command tells the modem whether or not it is to send responses to commands that are sent to it. Sending **ATQ0** to the modem will enable modem responses and sending **ATQ1** will disable modem responses.

Command: Sr?

The **ATSr?** command is used to tell the modem to return the value that is stored in one of its S registers where **r** is the S register whose value is to be returned.

Command: Sr=n

The **ATSr=n** command is used to set one of the modem's S registers. The S register is specified by **r** and the register's new value is specified by **n**. The following is a description of the S registers that are found in a typical Hayes-compatible modem:

S Register	Function
S0	The number of rings the modem is to answer the phone on. Setting this register to 0 will disable auto-answer.
S1	This register holds the number of rings detected and is reset between calls or when 8 seconds of silence has elapsed.
S2	The escape character. A typical value for this register is 43.
S3	The carriage return character. A typical value for this register is 13.
S4	The line feed character. A typical value for this register is 10.
S5	The backspace character. A typical value for this register is 8.
S6	The number of seconds the modem is to wait for dial tone.
S7	The number of seconds the modem is to wait after dialing for carrier to be established before returning to the command mode.
S8	This register specifies the number of seconds the modem is to pause for when it encounters a comma (,) in the dial string.
S9	This register specifies in tenths of a second how long carrier must be established before the modem recognizes that carrier is indeed actually present.
S10	This register specifies in tenths of a second how long carrier can be absent before the modem will recognize it as a true loss of carrier.
S11	This register specifies the number of milliseconds the modem is to delay between sending dial tones on a touch-tone line.
S12	This register specifies the number of 1/50ths of a second the modem is to wait both before and after an escape sequence to recognize it as a true escape sequence.
S13	Is a bit-mapped register and its contents vary a great deal depending upon the modem.
S14	Is a bit-mapped register and its contents vary a great deal depending upon the modem.
S15	Is a bit-mapped register and its contents vary a great deal depending upon the modem.

Command: V

The **ATV** command tells the modem what type of responses it is to return. Sending an **ATV0** to the modem will instruct the modem to return numeric responses and sending an **ATV1** to the modem will instruct the modem to return verbose (or word) responses.

Command: X

The **ATX** command tells the modem what type of responses are to be returned. Most modems support **ATX0** through **ATX4** and the following table illustrates what type of responses those commands will return:

Numeric	Verbose	X0	X1	X2	X3	X4
0	OK	*	*	*	*	*
1	CONNECT	*	*	*	*	*
2	RING	*	*	*	*	*
3	NO CARRIER	*	*	*	*	*
4	ERROR	*	*	*	*	*
5	CONNECT 1200		*	*	*	*
6	NO DIALTONE			*		*
7	BUSY				*	*
8	NO ANSWER	*	*	*	*	*
9	Reserved					
10	CONNECT 2400		*	*	*	*

Command: Y

The **ATY** command tells the modem how it is to deal with a BREAK condition. Sending the modem an **ATY0** will cause the modem to ignore a BREAK and sending the modem an **ATY1** will cause the modem to send a four second BREAK before disconnecting.

Command: Z

The **ATZ** command tells the modem to reconfigure itself to a previously saved profile in NRAM.

Command: &C

The **AT&C** command tells the modem how it is to control the DCD line. Sending an **AT&C0** to the modem instructs the modem to always assert the DCD line and sending an **AT&C1** to the modem instructs the modem to only assert the DCD line when carrier is actually present.

Command: &D

The **AT&D** command tells the modem how it is to respond to the DTR line. Sending an **AT&D0** to the modem tells it to ignore the DTR line, sending an **AT&D1** tells the modem to return to the command mode when the DTR line goes from an on to off state, sending an **AT&D2** to the modem tells the modem to disconnect and return to the command mode when the DTR line goes from an on to off state.

Command: &F

The **AT&F** command tells the modem to change its configuration to the factory settings.

Command: &G

The **AT&G** command tells the modem what type, if any, guard tone it is to use. Sending an **AT&G0** to the modem disables the guard tone, sending an **AT&G1** to the modem enables a 550 Hz guard tone, and sending an **AT&G2** enables a 1800 Hz guard tone.

Command: &J

The **AT&J** command sets the type of telephone jack the modem will use. Sending an **AT&J0** to the modem sets it for an RJ11, RJ41S, or RJ45S telephone jack and sending an **AT&J1** to the modem sets it for an RJ12 or RJ13 telephone jack.

Command: &L

The **AT&L** command sets the modem for the type of telephone lines it will be using. Sending an **AT&L0** to the modem sets it for dialup operation and sending an **AT&L1** sets the modem for leased-line operation.

Command: &M

The **AT&M** command sets the modem for either asynchronous operation or synchronous operation. Sending an **AT&M0** to the modem sets it for asynchronous operation and sending an **AT&M1** to the modem sets it for synchronous operation.

Command: &P

The **AT&P** command sets the modem for the type of pulse dialing it will perform. Sending the modem an **AT&P0** will set the modem for the type of pulse dialing that is used in the United States and sending the modem an **AT&P1** will set the modem for the type of pulse dialing that is used in the UK and Hong Kong.

Command: &R

The **AT&R** command tells the modem how it is to deal with the RTS/CTS lines. Sending an **AT&R0** to the modem tells it to assert CTS whenever the RTS line is asserted and sending an **AT&R1** to the modem tells it to ignore RTS.

Command: &T

The **AT&T** command is used to test the modem as follows:

Command	**Function**
AT&T0	End the test in progress.
AT&T1	Perform a local analog loopback test.
AT&T2	Reserved.
AT&T3	Perform a local digital loopback test.
AT&T4	Modem acknowledges a remote digital loopback test.
AT&T5	Modem denies a remote digital loopback test.
AT&T6	Perform a remote digital loopback test.
AT&T7	Perform a remote digital loopback test and self-test.
AT&T8	Perform a local analog loopback test and self-test.

Command: &V

The **AT&V** command tells the modem to display its current configuration.

Command: &W

The **AT&W** command tells the modem to saves its current configuration in NRAM.

Command: &X

The **AT&X** command sets the modem's synchronous timing source as follows:

Command	**Function**
AT&X0	Uses the modem's transmit clock.
AT&X1	Uses an external clock.
AT&X2	Uses the modem's receiver clock.

Command: &Zn=

The **AT&Zn=** command is used to store a telephone number in NRAM. Where **n** is the number's NRAM number and the dial string follows the = character.

Appendix C

An ASCII Code Table

The following table details the ASCII character set:

	0	1	2	3	4	5	6	7	8	9	A	B	C	D	E	F
0	NUL	SOH	STX	ETX	EOT	ENQ	ACK	BEL	BS	HT	LF	VT	FF	CR	SO	SI
1	DLE	DC1	DC2	DC3	DC4	NAK	SYN	ETB	CAN	EM	SUB	ESC	FS	GS	RS	US
2	SP	!	"	#	$	%	&	'	(	)	*	+	,	-	.	/
3	0	1	2	3	4	5	6	7	8	9	:	;	<	=	>	?
4	@	A	B	C	D	E	F	G	H	I	J	K	L	M	N	O
5	P	Q	R	S	T	U	V	W	X	Y	Z	[	\	]	^	_
6	`	a	b	c	d	e	f	g	h	i	j	k	l	m	n	o
7	p	q	r	s	t	u	v	w	x	y	z	{	|	}	~	DEL

Appendix D

Compiling the Serial Toolbox

Compiling the Serial Toolbox with Microsoft C 6.0A

Batch File Listing: compmc.bat

Listing D.1, **compmc.bat**, is a batch file for compiling the SERIAL toolbox, **mserial.lib**. In addition to constructing the SERIAL toolbox, **compmc.bat** compiles and links Simple Comm.

Listing D.1: compmc.bat

```
echo off
echo Assembling SERASM.ASM
masm /mx serasm;
echo Compling SIMPLE.C, SERIAL.C, PROTOCOL.C, and ANSI.C
cl /AL /D__MSC__ /Od /Gs /c simple.c serial.c protocol.c ansi.c
echo Creating MSERIAL.LIB
lib mserial.lib +serasm +serial +protocol +ansi;
echo Creating SIMPLE.EXE
link /NOI /INCR simple,,,mserial.lib graphics.lib;
```

Compiling the Serial Toolbox with Microsoft QuickC 2.51

Batch File Listing: compqc.bat

Listing D.2, **compqc.bat**, is a batch file for compiling the SERIAL toolbox, **qserial.lib**. In addition to constructing the SERIAL toolbox, **compqc.bat** compiles and links Simple Comm.

Listing D.2: compqc.bat

```
echo off
echo Assembling SERASM.ASM
masm /mx serasm;
echo Compling SIMPLE.C, SERIAL.C, PROTOCOL.C, and ANSI.C
qcl /AL /D__MSC__ /Od /Gs /c simple.c serial.c protocol.c ansi.c
echo Creating QSERIAL.LIB
lib qserial.lib +serasm +serial +protocol +ansi;
echo Creating SIMPLE.EXE
qlink /NOI /INCR simple,,,qserial.lib;
```

Compiling the Serial Toolbox with Turbo C++ 1.01

Batch File Listing: comptc.bat

Listing D.3, **comptc.bat**, is a batch file for compiling the SERIAL toolbox, **tserial.lib**. In addition to constructing the SERIAL toolbox, **comptc.bat** compiles and links both the C and C++ versions of Simple Comm.

Listing D.3: comptc.bat

```
echo off
echo Assembling SERASM.ASM
tasm /mx serasm;
echo Compling SERIAL.C, PROTOCOL.C, ANSI.C, and ANSI.CPP
tcc -ml -c serial.c protocol.c ansi.c ansicpp.cpp
echo Creating TSERIAL.LIB
tlib tserial.lib +serasm +serial +protocol +ansi +ansicpp
echo Creating SIMPLE.EXE
tcc -ml simple.c tserial.lib
echo Creating SIMCPP.EXE
tcc -ml simcpp.cpp tserial.lib
```

Index

S

T

U

X

Y